D1528512

FOLKLORE OF
LAKE ERIE

Judith S. Neulander

FOLKLORE OF
LAKE ERIE

INDIANA UNIVERSITY PRESS

This book is a publication of

Indiana University Press
Office of Scholarly Publishing
Herman B Wells Library 350
1320 East 10th Street
Bloomington, Indiana 47405 USA

iupress.org

Manufactured in the United States of America

First printing 2024

Cataloging information is available from the Library of Congress.

ISBN 978-0-253-06977-1 (hardback)
ISBN 978-0-253-06978-8 (paperback)
ISBN 978-0-253-06979-5 (ebook)

This book is lovingly dedicated to my son and daughter, Rick and Stephanie,
and in memoriam to Steve Levine 1959–2016
A friend in all weather

CONTENTS

ACKNOWLEDGMENTS

S pecial thanks are due to Jared Bendis, creative new media officer at the Freedman Center for Digital Scholarship, Kelvin Smith Library, at Case Western Reserve University. His technical assistance was invaluable, and without him, this would not be an illustrated volume.

I owe a great debt of gratitude to the many generous people who shared their materials, their expertise, and their photos with me as this book came into being. Rather than print a voluminous list of names, each of them is credited on the same page as their contribution.

Finally, my heartfelt thanks goes out to the hardworking team at Indiana University Press, who believed in the book and patiently guided me through the process of publication.

FOLKLORE OF
LAKE ERIE

INTRODUCTION

Folklore enchants and delights its audience with fantasy and fiction, but embedded in all folklore is a perfectly accurate account of the assumptions, aesthetics, aspirations, and animosities held by those who generate, modify, and maintain these traditions. A tale, for instance, will enter tradition only if it reflects and reinforces the way a given community makes sense of the world and feels about things—otherwise the tale wouldn't be considered a "good" story; it would disappear as fast as a magician's bouquet. A community's general way of thinking, its shared understanding of the world, is called its worldview—its own communal point of view. And this point of view will always be reflected, consciously or unconsciously, in the community's own expressive behavior.

Science tries to impart awareness of what is objectively, systematically, and universally true. Journalism aims to explain events with objective, unadorned facts. Conversely, folklore is richly adorned with cultural specificity; it reflects and reinforces a native, *subjective* point of view about what is right or wrong, true or false, good or evil, ugly or pretty—about what should or shouldn't be eaten (and when); what is or isn't funny; who should or shouldn't do what kind of work; what, and who, we should (or shouldn't) fear; what really matters and what doesn't. In short, folklore reflects a community's shared worldview—not just its own distinct view of "the way things are" but also its vision of how things ought to be. Folk tradition is so rich in this information it can give us unrivaled access to the spirit and mentality of any community, in any age, whose traditions come under our scrutiny.

For this reason, folklorists have no interest in the scientific validity or journalistic truth-value of folklore. It makes no difference to a folklorist if fairy godmothers really exist, divining rods locate buried gold, or ghosts ride up and down the nation's highways. What counts, to a folklorist, is gaining access to the spirit and mentality of the community, as embedded in its traditions—whether spoken, sung, expressed in material form, or otherwise performed.

Contrary to what most of us are taught to think, tradition is not a static thing. As times and generations change, any tradition that stops being timely and relevant is likely to be dropped and forgotten unless it, too, can change; alternatively, we may simply change the way we interpret it. For example, one hundred years ago, most Americans thought of the Adam and Eve story as the natural history of the world. Today, most people think of it as an allegory, a poetic way of describing the relationship between people and the deity, in Western civilization. Tradition is generally conservative, but it does—and often must—change, or its interpretation must change, for it to survive. Therefore, any sample of a region's traditions is a snapshot of what was timely and relevant to that particular generation, in that particular place, at that particular time. These patterns, changing over time, help distinguish one time period from another, holding true for all genres of tradition, for which the folktale is a representative example.

According to folklorist Stith Thompson, the smallest element of a tale that is striking or unusual and occurs in more than one telling is called a motif. Therefore, "mother" is not a motif, but "cruel stepmother" is. A number of traditional motifs in folk tradition, along with some folkloristic theories, methods, and techniques, will be cited as they become pertinent in this volume. Elements of folkloristic study, cited in this volume, are meant to help readers gain greater insight by revealing which patterns were prevalent in the culture at any given time, as well as what these patterns reflect over time and how they functioned, or ceased to function, for the community.

For example, we will find that, over time, changing motifs in local "Bloody Mary" narratives reflect and reinforce rapidly changing gender roles. We will learn how ghost narratives like "The Black Dog of Lake Erie" and "Gore Orphanage" help communities come to terms with senseless tragedies. We will see modern ice fishermen connecting with Native American forebears through material culture, and we will come to understand why today's skilled practitioners of anonymous, electronic communication still gather together, face to face, to wait for a "Ghost Train" that never comes.

This book will give us a glimpse of the spirit and mentality of the people surrounding Lake Erie from colonial times to the present. It recalls them in their own words, from the seventeenth century through our own time, up to and including their current voices on the internet. Although narratives tend to be carried in oral tradition long before they are written down, the book is arranged in historical order, moving forward from what was current in the seventeenth century to what is current in the present.

The most recent time period, the early twenty-first century, will carry the most folklore—not because there was less folklore in the past but because the items that remain relevant over time will join with new items accumulating in the ongoing present. Because items of folklore can drop in and out of tradition, any collection of traditions will have to be somewhat fluid and inexact—and certainly incomplete. But through this effort, we gain a general overview of traditions that have persisted in each generation, including our own.

Divisions in time can cloud the issue of where to find a tradition in this book—where to find the legend of Mad Anthony Wayne, for example. Wayne was an eighteenth-century Revolutionary War hero who died on Erie's shore, but the nineteenth-century tradition that developed around him persists in our own time. Hence, readers will find the entry on Mad Anthony Wayne in part 4, "Folklore in the Early Twenty-First Century," because his tale is still being told—is still current—at this time. A historical background will be given for each entry in the book, but each entry will appear only in the century of its latest appearance.

It would have been a lot easier to list each item according to the century of its earliest known appearance, not in the century when it last appeared. But by looking at what is or isn't current from century to century, we can see what did or didn't last across generations and how some lasting traditions have been modified, or reinterpreted, in order to be maintained. In this way, we can challenge the notion that traditional fairies did not cross the Atlantic to the New World; we can watch them morph into modern space aliens, displacing the evil water sprite Jenny Greenteeth as underwater inhabitants of the lake, and doing so alongside the infamous round goby—an invasive fish species currently giving human lake dwellers "The Galloping Goby Blues."

There is no best, or one, way to conduct professional folkloristic research, depending on what the researcher wants to know. But there are wrong ways to collect, wrong ways to interview, and wrong ways to both classify and interpret folklore. These activities are "wrong," not because naivete about folklore is ill intentioned but because lack of professionalism in ethnographic context too easily results in mis- and disinformation, and sometimes in social and academic dysfunction. The conduct of trained folkloristic inquiry, developed over more than a century, is designed to limit naive adventurism and avoid its negative consequences. In this volume, I have applied the theories, methods, and techniques of my discipline. I have used history as an essential context for memorializing and understanding the people of Lake Erie, listening for their voices from the seventeenth century onward. It is hoped, as you turn these pages, that you too will hear them calling, over time and across space.

PART ONE

FOLKLORE IN THE SEVENTEENTH AND EIGHTEENTH CENTURIES

Figure 1.1. *Comet Neowise* by Joël Kuiper via Flickr. (CC BY 2.0)

ORIGIN OF THE NAME ERIE IN MYTH AND HISTORY

Before the arrival of Europeans, the greater part of Lake Erie's southern shore was occupied by a Native American clan called the Erielhonan (pronounced *Erie-el-honan*). Their origin is unknown, but they belonged to the League of Iroquois Nations and apparently spoke an Iroquois language influenced by Wyandot. The Erie in Erielhonan means "long tail," linking the Erielhonan clan with a long-tailed comet, believed to be a white panther that streaked down from the night sky and made the lake its underwater home (see "Long Tail: The Underwater Panther of Lake Erie," this volume).

The French were the first Europeans to make contact with the Erielhonan people. Struggling with the local language, the French took the "long tail" description to mean some sort of cat. But they misunderstood its reference to a specific wildcat: the white, long-tailed panther-comet of Erielhonan mythology. Consequently, the French translated the lake's name to *Lac du Chat* (Cat Lake).

Starting out from Canada on the St. Lawrence River, French explorers extended the borders of New France to include an enormous portion of North America, their armies clashing with Iroquois resistance all along the way. The French defeated the Iroquois at Lake Champlain and would eventually lay claim to a vast territory that reached from Hudson Bay in the north to the mouth of the Mississippi River in the south and from the Canadian east coast to the foothills of the Rocky Mountains.

But European expansion did not always translate into control of internal Iroquois politics. In the mid-1600s, the League of Iroquois Nations turned against, and conquered, the smaller Erielhonan clan. By 1654–56, the Seneca had fully absorbed the Erielhonan, whom they called the Long Tail people, or Erie for short (Hamell 1998: 273). Since the Erielhonan clan was assimilated into the Seneca, the name Erielhonan, and even the name Erie, fell out of use for the people. But Erie remained the name of the lake.

By the time English-speaking settlers arrived at the lakeshore, all that remained of the Erielhonan was their memory. The old French name, *Lac du Chat*, had disappeared along with the French. But to this day, the lake is still called Erie, or "Long Tail," the same name once used for the clan that saw the long-tailed panther fall from the sky to make the lake his home.

Reference

Hamell, George R. 1998. "Long Tail: The Panther in Huron-Wyandot and Seneca Myth, Ritual and Material Culture." In *Icons of Power: Feline Symbolism in the Americas*, edited by Nicholas J. Saunders, 258–91. London: Routledge.

Figure 2.1. *Wild Puma Panther*, US Fish and Wildlife Service. (Public Domain)

LONG TAIL

The Underwater Panther of Lake Erie

anthers have lived in North America for roughly one hundred thousand years. They are members of the big cat family native to Asia, Af-
rica, and the Americas. The name *panther* does not refer to a distinct
species of animal but to any long-tailed feline of the big cat family, including
leopards, jaguars, cougars, mountain lions, and pumas. Panthers were once
plentiful in the Great Lakes area, but white panthers are rare everywhere on
earth. They share the same natural history as other long-tailed cats but differ
in their color and in their "supernatural" history on Lake Erie.

It seems that the long tails of awesome white panthers and awesome
white comets were fused in ancient Native American imagination. That is, in
Iroquois tradition, a mythical white panther, the clan that shared his habitat,
and the lake he made his home were all called Erie, meaning "long tail." (See
"Origin of the Name Erie in History and Mythology," this volume.)

According to historian George Hamell (1998: 264), the name referred
specifically to a white, mythological "panther/comet man-being" recognized
by different northern tribes who shared some of the same mythological beings, or "grandfathers, sleek of body and long of tail" (1998: 258). Some of
these were underwater dwellers, including the Iroquois panther/comet being, who—like many natives of the supernatural realm—arrived by falling
from the sky.

It was said that one winter night, Long Tail (Erie) the panther/comet
dropped like a thundering white stone through the ice, entering the lake
through the fissure he created, to become "chief resident" among other
mythological beasts that dwelled beneath the surface. According to Barbeau,
Long Tail's specific abode was in "Lake Erie, which reputedly takes its name
from its chief resident" (quoted in Hamell 1998: 264).

In the myth cycles of the Iroquois nations, phenomena like panthers,
serpents, comets, and eagles were conflated, or swept together, into one

11

Figure 2.2. *Canoe, Underwater Panther "Michipeshu," and Two Giant Serpents "Chignebikoogs"* on Agawa Rock, Lake Superior Provincial Park, Ontario, Canada. Photo by D. Gordon E. Robertson. (CC BY-SA 3.0)

fantastic long-tailed being. It seems to be a pattern, in almost all mythologies, to combine into one being a number of different biological species that never combine in the natural world, thereby signifying creatures that stand above the laws of nature, in the *super*natural world.

The Iroquois peoples in general, and specifically the Wyandot-related Erielhonan clan, believed in a supernatural, long-tailed being with "the head, breast and shoulders of a panther, the wings and claws of an eagle, and the body of a serpent" (Hamell 1998: 265). Hamell also quotes a description by Luckhurst and Thwaits, who suggest that on a long-forgotten winter's night, a meteorite crashed through the ice on Lake Erie, inspiring the notion that mythological beings like the panther/eagle/serpent/comet arrived from the sky, all of them fearsome to behold as they entered the lake, where "flames play over the entire lengths of their bodies and their mouths and eyes emit fire and balls of light. Their homes are at the bottom of great lakes, whose waters boil and hiss as they make their fiery nighttime entrances" (1998: 265). Along with such Euro-American speculation, some

Native tales of the underwater panther were eventually written down and, in that way, preserved.

Tales of Erie, the Underwater Panther

Hamell suggests that Lake Erie's Long Tail stories fall into a category of "charms derived from monsters" (1998: 266). In such tales, the charm resides in a small body part taken from the monster or in a small portion of his congealed blood; white items found in nature, even a white stone or piece of white flint, were closely associated with the white panther. Such charms were believed to bring good fortune in courtship, hunting, and warfare.

In one Wyandot tale, the sacrifice of a maiden was required to secure the charm. As the story goes, a Wyandot clan discovered the panther living in the lake. When powerful rituals overcame the beast, it agreed to provide a charm in exchange for a maiden to be left on the shore at rising tide. This was done, and when the water receded, she had disappeared. As promised, the panther then provided a blood charm and declared an annual holiday to memorialize the event (Hamell 1998: 266).

A tale called "White Panther," printed in 1870, refers to a sulfurous pool that emptied into the Huron River, not far from its confluence with Lake Erie. In this tale, a party of Wyandot from the Prairie Turtle clan threw valuables into the pool to see what would surface. After the emergence of some ordinary animals, the panther appeared just long enough to be shot with a red willow arrow. Blood was collected in a small pan, after which the beast submerged and headed downriver, "presumably to Lake Erie, his namesake" (Clark, quoted in Hamell 1998: 266–67).

The Underwater Panther and the Europeans

In Native American tradition, coats, leggings, robes, and pouches made of panther hide and other animal skins were thought to transfer powerful attributes from the animal to the wearer, usually a youthful hunter-warrior. Carved images, or effigies, of the panther were evidently potent as well. Nicholas J. Saunders notes that carved images "on smoking pipes and medicine pouches among the Seneca, for example, functioned as guardian spirits, protecting their owners from war and disease, which were at their height following European arrival" (1998: 35). This suggests that panther effigies were at the height of production in the seventeenth century, in response to the first confrontation with Europeans. It may be that European demand for such objects actually created the market or else stimulated a market that already existed. But either way, the symbolic meanings and qualities of the Native American panther would not fully survive the impact of European domination.

In the mid-1600s, the original panther clan, the Long Tail people, or Erielhonan, were defeated by the Iroquois and absorbed mainly into the Seneca. Erie is the short form of Erielhonan, used by the Seneca for the panther clan and also for the lake inhabited by the underwater panther. The Seneca clan clearly adopted Erie panther myths and rituals when the Erielhonan people assimilated into their midst. But by the 1700s, European colonists condemned panther traditions as "witchcraft" and considered the panther brotherhood devil worshippers, since two women were killed following negotiations for an alliance with the Seneca, after which "wholesale persecution was undertaken" (Rose 2001: 393). Carrying any panther paraphernalia was made punishable by death, and cult practices were extinguished.

Cultural Dominance: The Iroquois Panther Becomes a European Lion

According to Saunders, "Pre-contact mythic realities and their symbolic expression were reworked in the light of pressure from competing European imperial powers" (1998: 35). This helps explain the transformation of new-world *panther* tales into old-world variants of European *lion* tales, a prime example of dominant colonial influence. Transformation of the white panther into a white lion was generalized to all peoples of the Great Lakes region (Hamell 1998: 283). We can see this transition expressed in Native art forms and tales, as in a narrative of 1915, in which the mythical white lion howls in pain and extends his thorn-pierced paw to the hunter. The hunter then secures the charm by removing the painful object, a full eclipse of the Native American panther tradition by a classic European narrative known as *Androcles and the Lion*.

Hamell points out that in the spring of 1679, one of the first ships on Lake Erie was a sailing vessel, or bark, built by a French explorer (see "Ghost Ships of Lake Erie," this volume). Launched that summer, the French bark sailed across Lake Erie for ports on Lakes Michigan and Huron, only to disappear beneath the surface on its return voyage. The bark was named *The Griffin* (*L' Griffon*), and its mast was carved with an effigy of a griffin: a composite European mythical beast, its head and wings being those of an eagle and its body that of a lion. "What a cultural and historical coincidence," Hamell wrote, that a mythical European beast should grace the first bark to sail on Lake Erie, a lake that takes its name from a mythical Iroquois beast—a name used for the lakeshore clan, for the lake itself, and for the white, long-tailed panther/eagle/serpent/comet being that lived beneath its surface.

References

Hamell, George R. 1998. "Long Tail: The Panther in Huron-Wyandot and Seneca Myth, Ritual and Material Culture." In *Icons of Power: Feline Symbolism in the Americas*, edited by Nicholas J. Saunders, 258–91. London: Routledge.

Rose, Carol. 2001. *An Encyclopedia of Folklore, Legend and Myth*. New York: W. W. Norton.

Saunders, Nicholas J. 1998. "Architecture of Symbolism: The Feline Image." In *Icons of Power: Feline Symbolism in the Americas*, edited by Nicholas J. Saunders, 12–52. London: Routledge.

Figure 3.1. *Witch Holding Plant and Fan, Occult Symbols on Apron.* Woodcut, ca. 1700–1720. (Public Domain)

THE OHIO COUNTRY WITCH-WIFE

John Greenleaf Whittier is considered the greatest Quaker poet of the nineteenth century, and as noted by his biographer, some of his works were inspired by folk traditions heard in childhood: "While he was growing up Whittier heard much folklore from his own family, which was a particularly good source of folk narratives" (Whittier [1847] 1993: 2). But Whittier was born in New England in 1807, early enough in the nineteenth century that some legends he heard in childhood belonged more clearly to the 1700s. The tale of the Ohio country witch-wife appears to be one of them.

The Salem witch trials of New England had taken place in the 1690s, and while belief in witchcraft persisted well into the 1700s, it did so at a far less potent, nonlethal level, as we see in the tale of the Ohio country witch-wife. In addition, a number of obsolete terms unique to the seventeenth and eighteenth centuries also help date the narrative to the 1700s. The phrase *the Ohio country*, for example, was a pre–Revolutionary War term used only in the middle to late 1700s, referring to what was then the nation's western frontier, a region west of Pennsylvania and north of the Ohio River, extending to Lake Erie's shore. Similarly, *wind-broken* was a seventeenth-century term for breathing problems that afflicted horses, and in the same century, a "spavined" horse was one whose hocks (the spavins) had failed, rendering it lame, or useless. The tale seems to have entered the nineteenth century in Whittier's one literary rewrite, with no perceptible life after that.

By 1831, Whittier had published a number of his ancestral traditions in "prose and verse," and in 1847, he added items of "supernaturalism," including witchcraft. But Whittier himself discusses witchcraft as something belonging to an earlier generation, not his own. In his introduction to *Supernaturalism of New England*, he cautions against "self-congratulations" in his own age of "light and progress," lest future generations judge the nineteenth century "absurd and inhuman, as contrary to pure reason and Christianity, as we now consider the witchcraft and religious intolerance of our ancestors"

([1847] 1993: viii). Whittier seems to have consciously documented ancestral traditions, including those on witchcraft, hoping to preserve them as artifacts of an earlier age. If so, he was far from alone in his effort.

Intense interest in collecting and documenting folklore was typical of the nineteenth century. During the Industrial Revolution, it was widely believed that "folklore" was a product of the illiterate countryside and would vanish as large, rural populations migrated to cosmopolitan cities and literate factory centers. Although folklore did not vanish in the city as predicted, it is likely that some preindustrial traditions were indeed giving way to newly emerging traditions, the better to meet the new anxieties, aspirations, and animosities of a rapidly industrializing nation. Like that of many others in his day, Whittier's purpose may well have been to preserve traditions he thought had already vanished or were about to.

His untitled narrative below, which I have called "The Ohio Country Witch-Wife," is a case in point. It was told to Whittier during his childhood by an elderly relative—an old farmer—as Whittier himself confirms ([1847] 1993: 52), "When I was a boy I occasionally met at the house of a relative . . . an old farmer . . . when the cider mug got the better of his taciturnity, he would amuse me with interesting details of his early experiences in 'the Ohio country.'"

What follows is one of the old farmer's Ohio country tales. Although it is not about Lake Erie itself, it gives us a geographically focused overview of witch-related beliefs on the Ohio frontier in the eighteenth century. In addition, the narrative points to how the tale functioned socially, from the New England coast to Erie's shore. It appears below, abridged and edited for this volume, as told to young Whittier by the old New England farmer (Whittier [1847] 1993: 52–55).

The Ohio Country Witch-Wife

While a very young man, a native New Englander worked his way west and found himself in one of the old French settlements in Ohio. There, he found work on a farm owned by a widow. Despite some hints and warnings from the neighbors, all was cozy and compatible, and the mistress soon became his wife. The servant was legally promoted to head of household, and for a while things went well, but with the long winter months came a devastating change.

An evil and mysterious influence seemed at work in his affairs. Anything he did with his wife's permission, or at her suggestion, succeeded. Anything he did on his own failed. If he bought a horse, it was sure to prove spavined or wind-broken. His cows either refused to give down their milk or, giving it, perversely kicked it over. A fine sow, which had cost him dearly, repaid him by devouring her own children. By degrees, a dark thought forced its way into his mind. At last, he came to the melancholy conclusion that his wife was a witch!

One cold November morning, he was able to escape, and after a long, hard journey, he reached home. Although he was closemouthed about his life in Ohio, no one thought to pry. He soon married one of his schoolmates, and they made a comfortable home. But his evil star lingered above the horizon. One summer evening, when he returned from the hayfield, who should meet him but his witch-wife from Ohio! She came riding up the street on her old white horse, and behind her a pillion—an empty seat—attached to her saddle. She informed him that she had come all the way from Ohio to take him back again.

It was in vain that his other wife raised her shrillest remonstrations, mingled with expressions of vehement indignation at the revelation of her husband's real position. But the witch-wife prevailed; go he must, and speedily. Convinced of his witch-wife's supernatural power to compel obedience, and perhaps dreading the temper of his New England wife even more, he bade goodbye to the latter in a perfect hurricane of reproaches and mounted the white horse with his old wife on the pillion behind him.

Two or three years had passed with no tidings of the unfortunate husband when once again he appeared in his native village. He was not disposed to be very communicative, but for one thing at least, he seemed willing to express his gratitude. His Ohio wife, having no spell against intermittent fever, had paid the debt of nature and left him free. In view of this, his surviving wife, after manifesting a due degree of resentment, consented to take him back to her bed and board, and I could never learn that she had cause to regret her clemency.

In the 1950s, folklorist William R. Bascom (1954) noted that tales do not exist in a vacuum; they persist because they perform important functions for the communities that hold them in tradition. This tale, apparently one of witchcraft, might also be read (or heard) as the story of a young farmer who navigated the turbulent seas of bigamy—in this case, perhaps dreading the natural wife more than the witch-wife—possibly adding to its function as entertainment. It also seems to instruct the young, cautioning against leaving home, in accordance with well-known nuggets of folk wisdom: the grass may have seemed greener in "the Ohio country," but in the end, happiness lay in the young man's own backyard. In addition, it tells us that life on the Ohio frontier could be harsh enough to suggest uncanny influence. We can see how, in the eighteenth century, tales could still point to witchcraft as a plausible explanation for good or bad fortune, something apparently true on both the Canadian and the American sides of Lake Erie (see "Buried

Treasure and Witchcraft: Legends of Lake Erie's Canadian Loyalists," this volume). Finally, the tale clearly functioned as a social storytelling event, riveting the imagination of its audience. Some may find that it still does, more than two hundred years since a young boy heard it from an old New England farmer.

References

Bascom, William R. 1954. "Four Functions of Folklore." *Journal of American Folklore* 67:333–49.

Whittier, John Greenleaf. (1847) 1993. *Supernaturalism of New England*. With a new introduction by W. K. McNeil. Reprint, Baltimore: Genealogical Publishing. Reprinted for Clearfield.

Figure 4.1. *Tory Refugees on the Way to Canada* by Howard Pyle. *Harpers Monthly Magazine*, December 1901. (Public Domain)

BURIED TREASURE AND WITCHCRAFT
Legends of Lake Erie's Canadian Loyalists

David Ramsay (ca. 1740–1810) was a colonial adventurer of Scottish descent, loyal to Great Britain in Revolutionary times. He was therefore known as a Tory, or a loyalist. He settled in Canada and became the subject of legends told on the north shore of Lake Erie, in western Ontario. Ramsay has two conflicting story cycles: a flattering cycle of tales told by fellow loyalists and a number of accounts that more clearly reflect his own declaration of 1772, when he turned himself in to British authorities for crimes committed in Port Stanley and Long Point, on Lake Erie's northern shore. At the turn of the twentieth century, a member of the Ottawa Royal Society of Canada collected tales of eighteenth-century loyalists, including Ramsay (Coyne 1919). Tales of Ramsay, and later, of the infamous "Doctor" Troyer, are laced with folk beliefs of their own times.

Ramsay entered oral tradition with his testimony at Port Stanley, where he said he was taken captive by "thieving Indians" for refusing to provide them with whiskey and goods. Ramsay said he broke free of his bonds, killing a man and two women, scalping them, and kidnapping two children before he got away. According to Ramsay, a month later he was held captive by tribe members who demanded the return of the kidnapped children, but he again broke free, killing and scalping four adults and an infant.

In all cases Ramsay claimed self-defense, but he failed to convince Sir William Johnson, British superintendent for Indian Affairs. He was sent to Montreal and held on charges of inexcusable murder and wanton cruelty. British relationships with Native Americans were damaged by his actions, but tribe members were eventually compensated, and when the prosecution could not find witnesses, Ramsay was released. After that, it is said he befriended, and at times even defended, local tribes. Whether he did or not, he disappears from local history in 1810, at which time he would have been about seventy. But his legends, and those of the infamous Doctor Troyer, live on in written form.

Ramsay and Doctor Troyer Legends

Variants of Ramsay's story describe him as a fur trader who around 1790 sneaked a boat, filled with gold, past a large number of hostile Native Americans. It is said that he buried the treasure at Long Point, and mindful that Native tribes and Europeans both believed in the ghostly power of black dogs (see "The Black Dog of Lake Erie," this volume), he killed a black dog and buried the gold beneath the carcass. But according to legend, he never returned to retrieve the treasure.

At this point, the Ramsay legend is joined to that of "Doctor" John Troyer (1753–1842), the first white settler in Walsingham, near Long Point. Troyer was noteworthy as a farmer, a businessman, an unlicensed physician, and an artful practitioner of witchcraft.

Simpson McCall, aged eighty-five in 1893, retold a legend of Troyer's 1817 attempt to retrieve Ramsay's buried treasure. McCall, who had grown up as a neighbor of the Troyer family, told two different Troyer legends. The first paragraph below was recorded by James Coyne (1919: 111–12) in McCall's own words:

> Dr. Troyer believed in magic, and had a mineral rod by which he divined where gold was buried. . . . About 1817 Dr. Troyer and his son Michael, having found out by his divining rod where the [Ramsay] treasure was, went out towards evening to dig it up.

Coyne (1919: 111–12) repeated the remainder of McCall's story from memory:

> Having found the spot, they withdrew to the boat and waited until midnight, when they proceeded to the place, the Doctor leading the way with a lighted candle in one hand and an open Bible in the other, Michael following with pick and spade. Precisely at midnight they heard the clink of the spade on the iron chest, and Michael endeavored to pry open the lid, when the frightful apparition [of a black dog] rose up, expanding to an enormous size, and the daring intruders, brave as they had thought themselves, dropping book, candle and digging implements, fled to the boat, leaped in, and rowed with all their might for home.

Historically, Troyer was known to believe that he was persecuted by witches, some of whom he identified among his neighbors. But the consequences of these accusations did not fall on those he accused, as they might have in the 1600s. Times had clearly changed, since we learn that his strong-minded neighbor, Widow McMichael, not only found these claims amusing but also "made grimaces at the poor old doctor from some recesses or clump of bushes, just for the pleasure it gave her to tease and torment him" (Coyne 1919: 121).

Nevertheless, Troyer was convinced he was periodically kidnapped by witches who transformed him into animals, forced him to dance with them, and otherwise harassed him. His neighbors thought of him as eccentric but also believed he possessed "a thorough knowledge of witches, their ways and doings, and the art of expelling them"; Troyer's methods of expulsion included placing horseshoes over the door of his house. According to his former neighbor, Simpson McCall, "At the foot of his bed a huge trap was bolted to the floor where it was set every night to catch witches. The jaws were about three feet long, and when shut were about two and a half feet high. There are people in Port Rowan today who have a distinct remembrance of having seen this witch trap in Dr. Troyer's bedroom" (Coyne 1919: 122, 121).

As McCall informed his interviewer, Troyer owned witchcraft devices, including a magic stone: "Doctor Troyer had a stone, which he covered with a hat, and when one of the Pick girls put her head under the hat, she could see everything that was hidden—stolen money and goods, etc. Many things were recovered in this way, amongst others, some things stolen from my Uncle, Ephraim C. Mitchell" (Coyne 1919: 112).

Regardless of how the Pick girl was magically able to locate stolen goods, Troyer's stone would be put to use as late as 1829, as Coyne wrote (1919: 123): "Troyer's fame extended to the remotest parts of Lake Erie and northward to Lake St. Clair. It reached the . . . ill-fated Baldoon Settlement, where strange things were happening in 1829. . . . [For instance,] John McDonald's house stood on the banks of the Chenail Escarte. In or about November . . . stones and bullets crashed through his windows."

Fires also seemed to erupt spontaneously inside John McDonald's house, and some narratives note that a black dog was seen lurking on the premises. In addition, some of McDonald's outbuildings were burned down in January, and the family had to move to his father's house. But the inexplicable events, including being targeted by magic bullets, followed McDonald to his new location. For example, no matter how thoroughly the spent bullets were collected and bagged, carried off, or drowned, the very same bullets would come crashing back through the windows of his father's home.

Finally, when all the local ministers failed to help, Troyer was summoned. He traveled for three days, over one hundred miles, to perform the exorcism. The visit was successful, but not everyone gave Troyer credit for the outcome. "According to one version, it was Troyer's daughter, a sallow fragile girl of fifteen . . . who possessed the gift of divination. She used a stone, which, she said, was 'by some called a moonstone'" (Coyne 1919: 124). Before employing the "moonstone," she had already divined trouble between Mc-Donald and a neighbor to whom he had refused to sell land. Using the stone, Troyer's daughter accurately described both the neighbor and the neighbor's long, low-slung log house, much to the astonishment of all present. After retreating to recover from this effort, she returned and informed McDonald that the same conjuring neighbor had two hours earlier burned an additional property of his, and an investigation showed that the property had indeed burned down. As the tale goes, the Troyer girl also revealed a way to defeat the evil that afflicted McDonald and his real estate holdings:

> "Have you ever seen a gray goose in your flock?" she asked. He had; he had shot it with a leaden ball, and the fowl had escaped. She assured him "no bullet of lead would ever harm a feather of that bird." The bird was merely a shape assumed by his enemy. He must use a silver bullet, and if he hit the mark his enemy would be wounded in a corresponding part of the body. . . . Next morning the goose reappeared with the flock in the river. He fired, and the bird, "giving a weird cry like a human being in distress," fluttered into the reeds with a broken wing. Rushing to the low log house, he found "the woman who had injured him, with her broken arm resting in a chair, and her withered lips uttering half-ejaculated curses." From that moment the witchcraft ceased. The witch lived for some time, but continually suffered from racking pains throughout her whole body. (Coyne 1919: 125)

As McCall's interviewer wrote, "In the early days of settlement on Lake Erie no names were more widely known than those of David Ramsay and 'Doctor' Troyer," both loyalist settlers living at or near Long Point (Coyne 1919: 113). The Ramsay legends depict either an adventurous folk hero or a nefarious criminal, depending on the source. The Troyer legends depict an aging eccentric with a white, flowing beard—as McCall put it, a man who not only knew his way around witches but understood "also the use of the divining rod, with which he could not only find water, but could also tell how far below the surface of the earth precious metals were concealed, but [he] was never fortunate enough to discover any in the neighborhood of Long Point" (Coyne 1919:122).

Regarding the witchcraft narratives, Coyne also observed: "The legendary factors are old enough, to be sure. The witch doctor, the divining rod, the buried gold, the black dog, the exorcism with book and candle, the ghostly guardian of the treasure, the magic stone, the 'thinking cap'—these are some of the commonplaces of folklore. That Mr. McCall was firmly convinced of the truth of his story was manifest" (Coyne 1919:122).

Whether historical, fanciful, or some combination of the two, McCall's narratives recall motifs in folk literature held on the shores of colonial Lake

Erie that also appear in Stith Thompson's classic *Motif-Index of Folk Literature* (1956–58), as seen below:

Legend of Ramsay's Buried Treasure

V67.3	Treasure buried with dead [animal]
F401.3.3	Spirit as black dog

Legend of Troyer's Magic Possessions

D1385.9	Magic horseshoe keeps off witch
D1067.1	Magic hat/cap
D133.1	Object [stone] gives magic sight
D1314.2	Divining rod locates hidden treasure [water/gold]

Legend of Troyer's Treasure Hunt

D.1314.2	Divining rod locates hidden treasure
E434.9	Candle light as protection against ghost
E443.8	Ghost laid by Bible
F401.3.3	Spirit as black dog

Legend of Witchcraft against McDonald

G260ff	Evil deeds of witch
G229.4.2	Witch catches, sends back bullets
*D1271	Magic fire
D133.1	Object [moonstone] gives magic sight
G211ff	Witch in animal form [gray goose]
D1385.4	Silver bullet protects against witch
G270ff	Witch overcome or escaped

Although Troyer purportedly located Ramsay's buried treasure, it was never retrieved. Nonetheless, the combined Ramsay-Troyer legends unearth, for us, a priceless treasure of folk beliefs and magical practices held among early loyalists on Lake Erie's Canadian shore.

References

Coyne, James H. 1919. "David Ramsay and Long Point in Legend and History." In *Transactions of the Royal Society of Canada*, series 3, 13:111–26. Read aloud at May meeting 1919. Ottawa: Royal Society of Canada. http://archive.org/stream/davidramsaylong poocoyn/davidramsaylongpoocoyn_djvu.txt.

Thompson, Stith. 1956–58. *The Motif-Index of Folk-Literature*. 6 vols. Bloomington: Indiana University Press.

.

PART TWO

FOLKLORE IN THE NINETEENTH CENTURY

Figure 5.1. *Jenny Greenteeth*, drawing by author, Judith S. Neulander.

JENNY GREENTEETH
The Storm Hag of Lake Erie

Jenny Greenteeth, sometimes called Jinny, made her way to the Great Lakes from the Lancashire region of northeast England, an area dotted with stagnant ponds covered by a green aquatic plant called *Lemna minor*, or duckweed (Vickery 1983: 247). In summer, the growth was so thick, the water's surface could easily be mistaken for solid land, inviting accidental drownings, especially of children at play. Descriptions of Jenny as a malicious fairy, or water sprite, who lured children to watery graves served the region as a cautionary tale, saving lives by discouraging children from playing in these terribly dangerous places (Briggs 1976: 242).

Tales of Jenny Greenteeth vary greatly, but all retain certain core motifs—the smallest elements of a tale that are striking or unusual, as defined by Stith Thompson, grand old man of folktale classification (1977: 91, 96, 114). Using Thompson's striking-or-unusual definition, we can easily see that "mother" is not a motif but "cruel stepmother" is. Similarly, shared social functions and the use of names associated with Jenny, along with motifs of malevolent water spirits, especially those with green teeth, identify different tales as variants of the Jenny Greenteeth tradition and not some other.

Motifs from Thompson's *Motif-Index of Folk-Literature* (1956–58) include F420.1.4.8 (Water-spirits with green teeth) and F420.5.2 (Malevolent water-spirits).

Holding on to these motifs and the name Jenny (sometimes Jinny) Greenteeth, American mariners adopted the evil water spirit tradition to account for sudden storms and subsequent shipwrecks on Lake Erie, in which whole ships and crews frequently vanished without a trace. The Lake Erie variant recasts Jenny as a "storm hag," a malevolent spirit who conjures up violent storms that send her victims to the sandy lake bottom. She was said to live close to Presque Isle, and just before striking, she was heard singing to her prey:

Come to the water, love
Dance beneath the waves,
Where dwell the bones of sailor lads
Inside my saffron caves

Accounts of Jenny as the Lake Erie Storm Hag prevailed through the nineteenth century but did not persist into the twentieth. One author, not a trained folklorist, gives an example of a nineteenth-century storm hag account, followed by a twentieth-century ghost ship legend that he mistakes for a storm hag, or Jenny Greenteeth, variant. Apparently unaware of motif distinctions between the two, he misses the significance of this key difference, classifying the twentieth-century tale incorrectly and misinterpreting the spirit and mentality of the people and the age in which each tradition was held—in effect, falsifying the raw data of folklore. Nevertheless, his printing of the two tales is useful because it allows us to compare them from a trained folkloristic point of view and to reach a more accurate conclusion. The "Lake Erie Storm Hag" variant of "Jenny Greenteeth" follows:

> Local history has it that on a fall evening in 1782 an owler [smuggler] ship was caught in a bad storm on the lake and desperately tried to make it back to port at Presque Isle. It was tossed to and fro violently for more than an hour, and when it was in sight of land the storm abruptly stopped. The clouds dissipated and the moonlight from the full moon illuminated the water, and the sailors could see they were less than a mile from the northern edge of the Peninsula and home.
>
> Without warning, the water next to the boat foamed, and the Storm Hag burst from the surface. She spewed venom and attacked the crew, unleashing her fury upon them. Within seconds, the ship and its crew were taken beneath the waves to their doom. Witnesses on shore apparently heard the screams of the sailors echoing across the lake just before the vessel disappeared.
>
> To this day, some of those who sail the lake near Presque Isle claim to hear phantom screams of the victims who were taken long ago. (Swope 2011: 36)

By crediting no source, Swope becomes the narrator and subsequently gives this variant as local "history," but to a folklorist, it is instead a local *legend*: a tale always told as a true story, about real persons, places, times, or things, containing an ironic or supernatural twist, without any historical basis whatsoever (Brunvand 1981: xi–xiv). Legends are fictions; they are not history. It is extremely important to classify traditions correctly in order to study them productively. The truth-value or "historicity" of a confirmed legend is of no concern to a folklorist, who seeks the greater truths embedded in legends. That is, legends are extremely valuable as unique, accurate, and unselfconscious reflections of major concerns in the societies in which they circulate (Brunvand 1981: xii). As such, they are fictions that always give us perfectly accurate access to the spirit and mentality of the people and the age in which they were told.

The storm hag variant of the Jenny Greenteeth tradition informs us that in the nineteenth century, malevolent water sprites from the fairy lore of the British Isles were being held accountable for a panoply of mysterious maritime tragedies on Lake Erie. Moreover, "The Lake Erie Storm Hag" ends with a motif from Thompson's *Motif-Index* that is native to England, Scotland, and the English-speaking United States, reflecting Jenny's geographical origins: E402.1.1.3 (Ghost cries and screams).

The amateur who printed this variant should be credited for telling us that the term *owler* belongs to a nineteenth-century body of slang, used for the word *smuggler*. That seems to indicate he reprinted a narrative from the nineteenth century, when *owler* was still used. But he gives no information on his source, so we can't tell whether it is a nineteenth-century variant or his own twenty-first century variant, to which he added the word *owler* to make it *seem like* a nineteenth-century variant. Similarly, his phrase "local history holds" is a variant of a traditional folkloric formula—"this is a true story"—used in folk narratives (but not by professional folklorists) to frame fiction as truth (or as "history"). Because he leaves out his source, we can't tell if he is faithfully repeating a nineteenth-century folk narrative or modifying the story to meet his own twenty-first century literary goals. Consequently, his work leaves us unable to know which generation this narrative actually belongs to, rendering it unreliable as either a nineteenth-century or a twenty-first century narrative. Although innocent, this sort of dilettantism blocks, rather than gives access to, the people and the age responsible for the variant, so it remains entertaining but not useful for valid and reliable analysis.

Only two things remain certain and stable in the storm hag variant, as he gives it. First, the storm hag is a malevolent water spirit, and second, *if* the word *owler* was used by his source, "The Lake Erie Storm Hag" tale retained the same social function as the Lancashire "Jenny Greenteeth" tale: to scare an intended audience away from a dangerous activity in a specific place.

But his twenty-first century *Clevco* narrative, which he gives as a storm hag variant, is no such thing. It makes no mention whatsoever of Jenny Greenteeth or of the storm hag. Instead, it reveals the entirely different mentality of an entirely different generation in an entirely different age. The full narrative contains additional information not seen here, including the discovery of two bodies from the sunken *Clevco*. But the storm hag herself is consistently absent from all *Clevco* narratives—an absence that imparts distinct information about the people and the age to which the *Clevco* tale belongs. That tale follows:

> On December 1942 the oil tanker *Clevco* was being escorted with towline by the tugboat *Admiral*. They had left port at Toledo and were traveling east when just off the coast of Cleveland something strange happened. At 4am the *Clevco* radioed that the *Admiral* had disappeared without incident. The crew noted that the towline was no longer attached to the tugboat but it was at a sharp angle to the waves, as if the tugboat had somehow sunk to the bottom of the lake without a sound.
>
> The *Clevco* immediately stopped and radioed the Coast Guard and two cutters and a few motorboats were dispatched to the coordinates. However, arriving on the scene they found nothing.
>
> Both ships had vanished. (Swope 2011: 36–37)

We can see how the two defining motifs that actually identify a tale as a variant of Jenny Greenteeth (*water spirits with green teeth; malevolent water spirits*) are entirely absent from the *Clevco* narrative, confirming that the tale belongs to a completely different tale type and has nothing whatsoever to do with Jenny Greenteeth or her storm hag variant. Instead of confirming Jenny's, or the storm hag's, survival into the twentieth century, the *Clevco* legend reflects just the opposite.

The full *Clevco* tradition includes a haunting (see "Ghost Ships of Lake Erie," this volume), confirming a significant change in twentieth-century folk belief that actually banished the likes of Jenny and the storm hag from Lake Erie narratives. Instead, the *Clevco* itself enters the afterlife, persisting in tradition as a ghost ship, reflecting completely different anxieties and performing completely different social functions than the older storm hag tales.

According to historian Owen Davies (2007: 241), by the 1900s belief in ghosts had become more socially acceptable than belief in fairyland, fairy spirits, and fairy lore. Other folklore scholars have suggested that old-fashioned fairies, newly eclipsed by ghosts, would persist by morphing into modern space aliens, who despite their timely "high-tech" status still share a suspiciously large number of "low-tech" fairy motifs from the British Isles. In that case, we should expect that sky-based space aliens—having evicted Jenny Greenteeth from her "saffron caves"—would have moved in on her underwater territory. And upon investigation, we see that's exactly what happened (see "UFO Base under Lake Erie," this volume).

No matter how well-meaning they may be, amateur classifications and interpretations of folk traditions are often mis- and disinforming, and even more importantly, there are times when unprofessional fieldwork can have negative social consequences, for both specific individuals and even whole communities. Conversely, folklore specialists are trained to provide accurate classification and interpretation of folk materials and to act with professional integrity in the collection and dissemination of folkloric material.

Accurate classification and interpretation of the storm hag and *Clevco* legends tell us that by the twentieth century, fairy lore was no longer a popular explanation for disasters on Lake Erie. For one thing, the nineteenth century had suffered unusually high death rates brought on by waves of cholera (see "Cholera Cemetery," this volume), by often-lethal working and living conditions in industrializing areas, and, in the United States, by an additionally devastating loss of life to battle and disease in the Civil War. The need for coping strategies, like belief in an afterlife peopled by the spirits of lost loved ones, is reflected in the nineteenth-century rise of spiritualism and of the séances it introduced as a means to contact the deceased.

It may also be that by the twentieth century on Lake Erie, science and technology were explaining and predicting maritime disasters more accurately, helping to prevent them more efficiently than fear of the storm hag could do. In any case, the late nineteenth century shows us a diminishing interest in fairy lore to explain shipwrecks. Instead, it demonstrates that belief in fairies was edged out by belief in ghosts, confirming a heightened preoccupation with life after death. Not surprisingly, narratives of the twentieth-century *Clevco* designate the place where the ship went down as a kind of haunted ballroom (see "Fiddler on the *Clevco*" under "Ghost Ships of Lake Erie," this volume). But if we follow old, traditional fairy motifs into the twentieth and twenty-first centuries, we will find them with us still, recycled in contemporary tales of space aliens—a new variant of malevolent water spirit now in residence under Lake Erie, where the storm hag, Jenny Greenteeth, no longer rules.

References

Briggs, Katharine. 1976. *An Encyclopedia of Fairies.* New York: Pantheon Books.

Brunvand, Jan Harold. 1981. *The Vanishing Hitchhiker: American Urban Legends and Their Meanings.* New York: W. W. Norton.

Davies, Owen. 2007. *The Haunted: A Social History of Ghosts.* Hampshire: Palgrave Macmillan.

Swope, Robin S. 2011. *Eerie Erie: Tales of the Unexplained from Northeast Pennsylvania.* Charleston, SC: History Press.

Thompson, Stith, ed. 1956–58. *The Motif-Index of Folk-Literature.* Vol. 3. Bloomington: Indiana University Press.

———. 1977. *The Folktale.* Vol. 3. Los Angeles: University of California Press.

Vickery, Roy. 1983. "Lemna Minor and Jenny Greenteeth." *Folklore* 94 (2): 247–50.

Figure 6.1. *Battle of Lake Erie* by Henry Powell, US Capitol, Washington, DC. 1873. (Public Domain)

THE BALLAD OF JAMES BIRD

Death and Curse of a Lake Erie Deserter

The nineteenth-century "Ballad of James Bird" follows traditional oral formulas found in English and Scottish ballads, reflecting America's close cultural ties to the British Isles (Child [1882–89] 1969). On both sides of the Atlantic, ballads were the tabloid presses of their day. Lyrics were printed on affordable, one-sided panels called broadsides, some of them illustrated well enough to prompt those unable to read. Broadsides carried texts, poems, political cartoons and satires, and lyrics of popular songs and ballads. The ballads served as bearers of news, farce and scandal, crime, adventure, and romance, much of it written with an eye to moral guidance. For young people, moral guidance was easier to accept when sung as a tale than when preached from the pulpit or imposed by parental authority. "The Ballad of James Bird" is a prime example.

The ballad refers us to the War of 1812, fought in part on Lake Erie, against continuing British interference with American independence and western expansion. In August 1812, the American general William Hull had surrendered the city of Detroit to the British and to their Shawnee ally, Chief Tecumseh. Young volunteers like James Bird responded to the crisis, and Bird subsequently fought in the Battle of Lake Erie, under the command of Commodore Oliver Hazard Perry.

On September 10, 1813, Perry fought one of the most decisive battles of the war, gaining control of the lake for the Americans, allowing them to recover the city of Detroit and defeat Tecumseh's Native American confederation.

But in the same year, the young James Bird was executed for desertion. According to the ballad, he died on the shores of Lake Erie, where he had fought courageously on September 10, beside Commodore Perry. A neighbor of the man who betrayed Bird would later state: "After Perry's victory, Bird was idle for a long time, and seeing no further need of his services in the fleet, he deserted and went to work for a man named Waterman, in Gowanda, New York" (Schultz [1937] 1959: 8).

Waterman apparently owed Bird back wages and lured him to Erie's shore with a promise of payment there. Not suspecting betrayal, Bird traveled to Lake Erie with Waterman and, once there, was handed over to authorities. Waterman pocketed the reward for returning a deserter and left Bird to be shot. Bird's heroism in battle might have reduced his sentence, and the ballad's words "Spare him!" are said to have come from Perry himself, who reportedly rushed on horseback from Buffalo to save Bird's life, arriving just as the first volley was fired, executing the young man.

James Bird had no military or naval aspirations. He was a volunteer willing to step up in time of crisis. But he was certainly aware of breaking the law by deserting; much as he loved his parents and sweetheart, for example, he did not go home, probably aware that authorities were most likely to look for him there.

Yet, despite his desertion, it is significant that Bird is never criminalized or villainized in this ballad. Bird, his parents, and his sweetheart, Mary, are portrayed as entirely sympathetic figures. Bird and Mary are described as the kind of ordinary sweethearts whom many young folks could easily relate to. Therefore, the fate of James Bird was sung not as an outlaw ballad but as moral guidance to military youth who might also be tempted to desert their posts. Not surprisingly, we are told that the ballad was sung not only on Lake Erie but also "throughout the breadth of the United States" (Schultz [1937] 1959: 5).

Traditional ballads aimed at young people almost always begin with a variant of the same formula: "Come all ye young people and hear my tale." Following this tradition, the ballads impart warnings, wisdom, and guidance. This American ballad opens with a variant of the come-and-hear formula, asking "sons of pleasure" (probably meaning carefree youth) to "listen" and similarly asking daughters to "give ear":

The Ballad of James Bird

Sons of pleasure, listen to me
And ye daughters, too, give ear
A sad and mournful story
As e're was told you soon shall hear

Hull, you know, his troupes surrendered,
And defenseless left the west;
When our forces quick assembled,
The invader to resist

Among the troupes that marched to Erie
Were the Kingston Volunteers
Captain Thomas their commander,
To protect our west frontiers

Tender were the scenes of parting,
Mothers wrung their hands and cried;
Maidens wept their loves in secret;
Fathers strove their tears to hide

One sweet kiss he snatched from Mary,
Craved his mother's prayers once more,
Pressed his father's hand and left them
For Lake Erie's distant shore

Mary tried to say farewell, James,
Waved her hand but nothing spoke
Goodbye, Bird, may heaven protect you,
From the rest the parting broke

Soon he came where noble Perry
Had assembled all his fleet;
There the gallant Bird enlisted,
Hoping soon the foe to meet

Where is Bird? The battle rages;
Is he in the strife or no?
Now the cannons roar tremendous;
Dare he meet the furious foe?

Ah: behold and see with Perry,
In the self-same ship he fights;
See his messmates fall around him,
Nothing can his soul affright

But behold: a ball has struck him;
See the crimson current flow
"Leave the deck," exclaims brave Perry;
"No," cries Bird "I will not go

"Here on deck I take my station,
Ne'er will Bird his color fly;
I'll stand by you, gallant captain,
Till we conquer or we die."

So he fought, 'though faint and bleeding,
Till our "stars and stripes" arose,
Victory had crowned our efforts
All triumphant o'er our foes

And, did Bird receive a pension?
Was he to his friends restored?
No; nor never to his bosom
Clasped the maid his heart adored

And there came most dismal tidings
From Lake Erie's distant shore;
Better if poor Bird had perished
Mid the battle's awful roar

"Dearest Parents," says the letter
"This will bring sad news to you;
Do not mourn your first beloved,
Though this brings his last adieu"

"I must suffer for desertion
From the brig Niagara
[possibly pronounced in the vernacular Ni-a-ga-ree]
Read this letter, brothers, sisters,
"the last you'll hear from me."

Sad and gloomy was the morning
Bird was ordered out to die;
Whose is the heart, not dead to pity
But for him will have a sigh?

Lo: he fought so brave at Erie,
Freely bled and nobly dared,
Let his courage plead for mercy,
Let his precious life be spared

See: he kneels upon the coffin
Sure his death can do no good
Spare him! Hark, oh God, they've shot him,
See: his bosom streams with blood

Farewell, Bird, farewell forever.
Friends and home you'll see no more,
But his mangled corpse lies buried
On Lake Erie's distant shore.
(First published in Gleaner *[Wilkes Barre, PA], 1814)*

Figure 6.2. "Battle of Lake Erie" sheet music excerpt from Traditional Texts and Tunes. *Journal of American Folk-lore* 35, no. 138 (October–December 1922): 380. (Public Domain)

These lyrics were collected in 1855 along with a brief musical score from Mary Tannehill of Perrysville, Ohio (Tolman and Eddy 1922: 380).

Like all traditional ballads, this one became popular by doing its job well—in this case, by taking a socially dysfunctional situation and giving it a socially functional message. The message is clear: using James Bird's example, young men were encouraged not to desert under any circumstances, no matter how justified it might seem. And by example, young women were encouraged to speak up and caution their sweethearts (unlike Mary, who "nothing spoke"). Thus, no matter how accurate or inaccurate the storyline may be, the young defector is not the villain of the story, and he would live on through the ballad that bore his name, continuing, in this way, to serve the nation he once fought for.

Bird's treacherous employer also lived on in tradition, but as a villain who suffered the worst fate that can befall any farmer: land made barren through a curse, as noted by Lydia J. Ryall soon after the tragedy: "One singular circumstance remains to be told concerning this tragic affair." Ryall wrote in the 1800s, confirming that the farmer suffered grave consequences in folk imagination: "The land which Bird had assisted in clearing for his treacherous and heartless employer never produced aught of vegetable life, remaining a desert tract of barren soil. The truth of this statement has been amply verified by those who have visited the spot, strangely branded with a curse" (Ryall 2004: 45). Once again, where history is not clear that justice prevailed for Bird, folk tradition reassures us that poetic justice triumphs in the end.

References

Child, Francis James, ed. (1882–89) 1969. *The English and Scottish Popular Ballads*. 5 vols. New York: Dover.

Ryall, Lydia J. 2004. *Sketches and Stories of the Lake Erie Islands*. Perry Centennial ed. 1813–1913. In *Lake Erie Islands: Sketches and Stories from the First Century after the Battle of Lake Erie*, edited by Michael Gora. N.p.: Tafford.

Schultz, Dr. John Richie. (1937) 1959. "The Ballad of James Bird." *Keystone Folklore Quarterly* 4, nos. 3–4 (Autumn/Winter): 3–9.

Tolman, Albert H., and Mary O. Eddy. 1922. "Traditional Texts and Tunes." *Journal of American Folk-lore* 35, no. 138 (October–December): 335–432.

Figure 7.1. *Grain Boat on the Erie Canal* from *America Illustrated*, edited by J. D. Williams. Boston: DeWolfe, Fiske, 1893. (Public Domain)

TALL TALES OF THE ERIE CANAL

The human-made Erie Canal opened in 1825, an engineering marvel that some considered the eighth wonder of the world. The canal stretched 363 miles (584 km) across New York State, from Albany on the Hudson River to Buffalo on Lake Erie. A ten-foot tow path was built along its banks for mules or horses to pull boats from one destination to another, usually led by a lad called a hoggy.

The canal linked the Great Lakes to the Atlantic Ocean, causing the population to surge in western New York State, opening regions farther west to settlement and transforming New York City into the nation's busiest shipping port. The waterway was enlarged between 1832 and 1864. Its importance was diminished first by the New York State Barge Canal and finally by the railroad. Today its value is mostly historical and recreational.

But in its time, the Erie Canal generated a huge body of folk traditions, mostly in work-related vocabulary (e.g., the word *hoggy*), along with many songs and stories. Like the huge size of the canal and its monumental impact on the nation, Erie Canal stories often dealt with events and personalities larger than life. Called tall tales, or sometimes windies, such stories are deliberate, exaggerated fabrications that are "told with a straight face to humorous effect" (Schoemaker 1990: 240). Below are four variants, taken from the collection of Lionel D. Wyld.

The first tale is about the largest fish actually found in Lake Erie, the sturgeon. A natural subject for tall tales, Lake Erie sturgeon can grow to be ten feet long and weigh as much as three hundred pounds. Today they are an endangered species hovering on the lake bottom, but in the 1880s, the spill of huge Lake Erie sturgeon into the canal fed the imagination along with the appetite.

Mighty Sturgeon in the Erie Canal

In the 1870s, near Medina, a blacksmith made a hook of a crowbar, placed it on a length of old tow rope, and baited it with a young pig. A sturgeon grabbed the hook and hauled the boat all the way back to Lockport, where it had started out for Rochester loaded with barley. Before the rope snubbed on an abutment, the sturgeon pulled three mules into the canal, and "for weeks after," a crewman said, "we had to harness those mules facing the boat, they were so used to going backwards!" Later, the captain decided to use sturgeon-power to get from Lockport to Buffalo, but the fish wouldn't stop, and he wound up in Detroit. (Wyld 1962: 111)

Joshua, Giant Frog of the Empeyville Pond

In the early 1850s a young lad named McCarthy took a polliwog from the Erie Canal and named him Joshua. Joshua grew to be a 100-year-old giant with hind legs six feet long and an appetite for chipmunks, squirrels, and sometimes rabbits. For a time after his polliwog days, Joshua went missing, but he turned up later in the Empeyville Pond, where every time he jumped, the water sprayed 30 feet in the air and the pond got six feet wide. (Wyld 1962: 115)

The Erie Canal Squash Blossom

One year a big drought hit the Erie. The canal and its feeders were so dry a woman in Weedsport was arrested for filling her washtub and stranding fifteen canal boats. Tow path workers carried shotguns to fire at crows and sparrows that tried to drink. One fellow from Eagle Harbor kept a squash alive by spitting. When he finally stuck the roots in the canal, the vine sucked ten miles of the canal down to the bare bottom. The plant swelled so fast the fellow had to run to keep from getting *squashed*. The plant swelled like a rubber balloon and one vine passed him by like a racer snake. He grabbed at a flower bud, and it blossomed so fast and into such a big squash, he made a living for years selling sections of the leaves, since the veins made excellent drainage tiles. (Wyld 1962: 110)

Captain Darling and Redheaded Sal: Romance on the Erie Canal

John Darling was captain of the *Erie Queen*, and his cook was a woman named Sal. So many fellows sought Sal's hand in marriage, she proposed a contest. From midnight to midnight, the one whose boat was filled with the most bass would win her hand. But Sal really favored John, and when she found him at sundown with no fish, she joined forces with him.

Now, Sal was a fiery redhead, so John Darling figured a way to fool the bass. "Put your head down in the water!" he shouted to Sal, and a school of bass, scared by the fiery red glow, jumped clear out of the water. He swung the boat under as they all came down for a full count of two hundred and thirty-three. Redheaded Sal and John Darling were married the next morning and honeymooned at Niagara Falls. When they returned, the *Erie Queen*, gaily decorated, hosted a party that lasted all night, with 20 canal boats and 20 span of mules lining the Canal on both sides. (Wyld 1962: 116)

References

Schoemaker, George H., ed. 1990. *The Emergence of Folklore in Everyday Life: A Fieldguide and Sourcebook*. Bloomington, IN: Trickster.

Wyld, Lionel D. 1962. *Low Bridge! Folklore of the Erie Canal*. Syracuse, NY: Syracuse University Press.

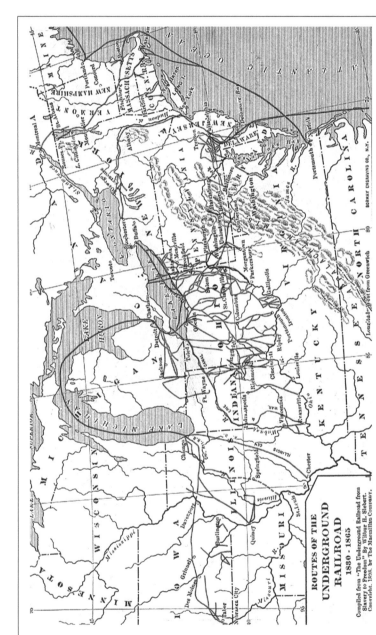

Figure 8.1. Wilber H. Siebert, "Routes of the Underground Railroad 1830–1865," in *The Underground Railroad from Slavery to Freedom,* 1898. (Public Domain)

UNDERGROUND RAILROAD
The Lake Erie Waterway to Freedom

The term Underground Railroad came to use around 1830, referring to secret routes to freedom used by African Americans fleeing enslavement in the South. In 1834 Canada abolished slavery, and the Great Lakes became a gateway to freedom on the Canadian shore. Traffic on the Underground Railroad reached its peak in the mid-1800s and stopped with the end of the American Civil War in 1865. An Indian trail known as Bullskin Trace was a critical route from southern states to the Ohio River and from there to the Great Lakes. Many escapees followed the tow paths of the Erie Canal to reach ports that gave passage to Canada.

Code words associated with the Underground Railroad constitute part of its folklore. Helpers along the way were called conductors, and hidden places of refuge were the Underground Railroad "stations." Ports receiving fugitives on Lake Erie's Canadian shore included Colchester, Gastfield, Buxton, Burwell, and Port Stanley. According to a map of 1830–65, Lake Erie offered fugitives more routes to Canada than the other Great Lakes combined.

The lighthouse on Lake Erie's Fairport Harbor was often the final stop on the American side of the lake. Historically, Fairport Harbor was an antislavery town, opposed to the Fugitive Slave Law, which called for the capture and return of escaped slaves. According to the Lighthouse Friends (n.d.) website, Fairport was a hub of antislavery activity: "In 1850, tavern owner Samuel Butler became chairman of a citizen's group that sought to repeal the law, and soon his Eagle Tavern was a haven for escaping slaves and headquarters for those willing to help. Anti-slavery captains, seamen, townsfolk and lighthouse keepers colluded to hide runaway slaves and smuggle them aboard ships bound for Canada."

The Ohio River separated the Confederate South (on the Kentucky side) from the Union North (on the Ohio side). Many tales that involve fugitives are also stories of narrow escape by crossing the Ohio River from Kentucky to reach the northern shore. Perhaps the best-known Ohio River escape is that of Eliza Harris. The story is compelling, as told by Harriet Beecher Stowe in

Figure 8.2. *Uncle Tom's Cabin, Eliza's Escape*, theatrical poster. Copyright ca. 1899 by Courier Litho, Buffalo, New York. (Public Domain)

her famous novel *Uncle Tom's Cabin*. But the book gives an almost saintly and rather saccharine portrait of Eliza, including miraculous reconnections with her husband in Ohio and with her mother in Canada, which were historically unlikely. But the escape scene in Stowe's variant has historical validity, as well as intense drama. Largely because of its intensity, it became the centerpiece of countless theatrical performances, and in 1878, it received further literary embellishment by Levi Coffin, the purported "President of the Underground Railroad." But it is Stowe's variant that endures, in part because it has historical value and in part because Stowe's Eliza embodies the spirit and mentality of the runaway slaves who risked their lives for freedom.

The stable core of the story involves Eliza, a slave owned by a Kentucky family that was purportedly kind to her until their circumstances changed. Then her master decided to sell her one surviving child, a toddler, to an unscrupulous slave dealer. Under cover of darkness, in the bitter cold, Eliza escaped to the banks of the Ohio River, planning to flee on foot across the frozen surface, only to find the ice breaking up underfoot. Carrying her child, and pursued by dogs and bounty hunters, Eliza refused to be taken. Leaving her pursuers behind, she jumped from one treacherous ice floe to another, sometimes up to her waist in freezing water, to save her child and reach freedom. Eliza was rescued by a bystander on the Ohio side and reached Canada by the Underground Railroad. According to one chronicler, she crossed Lake Erie from Sandusky Bay to arrive safely in Canada (Coffin 1876: 147–50).

Like Eliza, fugitives from slavery traveled by night to best avoid capture. But even Canada was not always hospitable, preferring to hire Irish immigrants and forcing many desperate fugitives back across the border to find work. A spate of imaginative overinterpretation about secret messages embedded in slave songs and quilts has done more to cloud than to clarify the meaning of images and lyrics, but north was the general direction of freedom, as suggested in the lyrics of "Follow the Drinking Gourd" (the "gourd" being the Big Dipper, which points to the polestar, the North Star). Much has been written about the song, which was first published in 1928 by the Texas Folklore Society. To date, its origin remains unknown, and its meaning is debated. At the popular level, the lyrics are said to have guided runaway slaves to safety, perhaps most convincing in the first stanza and chorus:

> When the sun come back, when the first quail call [spring season]
> The time is come, follow the drinking gourd
> Chorus: *Follow the drinking gourd, follow the drinking gourd*
> *For the old man say, follow the drinking gourd*

Common misconceptions about the Underground Railroad include the notion that it originated with, and was primarily maintained by, white abolitionists, or whites who wished to abolish slavery. In reality, most accounts of incidents were written and published by literate whites, making white abolitionists more noticeable than the fugitives. But escaped slaves and free African Americans were the driving force behind the flight northward. Because of its hidden and dangerous nature, the Underground Railroad could not be openly acknowledged by those who ran it, nor could it be tightly organized, but it is believed to have moved roughly one thousand people to freedom in every year of its existence (1830–65).

Many white abolitionist stations along the way are still standing on Erie's Ohio shore, including the Hubbard House in Ashtabula and Rider's Inn in Painesville. Often less well known, and therefore less celebrated, are the African American stations along the route, including the shop of Sandusky carriage maker George J. Reynolds, where Eliza Harris may have taken

Figure 8.3. *Harriet Tubman*, photo ca. 1860–75. (Public Domain)

refuge. Among the best-known conductors on the Underground Railroad is Harriet Tubman, a woman of heroic proportions who made thirteen perilous trips to the South and back, helping to free a great many runaway slaves.

In the absence of surviving documentation, there has been much romantic speculation about traditions associated with the Underground Railroad. Secret codes supposedly embedded in slave songs and quilt designs are cited informally, but to date, serious scholarship holds that while slave culture certainly expressed yearning for freedom and hope for the future, suggestive communication is not the same as hard evidence. Traditions like "Song of the Free" are more clearly and specifically about flight to freedom in Canada (the first stanza and chorus are sung to the tune of "Oh! Susanna"):

I'm on my way to Canada, that cold and dreary land
The dire effects of slavery I can no longer stand

My soul is vexed within me more, to think that I'm a slave

I'm now resolved to strike the blow for freedom or the grave

Chorus: *Oh, righteous Father, wilt thou not pity me*

And aid me on to Canada, where colored men are free

Although this song does speak directly of flight to Canada, it, too, raises more questions than it answers. The melody, written in 1847 by the famous white composer Stephen Foster, does not employ the musical signatures or regional dialect of African American slave songs. Moreover, some of Foster's original lyrics contained overt racist content, and the melody then became a popular means to belittle African Americans, especially in blackface minstrel theater. While folklore can (and often does) turn racist material against itself, subverting the racist messages originally intended, the lyrics to "Song of the Free"—as written, and presumably as sung—do not employ the vernacular speech or syncopated rhythms of African American compositions. Nevertheless, the lyrics clearly record the flight to freedom in Canada.

Songs like "Follow the Drinking Gourd" and "Song of the Free," whoever may have contributed to their composition and whoever may have sung them, now contribute to the historical consciousness of the Underground Railroad, reflecting the power of tales, whether sung or narrated, to convey the difficult struggle the fugitives knew they must face. These traditions make clear their resolve to go the distance, their willingness to die for freedom, and their abiding faith in the compassion of a loving God. For the duration of the Underground Railroad, Lake Erie prevailed for them as a gateway to Canada and to freedom from pursuit.

References

Coffin, Levi. 1876. *Reminiscences of Levi Coffin, Reputed President of the Underground Railroad*. Cincinnati: Western Tract Society.

Lighthouse Friends. n.d. Accessed August 7, 2019. https://www.lighthousefriends.com/light.asp?10=285.

Figure 9.1. Photo of John Yates Beall, taken the day of his execution, February 25, 1865. (Public Domain)

LAKE ERIE PIRATES AND BELIEF IN A TERRIBLE REVENGE

One should never underestimate Lake Erie's potential for intrigue, including its history of spying and piracy, from the fifteenth through the nineteenth century. Both the French and the British hired pirates on the lake during the French and Indian War (1854–63). Canadian pirates were notorious for a practice known as blackbirding, or mimicking lighthouse beacons and luring ships to crash on Long Point Peninsula, where their cargoes were then looted. Similarly, Americans were known to pirate fish from Canadian waters, where some desirable species were more plentiful.

During the 1860s, as the South struggled in the Civil War, plans were made to overtake the only federal gunboat on the Great Lakes, located on Lake Erie. The boat was to be used to attack Johnson's Island to free thousands of Confederate soldiers imprisoned there (see "Confederate Lookout at Johnson's Island Cemetery," this volume). Together with the freed prisoners, Confederate pirates planned to take the city of Sandusky, attack the city of Cleveland, and then escape to West Virginia. They intended to attack the region to draw General Grant northward, away from the vulnerable South. As it turned out, the plan failed, but some believe it set the stage for one of the most terrible acts of vengeance ever suffered by the nation.

On September 19, 1864, Confederate spy John Yates Beall and a band of Confederate pirates commandeered the steamer *Philo Parsons* on Lake Erie. Fully armed, they waited for a signal to attack the federal gunboat *Michigan*. But unbeknownst to them, the mission had been sabotaged. When no signal came, they docked at Middle Bass Island to take on fuel, and while there, they seized the unsuspecting steamer, *Island Queen*. Finally, aware that something had gone wrong, they scuttled the *Island Queen* four miles offshore and made a quick escape to Canada.

Beall would find his way back to the United States to continue his efforts on behalf of the South. But four months later he was arrested for trying to explode a railroad bridge over the Niagara River. Consequently, the Southern

Figure 9.2. *Steamer Philo Parsons*, 1861, from Alpena County George N. Fletcher Public Library, Great Lakes Maritime Collection. (Public Domain)

Figure 9.3. *Steamer Island Queen*, 1855, from Alpena County George N. Fletcher Public Library, Great Lakes Maritime Collection. (Public Domain)

hero was tried and found guilty of espionage and piracy on Lake Erie. According to the *New York Times* (1865), he was executed in New York, on Governor's Island, at the age of thirty.

Legend has it that a zealot named John Wilkes Booth was so incensed by Beall's execution, he hatched a plan to assassinate President Lincoln. He carried out his plan two months later, at Ford's Theatre in the heart of the nation's capital, on April 14, 1865.

Nothing known about John Yates Beall, or John Wilkes Booth, can either confirm or deny that Lincoln's assassination was an act of revenge for the Southern hero's execution, but the two tragic deaths remain connected in popular belief.

Reference

New York Times. 1865. "Military Execution: Execution of John Y. Beall, the Lake Erie Pirate and Rebel Spy." February 25, 1865. http://www.nytimes.com/1865/02/25/news/military-execution-execution-john-y-beall-lake-erie-pirate-rebel-spy-details.html.

MEDICINAL MAGIC
Lake Erie Folk Medicine

Sir James Frazer was an early Scottish anthropologist whose voluminous work has long been outdated, except in one important area: magical thinking (1913–22). Frazer identified two categories of magical thought: *sympathetic* magic (also called *homeopathic* magic) and *contagious* magic. Both are the major building blocks of folk medicine.

Sympathetic magic operates on the principle that like makes like. For example, if a voodoo doll, or "poppet," is made in the likeness of a person, whatever happens to the doll is supposed to produce the same experience in the person it looks like. Another example would be a rain dance, where dancing in a way that imitates (or is *like*) rain is supposed to bring rain.

Contagious magic operates on the principle of transfer by touch. Belief that touching a bumpy frog will give you warts or belief that holding a lock of someone's hair will give you power over them is an example of contagious magic.

Premodern folk remedies were rarely a product of systematic, scientific inquiry. But they did sometimes benefit from trial and error, and sometimes, by coincidence, magical thinking can produce the same remedy as a scientific finding. But most of the time, premodern folk medicine had no real medicinal value and could even be harmful. Folk medicine that used local plant life, easily available to everyone, is a good example of nineteenth-century remedies widely used on Erie's shore.

The plant life around Lake Erie is found over an extended geographical area of the United States and varies with the seasons. In addition, different locations around the lake might prescribe and prepare the same plants differently. But as a general rule, we find folks in the nineteenth century using spring flowers as home remedies for the following health problems (Allen 2013):

Figure 10.1. *Toothwort:* H. *Dentaria enneaphyllos,* L.—Neunblättrige Zahn-
wurz. Dentaire à neuf feuilles.—Nineleaves Toothwort. Image from page 88 of
"Atlas de la flora alpine," 1899. (Public Domain)

—For tooth problems, especially loose teeth, eat the greens, or drink a
tea made from toothwort.

In this case, sympathetic magic links the cure for tooth-related issues to
a plant that has the word *tooth* in its name and whose white blossoms can be
said to look like teeth. Contagious magic applies to the physical consumption of the plant's leaves in a tea brewed from them. Similarly, in each case
below, one or both types of magical thinking will apply.

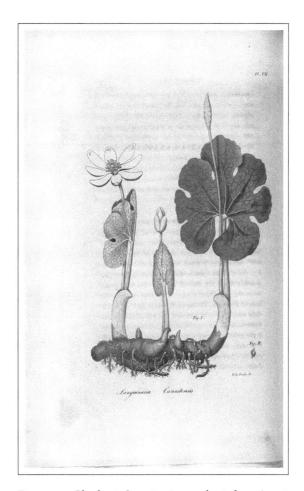

Figure 10.2. *Bloodroot: Sanguinaria canadensis* from *American Medical Botany, Being a Collection of the Native Medicinal Plants of the United States, Containing Their Botanical History and Chemical Analysis, and Properties and Uses in Medicine, Diet and the Arts*, with colored engravings by Jacob Bigelow, 1817–20. (Public Domain)

—If coughing up blood, use the sap of *bloodroot [now known to be poisonous].

The US Food and Drug Administration lists bloodroot as unsafe; neither its sap nor any other part of the plant should ever be consumed or applied to wounds.

In this case, color also has a role to play. Not only is the word *blood* included in the name of this plant once used for relief from bleeding, but the root from which the sap is taken is a bright or deep blood red.

Figure 10.3. *Anemones:* Page 1 of main content from a limited edition book containing an illustrated poem, "In Flanders Fields," 1921, by John McCrae and Ernest Clegg. (Public Domain)

—To avoid plague, or any life-threatening illness, avoid anemones (especially red poppies) because they frequently grow on graves.

If this belief actually predated World War I, it was certainly reinforced by a large cemetery cleared for American war dead in Flanders, Belgium. There, anemones cover the ground like a magic carpet. The Flanders cemetery inspired John McCrae's famous poem "In Flanders Fields," as well as the wearing of red poppies on Memorial Day.

Figure 10.4. *Skunk Cabbage:* Eastern Skunk Cabbage—*March Flowering* by Vasenka Photography via Flickr. (CC BY 2.0)

On occasion, remedies did meet expectations, but not always for the reasons people thought they did. For example, see the use of skunk cabbage:

—To avoid pregnancy prepare an elixir of skunk cabbage and drink three tablespoons, three times a day, for three weeks.

This might well *delay* a possible pregnancy, but only because many intimates would have kept their distance from the patient, given the foul, skunk-like odor emitted by the elixir and the digestive odors emitted by the patient.

Figure 10.5. *Violets: "Viola pedata"* in *Fieldbook of American Wildflowers*, by F. Schuyler Mathews, G. P. Putnam's Sons, 1911. (Public Domain)

Inevitably, by trial and error, or just by coincidence, some folk remedies proved medically useful. Violets, for example, were used for a wide variety of maladies. They would not have cured anything, but they might have soothed some symptoms, since we now know that some varieties (not all) contain salicylic acid, a common ingredient in modern-day aspirin.

Current studies show that some people seen in a modern doctor's office would eventually get well even if they weren't treated. Similarly, many people who used folk remedies would have recovered without them, and as we have seen, some folk remedies did have some medicinal value. More importantly, most of these remedies did no good, and some could be harmful—even lethal. But the fact that many sick people did recover after using folk medicine would have made these remedies seem more effective than they really were. Ironically, this would have prolonged the life of magical thinking rather than the lives of those who were treated.

When we're sick, especially when we're desperate for a cure, we can think of almost nothing except how to restore our health. Even in anxious, uncertain times, when we're not physically ill, we may seek ways to gain better control of our minds and bodies. But when we have no access to professional care or when current medical knowledge isn't enough (both problems typical of the nineteenth century), that's when we're most susceptible to pseudoscience and magical thinking. It is extremely important to be aware of when we're thinking magically and when we're not; rational, critical thought is the only way to be sure we receive beneficial care and remain safe from harm.

References

Allen, Stacey. 2013. "Wildflower Folklore." Garland Park Nature Center. Cleveland Metroparks. http://www.clevelandmetroparks.com/Main/Wildflower-Folklore.aspx.

Frazer, James G. 1913–22. *The Golden Bough: A Study in Magic and Religion*. 12 vols. 3rd ed. London: Macmillan.

Figure 11.1. *L'Amerique*, drawn by Jules-Antoine Vauthier, engraved by Bertrand. Paris, ca. 1820. (Public Domain)

HULDAH'S ROCK

An "Indian Legend"

S ubtitled an "Indian Legend," the poem below retells an oral tradition much older than the poem itself. It was penned by an author from Pelee Island, in the Canadian waters of Lake Erie. A shortened prose version of the Pelee Island legend was printed in a nineteenth-century publication by Thaddeus Smith, which also included the poem "Huldah's Rock." In his book, Smith identified the poem's author as a "young girl," but he inexplicably withheld her name: "The lines were written by a young girl of the Island while she was away attending boarding school as a contribution to a school paper published by pupils of the school" (1899: 6–7).

Others have attributed the poem to Thaddeus Smith's daughter, Bertha. In 1865, Smith and his partners built the first commercial winery on Pelee Island. He; his wife, Adelia; and their two daughters, Bertha and Minnie Bird, built "Vin Villa" and made it their home. On island websites, "Bertha Smith, daughter of Thaddeus Smith" is sometimes credited with the poem. But while Smith's book was published in 1899, it is unclear at what time Bertha actually wrote the poem. The only certainty is that the poem is a young girl's poetic account of a local legend told in the nineteenth century.

The name Huldah is given to a female prophet in the Hebrew scriptures (2 Kings 22:14). In the nineteenth century, the name could be found among Europeans but not clearly among Indigenous peoples of the Great Lakes region. This raises the issue of whether the oral tradition was really a Native American legend or whether it was simply a Euro-American cautionary tale meant to discourage intermarriage on an island closely shared with Native Americans.

As a literary convention, the poem's tragic theme conforms to typical nineteenth-century Christian-pagan tragedies, much like Puccini's *Madama Butterfly*, which was based on a short story of 1898 that was based, in turn, on a novel of 1887. All such romances condemn the white, Christian hero for general thoughtlessness in committing himself to a non-European or

Figure 11.2. *Manifest Destiny* by John Gast, 1872. (Public Doman)

"pagan" woman. The supposedly inevitable lure of his Christian roots eventually leads him to abandon his "noble savage" sweetheart, a common figure of nineteenth-century Romanticism.

Allegorical art renditions of Indian maidens, often in fanciful Indigenous costume, gave full expression to the Romanticism of the age. The images were typically depicted as Native royalty: the "Indian princess" meant to symbolize a noble, pagan, and "virgin" land. The French example in figure 11.1, titled *L'Amerique* (America), was published circa 1820.

In the Huldah tale type, the pagan Native American sweetheart is ultimately rejected in favor of white, Christian society. The image of a Bible-toting woman, seen in figure 11.2 in a flowing toga, symbolizes this white, Anglo-Protestant ideal. Known as *Manifest Destiny*, she is seen as bringing civilization to an expanding, increasingly Europeanized, American frontier.

A much later variant of the Huldah legend, written in broken English (or poorly translated from German), is also set on the shores of Pelee Island. This unlovely variant was written by a male European author whose hero is drawn back to his civilized roots when he becomes "sick of the wilderness," or more clearly, sick of the uncultivated wilder-ness of pagan America, specifically, of his pregnant, "simple half-breed" wife (Segers 1960: 65).

But in the classic nineteenth-century romance, as penned by schoolgirl Bertha Smith, the pagan wife is a full-blooded Native American princess, and there is no pregnancy. The lure that draws the hero away from her is his dear old mother, who calls him home as she lies dying. According to the literary genre, the subsequent lure of white, Christian society eclipses the "faithful heart" of Huldah, the pagan wife, who in this type of tale (as in *Madama Butterfly*) is destined to be abandoned for a Christian counterpart, or rival. True to the genre, it is the initial acceptance of the Indigenous woman, by the white Christian man, that accounts for her tragic end. Thus, Christian men are held responsible for such tragedies and are meant to avoid them by avoiding the "perfidy" of a racially mixed marriage:

Once there lived in Point au Pelee
An Indian maiden blithe and gay
Who often from her birch canoe
Would spear the spotted salmon through

Pride of her Chieftain father's heart
She oft would through the wildwoods dart
And with her bow and arrow raised
Would pierce the deer that calmly grazed

Joy of her mother's loving eyes
This dusky maid was a household prize
Whose beauty, grace and gentle arts
Won her a place in manly hearts

A pale face to the island came
To catch the fish and kill the game
And when this lovely maid he knew
She won his heart—she loved him too

"Be mine, dear maiden," then he cried
"Let me but win thee for my bride,
And on this isle I'll gladly stay"
The maiden did not say him nay

Happy they lived from year to year
Then tiding came of a mother dear

Who dying lay on a distant shore
And longed to see her son once more

Then with the pledge to come again
Before another moon should wane
The pale face parted from his bride
And o'er the waves his oars he plied

But many moons did wax and wane
The young wife's heart grew sick with pain
And all her life grew dark and chill
Her recreant husband tarried still

At length a boat approached the shore
Her heart beat high with hope once more
But ah! For her that small white yawl
Bore a brief letter—that was all

A letter that brought a withering blight
And broke a faithful heart that night
And told a tale of broken trust
And hurled bright hopes down in the dust

Hark! Hark a wail of dark despair
Floats out upon the midnight air
A splash is heard and Pelee's pride
Floats out upon blue Erie's tide

Upon the north of Pelee Isle
Three strangers linger but awhile
View "Huldah's Rock," the mariner's guide
That marks the fate of the Indian bride

It marks that death-leap into the sea
And marks a white man's perfidy
The waves that 'gainst it foam and surge
Seem chanting e're a funeral dirge

—Bertha Smith, daughter of Thaddeus Smith

References

Segers, Ladislaus. 1960. *The Song of Hulda's Rock: The Indian Legend of Pelee Island*. New York: Vantage.

Smith, Thaddeus. 1899. *Point au Pelee: A Historical Sketch of and an Account of the McCormick Family, Who Were the First White Owners on the Island*. Amherstburg: Echo Printing.

Figure 12.1. *Resurrectionists* by Hablot Knight Browne, 1847. (Public Domain)
This illustration accompanies an account of John Holmes and Peter Williams, who, for unearthing cadavers in 1777, were publicly whipped from Holborn to St Giles.

WILLOUGHBY BODY SNATCHERS AND
THE GHOST OF ELI TARBELL

From roughly 1780 to 1890, anatomy and dissection became essential to medical education in Europe and the United States. Even practicing physicians and surgeons needed cadavers to improve their skills. High demand for dead bodies caused a serious shortage and led to a period of widespread grave robbing. Because of public outrage and the threat of police action, this was always done under cover of darkness. The act was sometimes performed by entrepreneurial middlemen, or "resurrectionists," but body snatching was part of the curriculum at many medical colleges and became a common rite of passage for medical students. According to law professor Norman L. Cantor (2010: 249), before laws were passed to end body snatching, the crisis led many cemeteries to hire overnight guards, adding the term *graveyard shift* to the English language.

The Medical College of the Willoughby University of Lake Erie was incorporated in March 1834, one of the first medical colleges in northeast Ohio. Roughly ten years later, it would figure in the death of Eli Tarbell, who arrived from New York in 1845 to visit his stepdaughter, Phoebe Powell Burr, a resident of Concord Township (then known as Wilson's Corners). During his stay, Tarbell became seriously ill and died of typhoid fever. He was buried nearby in what is now Concord Cemetery. But not for long!

Soon after his burial, a disturbance was noticed in the ground above his grave. When the coffin was raised, it was empty, igniting a flare of public outrage. Tarbell's remains were quickly recovered from the medical college and returned to his resting place. That was how it happened according to newspaper accounts. But, despite—or perhaps because of—their accuracy, a different oral tradition arose.

Local legend recalls that on the third day of mourning, Tarbell's ghost rose up and appeared to his wife, telling of his dismemberment and giving the location of his mangled remains (Local Lore by Max 2012). It was said that Mrs. Tarbell demanded police intervention. When the truth was revealed, riots broke out in the streets, and according to tradition, the college closed, unable to withstand such scandal.

History confirms that the college closed, although it happened two years later, unrelated to the Tarbell incident. But history also confirms that "riots destroyed medical school buildings" in many places where body snatching and dismemberment were proved, as at the Medical College of Willoughby University of Lake Erie (Cantor 2010: 240).

Since the facts of the grave robbery and the return of Tarbell's remains are the same in both the local newspaper and the local legend, why did a legendary ghost tradition emerge at all? The most likely reason is that, while newspaper accounts did give accurate journalistic information, they gave no expression to something the people of Willoughby valued more than accuracy.

As many a scholar has noted, ghost stories may scare us, but they also reassure us that all does not end with death; the soul, at least, has a future—a significant comfort to the living. But in the case of grave robbing, the fate of the soul is in question. As Cantor writes, for many Americans, "the fate of the soul is affected by the treatment of bodily remains. That is, a soul is deemed to be attached to the body for an unspecified period after death, so abuse or disinterment interferes with the deceased's spiritual journey" (2010: 239).

In the nineteenth century, the integrity of the buried body would have symbolized a secure future for the soul, making any interference an intolerable offense. But the newspaper accounts gave no voice to interference in the fate of Tarbell's soul. And historically, there were no direct consequences to the medical college. But, when formal institutions fail to satisfy, legends often step in to do the job. Perhaps predictably, an oral tradition emerged, providing an act of poetic justice toward the college and venting the peoples' outrage through the disembodied voice of Tarbell's ghost.

The grave-robbing business came to an end by the turn of the twentieth century, when anatomy laws ensured a lawful supply of cadavers (Cantor 2010: 249). To this day, people still tell ghost stories, but body-snatching ghost stories came to an end when body snatching did. Like spectral remains, the tales disappeared when there were no more voices, dead or alive, demanding to be heard.

References

Cantor, Norman L. 2010. *After We Die: The Life and Times of the Human Cadaver*. Washington, DC: Georgetown University Press.

Local Lore by Max. 2012. "The Ghost Stories of Lake County." *Local Lore* (blog), October 22, 2012. http://wwwnews-heraldcom.blogspot.com/2012/10/the-ghost-stories-of-lake-county_22.html.

Special thanks are due to Dr. Ronald J. Taddeo of the Willoughby Historical Society, who graciously supplied accurate information on the history of the Tarbell grave robbery.

PART THREE

FOLKLORE IN THE TWENTIETH CENTURY

Figure 13.1. *The Griffin (Le Griffon)*, woodcut from Father Louis Hennepin's Nouvelle Decouverte, Utrecht, 1697. (Public Domain)

GHOST SHIPS OF LAKE ERIE

Ghosts Eclipse Fairies on Lake Erie

Over the course of the nineteenth century, traditional fairy lore was fully eclipsed by a marked rise in ghost stories (Davies 2007). This holds true not only in tales of human and animal ghosts (see "The Black Dog of Lake Erie," this volume) but also in tales of ghost ships, ghost trains, and other forms of spectral transportation. One possible reason for the ascendance of ghosts is that although they may scare us, they are a reassurance of life after death. This was a much-needed comfort in the nineteenth century, when serial waves of cholera killed thousands, as did work-related accidents in new industrial centers and diseases in overcrowded city slums, alongside pestilence and battle in the Civil War—all of which seem to have inspired Americans to abandon the fairy circle for the séance table. We can see the trend extend into the mid-twentieth century in sightings of ghost planes that disappeared in the battles of World Wars I and II. Ships might also enter the afterlife, and on Lake Erie, the oldest such ghost ship was *The Griffin*. It disappeared mysteriously in the 1600s but was still being sighted well into the twentieth century.

The Griffin and the Curse of the Iroquois Prophet

The Griffin was a seven-cannon, forty-five-ton bark—the first full-size sailing ship on Lake Erie and the first recorded shipwreck on the Great Lakes. It was built in the 1690s in Niagara by the French explorer Robert Cavelier, Sieur de la Salle, as part of a grandiose plan to connect all the continents in trade, starting on the Great Lakes.

According to some accounts, the Iroquois prophet Metiomek thought *The Griffin* was meant to destroy *Gitche Manitou* (the Great Spirit), and he put a curse on the sailing ship. But cursed or not, neither de la Salle nor his men could have anticipated the treachery of the inland sea. *The Griffin* was doomed from the start.

On August 7, 1697, de la Salle boarded *The Griffin* for its first voyage, sailing across Lake Erie, Lake Huron, and Lake Michigan. He left *The Griffin* on September 18 and sent the ship back toward Niagara, loaded with furs. But on the way, like so many that would follow it, the ship vanished along with its cargo, passengers, and crew.

Controversy exists as to whether the remains of the ship have been found in Lake Michigan. But sailors on Lakes Erie, Huron, and Michigan have all reported sighting a tall-masted ship that appears to be *The Griffin*, perhaps following the route of its incomplete voyage. According to those who are believed to have seen it, the closer they got, the more it faded from view.

The Bessemer and Marquette No. 2

The *Bessemer and Marquette no. 2* was a huge, 350-foot car ferry that shuttled across Lake Erie between the United States and Canada. On the morning of December 7, 1909, the *B&M2* left Conneaut, Ohio, bound for Port Stanley, Ontario, and sailed directly into one of the lake's most horrific seasonal gales, usually occurring in the month of November and sometimes in early December (see "The Witch of November," this volume).

It was a terrible night. The *B&M2* blew its whistle, sounding a series of four quick blasts; some could hear the distress signal, but almost no one could see the ship. A woman living east of Conneaut reported: "I heard the car-ferry's whistle and I knew it well. I saw her lights—white in the middle and red and green on each side, like she was headed for the shore.... The next time only the green light was visible [indicating a sharp turn to port], and then I could see only the tall, white stern light as the ship turned safely back to sea" (Boyer 1968: 156). That was the last ever seen of the *B&M2*.

That night, the steamer *Clarion* was driven onto a shoal and caught fire, but the grain-filled steamer *Leonard C. Hanna* rescued some of the crew. The *W. C. Richardson* lodged on Waverly Shoal, where violent seas rolled right over it, sweeping five seamen and a female cook overboard. "More than 30 battered freighters took shelter behind Long Port," historian Dwight Boyer wrote, "many with heavy burdens of ice" (1968: 154). The *B&M2*'s one and only serviceable lifeboat made it to shore with the dead bodies of nine frozen sailors, carrying with them knives and cleavers they may have used to secure a place on board.

Despite many years of searching and some false reports of its location, the huge vessel has eluded discovery. But some reported seeing a distant ship, built with the same features as the *B&M2*, poised on the Erie horizon. Some claimed to have seen its lights as it headed in and then turned back, just as it did so long ago. And on stormy nights, some are said to have heard the whistle, just as it sounded on that fateful night: four quick blasts, and then silence.

Fiddler on the *Clevco*

Maritime tradition tells us that ships are referred to as *she*, even when they have male names, but perhaps more importantly, tradition warns us that to change a ship's name is an invitation to disaster. There are certainly many ships whose names were never changed that were lost at sea anyway. But a name change evidently preceded enough tragedies to encourage belief in a connection. The *Gotham 85*, a 250-foot, thirty-thousand-barrel-capacity oil barge, is a fitting example. The *Gotham* was sold in the early 1940s, and the new owner renamed it the *Clevco*. On December 1, 1942, it was towed by the *W. H. Meyer*, a tug that had just recently been renamed the *Admiral*. According to tradition, this was an open invitation to double trouble!

Together the ships steamed out of Maumee Bay onto Lake Erie and into a gale with mammoth winds and waves. They would soon be blinded by snow and burdened with ice. By four in the morning, the *Clevco* radioed that the *Admiral* had inexplicably gone down with all on board adding that they were anchored to it by the towline, trying to break loose. The Coast Guard set out to find them, but whether they actually broke loose or were never where they thought they were, they were not at the position they'd given. At some time during the night, the *Clevco*, and all on board, had also been lost.

Before the ships left port on December 2, one tipsy sailor, deemed unfit to sail, had been taken off the *Clevco* and replaced by a slight, olive-skinned fellow said to be a "Russian Gypsy." He was a welcome seaman who had earned the nickname Fiddler by fiddling on board through many a storm. After the tragedy, the *Clevco* partially surfaced from its watery grave, and the bodies of the entire crew were found trapped in the ship, except for one. The body of the Fiddler was never found. Because the drifting *Clevco* was a navigation hazard, it was towed to deeper water and allowed to sink again. The tragedy would have ended there, but through the twentieth century, many a sailor continued to see ghostly apparitions where the ship went down, dancing on the waves to the sound of the fiddle.

Whatever may account for the ascendance of ghosts over fairies, traditional bogies and goblins have not completely disappeared. Many "low-tech" fairy motifs now appear in tales of "high-tech" extraterrestrials (see "UFO Base under Lake Erie," this volume). Nevertheless, in the years flanking the turn of the twentieth century, shipwrecks on Lake Erie were no longer attributed to evil water spirits. Rather, different anxieties, animosities, and aspirations seem to have shifted regional attention from life in fairyland to life after death. To the extent that twenty-first-century technology ended deadly shipwrecks on Lake Erie, newer tales of ghost ships have failed to launch.

References

Boyer, Dwight. 1968. *Ghost Ships of the Great Lakes*. Cleveland: Freshwater.
Davies, Owen. 2007. *The Haunted: A Social History of Ghosts*. Hampshire: Palgrave Macmillan.

Figure 14.1. "Witch of November," 1913, from Ohio History Connection. (Public Domain)

THE WITCH OF NOVEMBER
America's Deadliest Maritime Disaster

The Great Lakes chain makes up the world's largest freshwater sea, so large it generates its own weather systems. The "Witch of November" is the local name given to brutal storms that blow across the Great Lakes every autumn, sometimes for days, usually around mid-November. Each year, as tropical air pushes north from the Gulf of Mexico and arctic air pushes south from Canada, the two systems clash and generate massive storms over the Great Lakes. Ice and snow can be paralyzing and blinding, winds can sustain hurricane strength, and waves can tower as high as a three-story building.

America's deadliest maritime disaster occurred in 1913, lasting from Saturday, November 8, through Monday, November 10, when a Witch of November descended with unprecedented fury on Lakes Superior, Michigan, Huron, and Erie (Brown 2002: 202). Of the seventeen large steel freighters known to have been on Lake Huron between 8:00 p.m. and midnight on November 9, only two survived, and both sustained serious damage. A Witch of November of this proportion unites all five lakes into a single major disaster area. According to the *Farmers' Almanac* of 2008, an estimated twenty-five thousand mariners had lost their lives on the Great Lakes, "with the vast majority of those casualties occurring within the icy grip of the November witch" (McLeod: 2008).

Officially, 250 sailors were killed across the lakes in the storm of 1913, but only large steel freighters were counted; there is no official record of the dead aboard commercial fishing boats, tugboats, and powered barges or among hunters and anglers caught in the storm. Miraculously, only six men were known to be lost on Lake Erie, but Cleveland was hit hardest of all by deep, paralyzing snow. Without electricity, the city plunged into frigid darkness for several days. Unable to move anything in or out, Cleveland lacked a food supply and took emergency measures to import and ration milk for babies.

Regional and seasonal events that rivet human imagination—extraordinary disasters in particular—are almost inevitably memorialized in folk art, rituals, narratives, and folk songs. The ways in which they are memorialized reveal local attitudes and coping mechanisms, helping explain what happened, indicting the guilty when indicated, honoring the dead, and bringing comfort to the living. The wreck of the massive freighter *Edmund Fitzgerald*, bound for Cleveland in 1975, was just such a disaster. In local terms, like the Ojibwa name *Gitche Gumee* (Great Water) for Lake Superior and the name Witch of November for the seasonal gale, the tragedy was powerfully memorialized in a folk song, "The Wreck of the *Edmund Fitzgerald*," by singer-songwriter Gordon Lightfoot, a folk artist who is surely one of Canada's national treasures. The song has become emblematic of all maritime disasters on the Great Lakes, an homage to all who were ever lost to the Witch of November (Hemming 1981).

The memorialization of lives once lost on the Great Lakes is ongoing. But advanced weather prediction and modern seafaring technology have all but erased the elements of chance, fate, and the unknown that in the past generated art, narratives, songs, rites, and rituals on the seasonal gales. Although Lightfoot's folk song lives on and can be heard on popular venues like YouTube, new folk traditions on Erie's Witch of November have not continued into the twenty-first century.

References

Brown, David G. 2002. *White Hurricane: A Great Lakes November Gale and America's Deadliest Maritime Disaster*. New York: International Marine/McGraw-Hill.

Hemming, Robert J. 1981. *Gales of November: The Sinking of the* Edmund Fitzgerald. Chicago: Contemporary Books.

McLeod, Jamie, ed. 2008. Farmers' Almanac, November 8, 2008. https://www.farmersalmanac.com.

Figure 15.1. Women's Christian Temperance Union, prohibition poster, ca. 1920. (Public Domain)

PROHIBITION, AL CAPONE, AND THE MIDDLE ISLAND MYSTERY

When Prohibition went into effect on January 16, 1920, it was a good idea in theory, but it backfired in practice. Prohibition levied a tax on alcoholic beverages and criminalized the manufacture, distribution, and purchase of beer and liquor in the United States. This was meant to relieve the nation's families, and its economy, of the devastating effects of widespread alcohol abuse.

But many families had distilled homemade whiskey for generations, making it the backbone of countless rural and mountain economies. Of necessity, local stills continued to manufacture whiskey, although illegally. Courts prosecuted local offenders, but it was almost impossible to get a local jury to convict the guilty parties. Yet Prohibition was not the private moral imperative of rural Bible thumpers and puritanical crackpots. Instead, the alcohol abuse of the early twentieth century was the equivalent of the opioid crisis of the early twenty-first century. According to journalist Mark Lawrence Schrad, Prohibition's advocates included not only many unknowns who had suffered the consequences of alcohol abuse but also leaders of social conscience and formidable stature, including Abraham Lincoln, Frederick Douglass, and Susan B. Anthony (2020: 6).

Tales, jests, and ballads vividly recall the times, in particular the clandestine manufacture of illegal whiskey. Illegal stills brewed the whiskey secretly at night, or by the light of the moon, lending it the nickname moonshine.

Prohibition and Criminal Activity

A variety of alcoholic products inevitably found their way into the lucrative black market, as did many hard-core criminals and corrupt police officials. The Great Lakes, and in particular Lake Erie, became a major waterway for illegal transport to the United States from Canada, where the manufacture of alcohol was still legal. Joe Roscoe, a petty thug from Toledo, Ohio, managed to purchase Middle Island, a small landmass just outside American waters in the middle of the lake. There he built a notorious nightclub with a landing strip and a loading dock. Nightclubs where one could drink alcohol were entered by giving a secret code at the door, spoken through a small transom, known as a speakeasy. Illegal establishments that controlled entry through a transom were themselves known as speakeasies, a moniker that eventually transferred to all illegal establishments, regardless of how entry was achieved. The identities of those who visited Middle Island's speakeasy, and their activities there, remain a mystery. But whatever they did, alcohol was both integral to being there and illegal off the island, on the American side of the lake.

Americans have a long history of "Robinhooding" famous outlaws—that is, of admiring them for defying authorities and laws that were popularly seen as unjust (Steckmesser 1966). Legends abound about the generous acts of American outlaws toward ordinary folks cast into poverty by oppressive legalities enforced in difficult times. One folk song, for example, puts these words in the mouth of outlaw Pretty Boy Floyd: "You say that I'm an outlaw, you say that I'm a thief—well here's a Christmas dinner for the families on relief." American tales and ballads include—but are not limited to—purported acts of sympathy and generosity by such notorious criminals as Pretty Boy Floyd, Jesse James, and Billy the Kid. But Prohibition spawned an underground economy ruled by at least one organized crime boss too vicious to inspire public affection: Alphonse "Scarface" Capone.

Capone Treasure Hidden at Middle Island's Speakeasy

Al Capone was different. More feared than admired, he never won public affection, even when he tried to buy it with charitable donations. He was the first criminal to be named public enemy number one, and his sinister reach would extend to Lake Erie's Middle Island.

Capone ran a Prohibition-era crime syndicate in Chicago, and his public image was doubly tarnished by his reputation for acts of extreme brutality, including his alleged involvement in the Saint Valentine's Day Massacre, a mass execution of his business rivals. Folklorist Ronald Baker writes that Indiana's storytelling traditions follow the same pattern as that of Capone stories told across the nation, explaining, "When Hoosiers do not reveal Capone's several hideouts to the police, it is not through love . . . but through fear" (1982: 17).

The legend of Al Capone on Lake Erie's Middle Island reflects that fear. Despite Capone's efforts to gain popularity through publicized charitable giving, the tale expresses no admiration or affection for him. It simply speculates

Figure 15.2. *Al Capone Mug Shot*. (Public Domain)

on the hidden proceeds of Capone's contraband. Chad Fraser alludes briefly to a narrative of Capone's visits to the notorious Middle Island speakeasy: "Al Capone was thought to have paid at least a few visits. For many years a rumor even circulated that Capone had hidden a large fortune in the walls at the club at Middle Island. But . . . the building now stands in ruins and no bills have ever been found there" (2008: 192).

It's not really known if Capone ever visited Middle Island before Prohibition ended on December 5, 1933. But it's well documented that Capone was finally imprisoned for tax evasion and eventually released. He died in 1947, riddled by syphilis, at his mansion on Palm Island, Florida. Joe Roscoe, the petty thug who bought Middle Island, spent a few years in prison, and then he, too, was released. He died in 1965.

In 1999, Middle Island was auctioned and reclaimed by Canada. The island is now part of a protected parkland. Prohibition had such a great impact on the waterways between Canada and the United States that it left its mark across the landscape in a wide variety of expressive behaviors and traditions. But those who may have visited Middle Island during Prohibition, and whatever they may have done, plotted, or hidden there, remain a mystery yet to be solved.

References

Baker, Ronald L. 1982. *Hoosier Folk Legends*. Bloomington: Indiana University Press.

Fraser, Chad. 2008. *Lake Erie Stories: Struggle and Survival on a Fresh Water Ocean*. Toronto: Dundurn.

Schrad, Mark Lawrence. 2020. "Prohibition's Centennial: Why Drinking Won." *New York Times*. https://www.nytimes.com. Quoted in *The Week* 20, no. 960 (January 31, 2020): 16.

Steckmesser, Kent L. 1966. "Robin Hood and the American Outlaw: A Note on History and Folklore." *Journal of American Folklore* 79, no. 312 (April–June): 348–55.

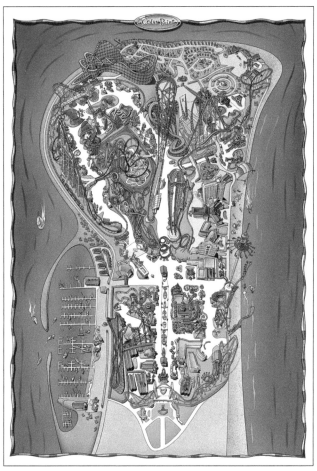

Figure 16.1. *Illustrated Map of Cedar Point Amusement Park* from Cedar Point. (Copyrighted content used with permission)

GHOST HORSE ON THE CEDAR POINT CAROUSEL

The Cedar Point Amusement Park opened in 1870, when leisure time first became a reality for the American working class. It is the second-oldest operating amusement park in the US. Located on a peninsula that juts out into Lake Erie, Cedar Point attracts more than three million people a year, and for more than twenty years, it has won the Golden Ticket Award for Best Amusement Park in the World.

Over the course of its lifetime, Cedar Point has boasted four simultaneously running roller coasters taller than two hundred feet, seventy-two additional rides, a magnificent water park, a mile-long beach, two marinas, two museums, two miniature golf courses, several hotels, a number of landmark buildings, and the only haunted carousel on the planet.

The first carousels in the United States were unremarkable, just as their European models were fairly commonplace. But around 1860, with the arrival of Gustav Dentzel to Philadelphia, the Philadelphia Style was launched, ushering in a golden age of highly skilled, realistic carousel carving. When his partner, Johann Muller, died, Dentzel raised Muller's two young sons, Albert and Daniel, and taught them the craft. When in 1903 they left him to strike out on their own, Dentzel was unable to forgive them, and he refused to hire them back. Although Muller's son Daniel (1872–1951) became one of the premier carousel carvers of his time, the Muller shop was unable to compete with older, more established businesses like the Dentzel Company. When Dentzel died in 1918, his son William rehired the Muller brothers, and they went on to complete the careers they had started under Gustav Dentzel's tutelage.

Daniel C. Muller won many prizes as a young carver, and along the way, he developed an interest in the ornate regalia of military horses. With less regard for history than design, he was known to combine historically unrelated decor and flourishes to achieve the most fanciful and spectacular of displays. In 1917, just before returning to the Dentzel Company, he carved a

Figure 16.2. *Muller's Ghost Horse*, photo from Haunted Pittsburgh Facebook Group. (Copyrighted content used under US Code, Title 17, Chapter 1, Section 107, Limitations on exclusive rights: Fair Use)

magnificent military horse for the carousel at Cedar Point Amusement Park. According to legend, on some nights after the park closed, the ghost of a lone woman would mount the horse, the lights would softly come on, and the carousel would slowly start to turn (Mann, Shank, and Stevens 1990: 64).

In 1995, the carousel was moved to Dorney Park in Allentown, Pennsylvania, without Muller's masterpiece. Muller's original was put in storage at Cedar Point, and a fiberglass replica was placed on a new Cedar Point carousel. It may have been the original's disappearance that gave new life to the old legend. As the story went, Mrs. Muller was so taken by her husband's military horse that she fell in love with it, so much so that after her death she returned to ride it and would go to any length—even interfering with attempts to photograph it—to prevent others from viewing the horse she coveted as her own. In fact, after Muller's horse was removed from the carousel, Mrs. Muller's ghost showed no interest in the fiberglass copy that took its place.

Daniel C. Muller's original military horse is no longer stored away; at this writing, it is on display at the Town Hall Museum in Frontier Town at Cedar Point, and many still believe that Mrs. Muller's ghost keeps close vigil.

Museum attendants are happy to provide visitors with background on the carousel "ghost horse" of Cedar Point. Mrs. Muller's ghost seems to take no interest—but only because no one can see what happens at night when the museum shuts down.

Who knows? If Muller's hand-carved original should reappear on a carousel, perhaps the fairy lights will once again twinkle when the crowds go home, the platform will slowly begin to turn, and Mrs. Muller will ride again.

Traditional Motifs

E280.	Ghosts haunt buildings
T11.2.1.	Love through sight of statue

Reference

Mann, William, Peggy Shank, and Marianne Stevens. 1990. *Painted Ponies: American Carousel Art*. New York: Zon International.

Figure 17.1. Canadian sand dredger *The Sand Merchant*, ca. 1927. (Public Domain)

CURSE OF THE LAKE ERIE QUARRYMEN

K elley's Island, the largest island in Lake Erie's American waters, is four square miles long. It is named after Addison Kelley, who opened a limestone quarry there in the 1800s. It was a time of mass migration from Europe to the United States, and much of the country was experiencing economic stress.

Many Anglo-Americans had reached these shores long before the nineteenth century, and they saw themselves as "natives." Called nativists, they saw all newcomers as intrusive foreigners. In economically stressed areas, they resented immigrant competition for jobs, and being primarily Protestant, they reserved their worst animosity for immigrants of other faiths.

Tensions ran high at the Kelley's Island quarry since the supervisors were largely "native" Anglo-American Protestants and the laborers were almost all Italian Catholic immigrants. The laborers chafed under the demands made of them, sometimes even refusing to follow orders. The supervisors responded by demanding even more. The longer, harder, and faster the quarrymen were forced to work, the greater the chance that something could go terribly wrong. Eventually, it did.

According to the Ghosts of Ohio website (2008), the quarrymen were attempting to dig an underwater tunnel when a foreman ordered a laborer named Battaglia to set a dynamite charge to blast away a rock shelf suspended over a deep reservoir at one end of the quarry. Battaglia refused, claiming that the blast would be far too great. But the foreman threatened until the quarryman had to comply.

Battaglia's fears were justified. Part of the quarry wall exploded along with the rock shelf, all of which plunged into the reservoir, creating a tsunami-like water wall. The giant wave engulfed Battaglia and many of his fellow quarrymen, sweeping them out into Lake Erie, where their bodies were never found. Almost immediately, rumors spread that during storms on the lake, the quarrymen's ghosts were walking the same tunnel they had started to dig. Some said anyone on the lake during a storm would be dragged under—an event referred to as "the curse of the quarrymen." Such stories were repeated over the years, but no one could substantiate the dreaded curse.

Then, in October 1936, newspapers across the country reported a tragedy involving a Canadian sand dredger, stating, "The *Sand Merchant* was capsized by mountainous waves at 10:00 p.m. Saturday, 17 miles northwest of Cleveland in approximately 60 feet of water. She sank rapidly" (Newspaper Archive, n.d.).

Nineteen people, one of them the first mate's wife, were drowned despite their life preservers. Their bodies were later found bobbing in the choppy lake. Seven men managed to cling to an overturned lifeboat for eleven hours, and these were the only survivors. According to the Ghosts of Ohio (2008), "The survivors claimed to have heard ghostly voices, and said the waves appeared to be like hands reaching out for them." For those who accepted this testimony, the quarrymen's curse was finally confirmed.

References

Ghosts of Ohio. 2008. "Curse of the Quarrymen." http://ghostsofohio.org/lore/ohio_lore _16.html.

Newspaper Archive. n.d. Accessed October 11, 2023. https://newspaperarchive.com /moorhead-daily-news-oct-19-1936-p-1/

Figure 18.1. *Lake Erie Cow Monster*, drawing by author, Judith S. Neulander.

THE LAKE ERIE COW MONSTER
A Possible Origin for South Bay Bessie

The negative effects of manufactured pollution have long been a preoccupation across the nation. In the Lake Erie region, waste created by the Industrial Revolution is credited with spawning a number of monstrous animal mutations, including the Lake Erie Cow Monster, also known as the Lorain Ocean's Lake Monster. There is no ocean in the vicinity of Lorain, Ohio, but the cow monster dwells in Lake Erie's waterways, and since lake monsters descend from ancient, ocean-dwelling sea serpents, perhaps *ocean* crept into the lake monster's name. In any case, Lorain began as a peaceful, leafy farming community. The area raised mostly dairy cows, until a steel mill was built in the late nineteenth century. As soon as the mill opened, a wave of immigrants arrived to work there, and the industry prospered.

But soon after the mill opened, industrial waste entered the Black River, a tributary of Lake Erie. And at the same time, local farmers began reporting strange cow behavior, including the unexplained disappearance of cows from their fields. One day, according to a local farmer, all of his cows suddenly disappeared, only to reappear the next day as a single, monstrous, multiheaded cow.

The demon cow chased him all the way to downtown Lorain, where he assembled a posse that pursued the monster for weeks. When they finally caught up with it, they chased it into the Black River, where they thought it would drown. But to their amazement, pollution from the steel mill was so toxic, the cow had developed gills! Thereafter, the cow monster took up residence in Lake Erie's waterways.

One sighting, reported in 1907, confirmed that the cow monster "looks like a cow with multiple heads," while two brothers who spotted the cow in 1937 described it as a creature "made up of 100 cows combined into one, with arms" (Joe [creepybits] 2017).

There is some speculation online that the Lake Erie sea serpent (see "South Bay Bessie," this volume) may be a later mutation of the Lorain cow that morphed into the Lake Erie Cow Monster (Rock the Lake 2017). Actual sightings of the cow monster fade away after the 1930s. But the cow monster's kin, South Bay Bessie, is still spotted to this day.

References

Joe (creepybits). 2017. "Bessie (Lake Erie Cow Monster or Lorain Ocean's Lake Monster)." Tumblr, September 22, 2017. https://www.tumblr.com/creepybits/165623694162/bessie -lake-erie-cow-monster-or-lorain-oceans?source=share.

Rock the Lake. 2017. "South Bay Bessie." December 2017. http://www.rockthelake.com /search/bessie.

Figure 19.1. The Pioneer Fire, Boise National Forest, Idaho, 2016. Forest Service photo by Kari Greer. (Public Domain)

LAKE ERIE'S BLACK SUNDAY AND BLUE MOON

In the summer of 1950, a human-made fire was left to smolder about twenty miles northwest of Fort St. John in British Columbia, Canada. The event was reported by Norman P. Carlson (1986), a historian for the town of Busti, in Chautauqua County, New York. Carlson's dates are not always certain, but he was correct that within twenty-four hours, the fire had spread to one hundred acres, and by the time fire rangers arrived, it had doubled in size. According to Carlson, the area had already been scheduled for deforestation, and in that exceptionally dry season, other fires in neighboring Alberta were already demanding attention. This fire was left to burn itself out, doing the rangers' work for them. But the fire got out of hand, and other flare-ups joined it. The largest Alberta fire, in Chinchaga, burned actively from June through late September, producing a smoke tower so extraordinary, it reached to the troposphere and traveled far enough to be seen in the Netherlands and England.

It became devastating in combination with other fires that flared up at the same time. For example, about the same time the first fire started, another erupted near Wanham, Canada, about 250 miles northwest of Edmonton. Forty-mile-per-hour winds quickly whipped the flames across thirty square miles, forcing the evacuation of farms and homes across the region. Ten days later, with the fire still going in Wanham, a long-smoldering peat fire was activated by high winds 75 miles north of Edmonton. In another three days, the peat fire threatened to engulf an Edmonton settlement despite the best efforts of two hundred villagers who eventually had to flee. By then, the fire that began in British Columbia had spread 100 miles into Alberta, but according to Carlson (1986), it went unreported in that province since fires more than ten miles from roads, rail lines, and communities were left "free burning," following government policy at the time.

Once the magnitude of the problem was fully realized, and as winds subsided, backfires were lit to control the raging firestorm. But before it was over, thirty fires were burning across Canada, and smoke was accumulating heavily; seven hundred men were fighting fires in Alberta alone. Similar fires were burning over a two-hundred-mile stretch on the east side of the Alaska Highway. At one point, roughly sixty thousand square miles of timber and brush were on fire. Airline pilots were diverted from normal flight paths, unable to fly over vast areas entirely obscured by dense smoke. Over the summer, as some fires came under control, new ones broke out.

A few rain showers were forecast at the end of the dry season, but as Carlson (1986) later reported, the smoke was not affected: "The vast accumulation of smoke that was boiling high into the atmosphere began to ride the jet stream to distant areas where it created [a] memorable phenomenon. It traveled east northeast and reached the upper western shores of Hudson Bay on Saturday morning. Then it followed south."

The smoke rising from the massive fires was ten thousand feet thick and reached a height of three miles as it rose on the air current. On September 24, a sunny Sunday afternoon in 1950, communities around Lake Erie were suddenly plunged into darkness with no warning and with nothing but scant radio reports for information. The event became known as Black Sunday, and it was followed by the rare vision of a "blue moon."

The Blue Moon Phenomenon

The familiar phrase "once in a blue moon" refers to the infrequency with which the moon (not necessarily a full moon) sometimes appears to be blue. This occurs in nature when smoke or dust particles cloud the atmosphere, as occurred after the eruption of Krakatoa in 1883, which made the moon look blue for almost two years. In 1950, after a prolonged period in which the smoke from thousands of square miles of fire blocked out the sun over portions of Canada and the United States, a blue moon was seen wherever the smoke particles drifted. They drifted as far away as Europe, and as we are about to see, they are floating still through the memories of those who remember Lake Erie's Black Sunday.

Black Sunday Narratives

The event generated narratives so rich in creative expression they give us direct access to life on Erie's shore at a time when all stores closed on Sundays, first responders were the only ones at work, families went to church, and adults napped over Sunday papers. Folks went visiting or went for a drive in the family's one car, dads took kids to baseball games, and teens went to movie matinees, tinkered with cars, or curled up with good books. Schoolkids drifted freely across backyards, and little ones played out front, watched by parents gossiping on the porch. It was a time when the countryside was dotted with small, family-owned farms, no toys were electronic, and time was measured by the steady, predictable rhythms of nature. TV was so new, most people's only media connections were landline phones and plug-in radios. After dark on most family farms, the only visible electric light would have been from a nearby town. Narratives of Black Sunday take us back to that place and time, giving us extraordinary access to the traditional beliefs of ordinary folks on both sides of Lake Erie, exactly at the midpoint of the twentieth century.

Notably, it had been three months earlier, in June 1950, that the United States went to war against North Korea and was otherwise in the throes of a terrifying Cold War with the Soviet Union. The country was beset by the hysterical Red Scare, which saw communist bogeymen lurking in every shadow, including throughout the US Armed Forces, Hollywood, and the government. It is not surprising, then, that conspiracy theories were among the most frequent explanations for Black Sunday; they offered a compelling way to explain a mystifying and sometimes terrifying episode of sudden, unexplained darkness during the day.

Similarly, when any two significant events take place in proximity, we tend to assume a cause-and-effect relationship, whether one exists or not. Consequently—although to a smaller extent—Black Sunday was sometimes linked to significant events that followed in proximity, especially illnesses and birth defects.

Descriptive versus Explanatory Narratives

At this late date, most narratives are recalled by people who were still children in 1950, and their stories tend to fall into two categories: descriptive narratives and explanatory narratives. Descriptive narratives give us a much richer description of the experience than mere times and dates could possibly do, while explanatory narratives consist of homegrown explanations for the event. Descriptive narratives often reflect children's impressions, while explanatory narratives usually reflect traditional beliefs, as well as aspirations and anxieties typical of the time and place. Seemingly plausible causes and conspiracy theories were important sense-making strategies for people trying to explain the forest fire reports that most learned of only after the fact and after they had formed first opinions.

Fifty years later, on June 17, 2000, Betty Matteson Rhodes, who was eight years old in 1950, posted a query on the GoErie website asking folks to "write me regarding a mysterious 'Black Sunday' that occurred in the early 1950's." And write they did! The full account appears in Rhodes's book, *Black Sunday: What Really Happened on That Day on September 24, 1950?* (2012).

Excerpts seen in this chapter appear with permission from Betty Matteson Rhodes.

Descriptive Narratives

It should be noted that narratives rarely fall into neat subcategories. But for folkloristic purposes, descriptive narratives written to Rhodes fall into primarily three types of childhood memory: memories of sudden darkness, memories of grown-ups being frightened, and memories of strange animal behavior.

Occasionally, descriptions confuse Black Sunday with other events or seasons, and some include the emergence of stars in the midday sky:

> My father and I were in the backyard . . . playing badminton. . . . The *Spring weather* was rapidly alternating between cloudy and cold, and sunny and warm. . . . Suddenly it went from normal daylight to late evening darkness in about 20 seconds, then total night darkness. I asked my father "What's going on?" . . . My father didn't know. *Stars were visible*, and night insects or peepers—I'm not sure which—started chirping. I would say the total darkness lasted a minute. . . . The whole thing happened in the space of about two minutes. (Rhodes 2012: 18; my italics)

The memory is real, but it may be flawed, as sometimes occurs with childhood memories. In this case, the event of 1950—which took place in fall—is confused with spring, probably because of similarly mild weather. Also, although time estimates differ, the two-minute darkness doesn't conform to most reports of the event. The narrative seems reminiscent of an eclipse or some other event different from Black Sunday. But, as in this case, many others have also remembered Black Sunday as a "starry" night in the middle of the day.

The phenomenon that accounts for this type of memory is called habitual association (Lord 1960), which refers to items that we link together by habit because they go together in our minds. For example, almost all of us can add the final word to "where there's smoke there's—" associating smoke with fire just as we tend to associate mild weather with spring. As we grow older, experience teaches us that habitual association isn't always reliable; sometimes smoke does not indicate fire, and mild weather occurs in fall just as often as it does in spring.

But young children rarely make such nuanced distinctions. Hence, when Black Sunday's sky is recalled from childhood, it is sometimes remembered as a night sky complete with stars, most likely because the night sky habitually goes with stars in children's imaginations. Clearly, the brightest star in sight, the sun, was completely blocked out by the dense smoke aloft, leaving no possibility that weaker or more distant stars were visible in the same sky. But in the magical realm of childhood memories, the dark sky of Black Sunday will sometimes be studded with a myriad of stars that weren't there.

Writing in the 1980s, journalist Norman Carlson (1986) described that afternoon in New York State, which lay farther east of the cloud that had already cast western Lake Erie into darkness, saying, "Locally, for some people [eastward, in New York] the first hint of something strange was an announcement on the radio that the lights were being turned on at the ballpark in Cleveland."

The event would be experienced as either more or less dramatic depending on the geographical location of those who experienced it, their activities at the time, and the length and intensity of the darkness at their location. Some adults showed fear; others concealed their fear from their children, revealing it only years later. Ken, a ten-year-old, was at the Cleveland ballpark when the lights came on that day. Writing to Rhodes fifty years later, he remembered a crowd too distracted by the game to pay much attention! As we shall see, experiences varied greatly on that day and were reported accordingly. But in most accounts, we can hear the spirit and mentality of a mid-twentieth-century childhood, singing out with clear and perfect pitch.

Sudden Darkness

Ken: I was a ten-year-old watching a Cleveland Indians game with my father when this happened. . . . I remember the sky becoming progressively darker and then the stadium lights coming on in the middle of what minutes before was a clear afternoon. I don't recall anyone being alarmed by the event and I do recall some speculation at the time that it was caused by a forest fire in Canada. From what I can remember, the cloud seemed very continuous and I could not see the beginning or end of it in any direction. I don't recall when it ended but I don't think it was still overhead by the time the game was over.

JK: I was 5+ at the time of "Black Sunday" and lived in a suburb of Cleveland. I remember the event well and the official explanation of a fire in Canada. . . . My best friend was 3 at the time and thought it was night when her mother put her down for a nap. It was very dark—like the darkest of nights—and there was a yellow glow to the blackness. I don't remember anyone mentioning stars.

Toni: I remember it being a Sunday in September 1950 when, after my family had returned from Mass at our local church in Sharpsville, PA., we ate our dinner and at 2:30 p.m., my two younger teen age sisters went to the matinee at the Ritz theatre to see "Pride and Prejudice." I had a good book to finish, so I stayed home reading. Mom was napping, Dad was reading the paper and my brothers were out somewhere. I noted that the afternoon kept getting darker, and as I read I had to turn on a lamp.

I thought it would storm but the sky was a bright kind of yellow. It kept getting darker and within the hour, the sky and the general outside light seemed to be deep orange-yellow and getting darker! By the time my sisters returned and my brothers got back, about 5:30, it was like night . . . very dark with only a tinge of yellow . . . artificial lights outside (lampposts and car headlights) were unusually white-blue in this strange atmosphere, and it continued into the usual time for sundown. (Rhodes 2012: 21, 32, 30–31)

Grown-Ups Frightened

Charlie: I was born in 1941 so I was about 9 years old at that time. I remember that day, very well. . . .

I knew something was strange at that time; I wasn't very concerned until I noticed the older people. They were TERRIFIED, some were praying. When you are 9 years old and see 15 to 20 older people terrified, you don't forget that.

Sylvia: I was a little kid at the time driving with my parents back from Batavia to Buffalo, NY along Genesee Street. It had been a clear sunny day and then along the horizon the sky began to darken (as if a thunderstorm were approaching). The sky got darker and darker until my Dad put on the headlights. My Mom was rather afraid but my Dad said we would just keep going back to Buffalo. Along Genesee Street at this time there were dairy farms and I can remember seeing the cows' confusion and then some started walking back to their barns. We got to Buffalo and home and the streetlights were on. . . . Neighbors were out in the street and very frightened.

Brian: I remember it well, I lived in Jamestown, NY; I was 7 at the time. Initially the sky yellowed and I can remember darker streaks across the sky. We were playing in a neighbor's yard and we drifted back to our houses as parents came out to find us. It ultimately became totally dark, and then quickly lightened up to normal. As kids we took it in stride, but in later years, my parents admitted to being frightened. (Rhodes 2012: 35–36, 29–30, 10–11)

Strange Animal Behavior (and a Blue Moon)

Gene: I remember that day very well, I was with an aunt of mine, outside of Plumville, PA. . . . She had a farm and all of the chickens headed for the hen house, and the cows headed for the barn. I grew up in the hills of central PA., where there were no city lights. I never saw nights as dark as that Sunday afternoon.

Carroll: I was a 13-year-old living in rural Northwestern Pennsylvania . . . on my parents' small farm. . . . Early in the afternoon, the sun disappeared and it became as dark as midnight. Lamps were lit and lanterns brought out. I went outside to walk around and check the livestock, and found that the chickens had all gone to roost, all the wild birds had gone to sleep, and the farm animals had gone into their normal sleeping places in barns and coops. We could see the streetlights had come on in the nearby town. We had no Television at the time, but heard over the radio that there was a forest fire in Canada producing so much smoke it had blackened out the sun.

People were very frightened and some thought the world was coming to an end. Others thought the Russians had done 'something.' . . . Some thought the dreaded nuclear holocaust had come, but most people I knew thought it was a secret government smoke-screen experiment related to Cold War defense. The true believers in conspiracy never would accept the forest fire "cover up" story as they called it.

After nightfall, the moon, which was full that night, was blue. I read later that blue moons were seen as far away as Europe.

Most people who lived in Western Pennsylvania at the time remember that day vividly if they had any reason to be out-of-doors. We always called it "Black Sunday" afterward. Sometimes you read references from people who said they saw stars because it was so dark, but that is not true. Obviously no stars were visible because the smoke was so thick we could not even see the sun. I remember a sky that was totally black, smelled like smoke and was truly frightening. (Rhodes 2012: 34, 55–56)

Explanatory Narratives

Explanatory narratives seek other ways than a forest fire to account for the extraordinary event. These memories reflect peoples' speculations on cause and effect, and the four most notable explanations include God's hand at work; the cause of subsequent tragedies (such as illness and birth defects); conspiracy theories; and the end of the world. Examples of each appear below.

God's Hand at Work

Albert: I remember that Sunday afternoon well. In particular I recall looking out the front window and seeing the street lights on. Chucky and Richard, who lived across the street, played with a wagon on the sidewalk as their parents sat on the front porch. My mother, who used every unusual event as a control mechanism, told us something along the lines that God was behind it all and we better stay inside and behave. As best I can remember it was late afternoon and the darkness only partially abated before night fell. A few days later I heard the adults talking about forest fires in Canada—which was logical given Buffalo's proximity to Canada—but I was still concerned that God's hand was in it.

Larry: I was born in 1945 and I remember a Sunday when I was 5 or 6 when it got very dark in the middle of the afternoon. It must have been in September or early October because we were picking tomatoes and all migrant workers quit because they thought it meant they shouldn't be working on Sunday (Rhodes 2012: 20, 32).

Bill: In New Castle and many other places . . . some thought it was from tampering with the Lord's time because people had set back their clocks [for daylight saving time] the day before. (Burmester 1992–93).

Cause of Subsequent Tragedies

Sometimes noteworthy events do account for subsequent health issues, but they are not necessarily connected just because a health issue follows a noteworthy event. We tend to see cause-and-effect relationships between things that happen in proximity, even when there is no relationship—as if the sun rises because the rooster crows, even though roosters actually crow all day and night and the two events have nothing to do with each other.

Unfortunately, catastrophic health issues occur throughout the year in every year, but when these tragedies closely follow an unusual event, we tend to link the two. Moreover, when they happen to folks previously untouched by such misfortune, they become more aware of the frequency than ever before—as if it just started happening more often, although the frequency over time hasn't changed. Families that are personally affected are likely to suddenly be in contact with professionals, agencies, and others they were formerly unaware of, reinforcing the notion that the tragedy suddenly became more widespread, happening more often and to more people, although statistically nothing really changed. The phenomenon finds clear expression in Black Sunday narratives.

Lydia: My grandmother was telling me about this day and what the sky looked like. She was pregnant at the time with my aunt . . . who is mentally retarded. I am telling you this because almost every woman in our area that was pregnant at this time had a mentally retarded child. She seems to think that this had something to do with it and I do as well. It just seems strange that so many women had mentally retarded children after this occurrence.

Ron: I was born in 1941, and many of my classmates [who graduated from high school in 1959], and later 60, 61 etc., contracted MS [multiple sclerosis]. I always wondered if there wasn't a connection between the two.

I tried to link a "dirty" nuclear explosion for this event. If so the government covered it up pretty well. I could not find any information of a test on or around Sept. 1950. (Rhodes 2012: 27–29, 50–51)

Conspiracy Theories

Kirk: I wasn't born yet when this happened, but my parents told us about it several times. They too mentioned the explanation of a big fire in Canada, but also other explanations, like the CIA and so forth.

Commissioner Wm. L. Miller, Col. USAF (Ret.): My father later talked to an uncle who was an air force pilot. My uncle said that the event was the result of a government experiment using powdered silver nitrate to seed clouds as a cover for our bombers . . . and the cloud floated across the country from the desert in New Mexico. . . .

Interestingly, I have heard from several sources that they believed that an early version of a nuclear bomb was accidently detonated resulting not only in the darkening cloud, but in many military and civilian deaths. Unfortunately, we (the US government) are +all too capable of orchestrating cover-ups so well that truth becomes a non-sequitur. (I KNOW that this scenario was a possibility!) . . . You have no idea how much you have been deceived by those that you trust! I had to bite my tongue so many times I am surprised that I didn't bite it off!!!

Sally: Canadian forest fires were not cutting it with the adults I knew. They felt it was some government experiment we weren't supposed to ask much about. I tend to agree as I never smelled smoke but I sure remember the air having a strange smell.

Jack: Although I wasn't born until 1970, I had a high school chemistry teacher who told us about the day "they" turned the sky black. . . . Wish I had more details, but remember him saying that the experiment got a bit out of hand or something . . . seem to recall that it had to do with man-made weather . . . rain seeding or something like that.

Larry K.: I was five or six years old at the time and it made a lifelong impression. I checked with my father and he confirmed what little I'm able to tell you. . . . My dad didn't recall the Canadian forest fire explanation but he did say that many people thought it signaled the end of the world. (Rhodes 2012: 39–40, 40–41, 29, 14–15, 42)

The End of the World (and a Blue Moon)

Dorothy: I remember it was a Sunday in the early 1950's when this strange occurrence took place. I was living west of Oren Sound, Ontario at the time when the sun darkened around noon. It reminded me of twilight time. The atmosphere seemed eerie and the birds went to roost.

The adults talked of signs of "the end of the world." We eventually heard that forest fires in the west were so dense the smoke blew east, and blotted out the sun.

Neil: My [Salem, Ohio] memory is brief. My mother called my father, a minister, from the back porch, asking him to "Come look at this." Father and I went out with my brother. We found the sky an eerie color. From horizon to horizon the sky was a solid soft golden orange. . . . "What do you suppose is happening?" Mother asked. Father didn't reply; he was still taking it all in. "Listen," Mother said, "it's completely quiet." It was. There were no sounds whatsoever. No dogs barking, no traffic noises, no airplanes droning. Mother said, "The birds are silent. Do you think it's the end of the world?" she asked. Father stood gazing, looked at her, and shook his head slightly, "No."

We all stood in the backyard . . . for several minutes. Then we returned to the house. Father turned on the radio. I don't remember anything further. I do recall my mother discussing the event the next day with a neighbor, and saying the news had said it was a forest fire in Canada. She wasn't certain it was that, she said.

Jo Ann: I remember that day very well. It was September after I had graduated from high school in northwestern Pennsylvania. I was visiting my aunt and uncle who lived up the street from me and around 3 pm it got as dark as night. My aunt thought it was the end of the world. I remember running home as my mother was alone because my Dad was at work. We heard rumors of fires in Canada and also some government testing of some sort, but we never did hear anything for sure.

Tom: I was just a young boy . . . living in New Castle Pennsylvania. . . . It got really dark in the daytime; I remember the street lights came on in the early afternoon, like 1 or 2 pm, and you could smell the slight odor of smoke. Anyway, for a night or two, we just had this bluish-tinged near-full moon. I don't remember the exact year or month. I just remember we kids were all scared, and thought maybe the world was coming to an end—not because of the moon, but rather, the daytime darkness. (My one and only Real Blue Moon!) (Rhodes 2012: 65, 20–21, 35, 56–57)

References

Burmester, Bill. 1992–93. *Legends of Lawrence County.* Vols. 1–2. New Castle, PA: New Castle News.

Carlson, Norman P. 1986. "The Dark Day, September 25 [sic], 1950." *Jamestown Post-Journal.* http://the-red-thread.net/dark-day.html.

Lord, Albert. 1960. *The Singer of Tales.* Cambridge, MA: Harvard University Press.

Rhodes, Betty Matteson. 2012. *Black Sunday: What Really Happened on That Day on Sept. 24, 1950?* N.p.: Betmatrho.

Figure 20.1. *Wave destruction on clay cliffs during high stage of Lake Erie, winter of 1928–29. Camera standing in middle of former road. Man also. Waves breaking obliquely. Mentor Headlands, Painesville, O.* Slide 264.-.12 from the Jesse Earl Hyde Collection, Case Western Reserve University Department of Geological Sciences. (Copyrighted content used under US Code, Title 17, Chapter 1, Section 107, Limitations on exclusive rights: Fair Use)

HOW LAKE ERIE GOT ITS NAME
An Example of Onomastic Wordplay

The term *onomastics* refers specifically to wordplay with *names*, as occurs in games like the "banana-fanna" song, nicknaming, and wordplay referring to how places—like Lake Erie—got their names. The James T. Callow Folklore Archive was founded in 1964 at the University of Detroit, Mercy, and is available online. It has amassed a large collection of folk traditions associated with the Great Lakes, including an instance of onomastic wordplay on how Lake Erie got its name (for history of the name, see "Origin of the Name Erie in Myth and History," this volume).

The cities of Lackawanna and Buffalo, New York, both sit on Lake Erie's southern shore. In the 1960s, an explanation for the name Erie was collected in two parts, beginning with an interview on how Lackawanna got its name. According to the narrator, he was originally from Lackawanna but had moved to Buffalo a couple of years earlier, in 1962–63. He said he first heard the explanation of Erie's name in Buffalo, after he moved there. That explanation was directly linked to his explanation of how Lackawanna got its name, so both are given here, as they appear in the archive.

Notably, onomastic wordplay with the names Lackawanna and Erie share the same theme: the vast expanse of Lake Erie, which extends so far that no matter where you look, "all you can see is water."

Onomastic Wordplay on How Lake Erie
Got Its Name

Part I

There was this Indian tribe in New York (Oneidas, I think) who inhabited the Buffalo area. One of the Indians got up on this big old hill and surveyed the area. All the Indian could see was water, so he said "Lackawanna," which was that tribe's way of saying . . . "All I can see is water." And so that is how Lackawanna, New York, got its name.

Part II

Remember yesterday how I told you how Lackawanna got its name? Well, the next day that Indian brought the chief to that same hill. When the chief got up there he said, "You were right; all you can see from up here is water. Boy, is this ever *eerie!*" So that's how that particular body of water got its name—Lake Erie.

Reference

James T. Callow Folklore Archive. University of Detroit, Mercy. Item 3010. Collected May 14, 1965.

BIRTH OF A LAKE ERIE PROVERB

"A proverb is a short, pithy, traditional saying that sums up an argument or a point of view. Well-known examples include *A stitch in time saves nine, People who live in glass houses shouldn't throw stones,* and *You can lead a horse to water but you can't make it drink*."

George H. Schoemaker (1991: 238)

We can trace some proverbs back to their earliest known publication, but we rarely know where, when, or who uttered a particular proverb, how a statement may have been shaped into a proverb, or how a proverb may have been modified by persons unknown, over time and across space. But once a well-polished nugget of wisdom enters tradition, we gain a proverb. And in the case of one American-made proverb, that process began on Lake Erie.

According to Charles C. Doyle, Wolfgang Mieder, and Fred Shapiro (2012: 68–69), this particular proverb is based on a message sent in 1813 by Commodore Oliver Hazard Perry to President William Henry Harrison (see "The Ballad of James Bird," this volume). As the Battle of Lake Erie ended, Perry informed the president, "We have met the enemy and he is ours."

Walt Kelly (1913–73), a gifted American cartoonist, wordsmith, and social critic, was born a century after that statement was made. Kelly grew up to create Pogo, the lead character of an award-winning comic strip whose characters in *Pogo the Possum and Friends* were animals living in the Okefenokee Swamp, located in the southeastern United States. The high delight quotient of the strip was largely based on social and political satire. What would evolve into a proverb was first uttered in the foreword to Kelly's book *The Pogo Papers* (1953), where he described us as potentially our own worst enemy (my italics): "Resolve then, that on this very ground, with small flags waving and tinny blasts on tiny trumpets, *we shall meet the enemy, and not only may he be ours, he may be us."*

The version that would enter tradition appeared later on a Pogo environmental poster in 1970 and was repeated in an environmentally themed comic strip in 1971. In the strip, Pogo and his friend Porkypine sit on the edge of what was once a beautiful bayou that has become an almost impenetrably polluted blight. Porkypine complains, and Pogo identifies the culprit, as seen in figure 21.1.

Figure 21.1. Panel from 1971 *Pogo* comic strip, © Okefenokee Glee & Perloo, Inc. (Copyrighted content used with permission)

The statement enjoyed a long period of use in association with environmental and other human-made travesties of the times. Popular in the twentieth century, it is still likely to resurface at any moment if and when it becomes timely and relevant again, ready to serve us as a gem of insight—a gem that began as a message of triumph from a battle site on Lake Erie and later was polished as a perfect reference for all manner of human foibles for which we, ourselves, are guilty.

References

Doyle, Charles C., Wolfgang Mieder, and Fred Shapiro, eds. 2012. *The Dictionary of Modern Proverbs*. New Haven, CT: Yale University Press.

Schoemaker, George, ed. 1991. *The Emergence of Folklore in Everyday Life: A Fieldguide and Sourcebook*. Bloomington, IN: Trickster.

PART FOUR

FOLKLORE IN THE EARLY
TWENTY-FIRST CENTURY

Figure 22.1. Groundhog. Photo: *Chewie No. 9* by Gregory Laing via Flickr. (CC BY 2.0)

WEATHER LORE
The Groundhog's Spring Forecast

In the northern regions of Europe, the US, and Canada, winter is an infertile season of failing light and frigid cold. In premodern times, there was always a danger of freezing to death if fires could not be fed and a danger of starving to death if food ran out before plant and animal life could be replenished. Therefore, harvesting took place in fall, to be rationed and shared with important domestic animals over the winter. Some of these animals were raised for butchering at the winter solstice, halfway through the season, helping to sustain life until the return of spring.

Feast days were declared at the winter solstice, and festivals of light (called Candlemas by English speakers) took place against the darkest time of year. People looked everywhere for signs of spring, for weather-related indications of relief, or for enough patience to endure a long wait in case of prolonged winter weather. According to one English poem:

If Candlemas be fair and bright,
Winter has another flight.
If Candlemas brings clouds and rain,
Winter will not come again.

Modern meteorology has determined that spring arrives at Lake Erie on March 20, the time of the vernal equinox, when the sun's angle is directly above the equator, creating twelve hours of daylight and twelve hours of darkness. After that, the days grow increasingly longer and warmer, through spring and summer, until fall arrives and the cold cycle starts again.

In the last six or seven weeks of the Great Lakes winter, some would see spring in the first lengthening of daylight against darkness and others not until the length of days exceeded the length of nights. Across all wintery sections of the United States, a compromise came to embrace all factions. The

Figure 22.2. *Wiarton Willie Park* by Kevin M Klerks via Flickr. (CC BY 2.0)

compromise involved the native groundhog (or hedgehog), a robust marmot belonging to a family of large, local ground squirrels.

Every year, on February 2, Americans celebrate Groundhog's Day. Early-morning festivals are held based largely on traditions inherited from England and Germany. Participants gather to watch the groundhog emerge from its burrow. If the sky is overcast and the groundhog can't see his shadow, spring is forecast as coming early; if the sun shines and the groundhog can see his shadow, winter weather is forecast for six more weeks.

Groundhogs (also known as woodchucks) are given pet names from place to place across the nation. Among the best-known groundhogs are two named Chuck: Staten Island Chuck, from the island adjacent to New York City, and Buckeye Chuck, from Marion, Ohio ("Buckeye" because Ohio is known as the Buckeye State). But only Wiarton Willie is memorialized by a huge statue at Blue Water Park, in Wiarton, Ontario.

Yet the most famous of all groundhogs from the general Great Lakes area hails from Punxsutawney, Pennsylvania. This little fellow is known as Punxsutawney Phil, Punxsy, or just plain Phil. The annual Groundhog's Day celebration in Punxsutawney is sponsored by the local Groundhog Club, in a place called Gobbler's Knob. On February 2, as many as forty thousand people gather to watch local dignitaries (known as the Inner Circle) wearing top hats and standing beside the club president as he taps on Phil's burrow,

Figure 22.3. *Inner Circle* from the Punxsutawney Groundhog Club. (Copyrighted content used with permission)

waking the sleeping groundhog at approximately 7:30 a.m. to check on his shadow.

According to tradition, the club president then converses privately with Phil in "Groundhogese," after which Phil's prediction is proclaimed for all to hear. There's an obvious problem: clouds come and go, and the groundhog may or may not see his shadow at any point on the same day, depending on the moment he happens to appear. To no one's great surprise, the furry little fellow is wrong more than 40 percent of the time. In fact, in 2013, Punxsy forecast an early spring although most of the country shivered through a frigid March. In mid-March, a chilled Ohio prosecutor threatened to indict the groundhog for fraud. But before that could happen, Ohioans were relieved to hear that the groundhog had been right after all; it was simply that the club president had translated incorrectly.

Phil's handler, Club President Bill Deely, confirmed for reporter Soledad O'Brien (CNN, March 27, 2013) that a magic cane is passed from president to president, enabling effortless translation to Groundhogese, but misunderstandings can sometimes happen. Amid rumors of impeachment (and conspiracy theories that President Bill took the fall for Phil), Bill was reelected. He was interviewed on CNN along with Phil, who watched in silence and contributed by looking adorable.

Phil was onto something in 2015, when his prediction was correct and freezing weather broke records, lingering for weeks across the nation. Nevertheless, he was indicted that year for snow beyond a reasonable amount and—this time with absolute accuracy—for biting the mayor.

If Phil hadn't been making a political statement, the people of Pennsylvania certainly made one that winter. According to a Public Policy Poll taken during the election season of 2015, "50% of Pennsylvanians would rather be represented by the groundhog Punxsutawney Phil than by their current members of Congress" (*The Week* 2015).

For the American states and Canadian provinces surrounding Lake Erie, winter can be a long season. Folks appreciate events that ease the wait for light and warmth. Year in and year out, all around the lake's perimeter, locals gather faithfully on the second day of February (or simply turn to the media) for news of spring's furry little harbinger. Should winter's chill exceed all limits or prevail against a groundhog forecast, Great Lake dwellers see it through by keeping things light and bright until spring arrives to do it for them.

Reference

The Week. 2015. "Poll Watch: The Way We Were in 2015." December 25, 2015, 24.

Figure 23.1. *Woolly Bear* by Mike Keeling via Flickr. (CC BY-ND 2.0)

THE WOOLLY BEAR'S WINTER FORECAST AND FESTIVAL

The larval form of the Isabella tiger moth is a caterpillar known as the woolly bear. The fuzzy insect looks just as woolly as any bear and has two bands of color: black and rusty orange. The woolly bear is black at both ends, and according to folk belief, the width of the rust band in the middle (or bands, since there are sometimes more than one) can predict the nature of oncoming winter weather. The wider the rust band (or the more rust bands there are), the milder the coming winter will be. A narrow band of rust color is said to predict a harsh winter.

In the 1940s, C. H. Curran, curator of insects at the American Museum of Natural History in New York City, joined with some friends to enjoy the fall colors in upstate New York and to test the woolly bear color-band theory. They formed the original Society of the Friends of the Woolly Bear while they experimented and to some extent legitimized the folklore, their main objective was to have fun.

A PhD is not required in order to grasp the fun concept on Lake Erie. Woolly bear festivals are now held on both Canadian and American shores; they are always fun, but none is more successful than the festival at Vermilion, Ohio, a town that first developed in the 1800s as a small boat and fishing harbor on Erie's shore. Ohio's annual Woolly Bear Festival actually began nine miles away in 1973 and was meant to benefit an elementary school in tiny Birmingham, Ohio. The festivity was inspired by local meteorologist and TV weatherman Dick Goddard, who occasionally added color to his broadcasts with tidbits of local weather lore. By 1980, Goddard's Woolly Bear Festival had grown to such proportions that tiny little Birmingham could no longer contain it. It was on its way to becoming a local tradition.

According to the Vermilion Chamber of Commerce (2023), the Woolly Bear Festival was relocated to Vermilion because the resort town was better equipped to manage large crowds and celebrations. The festival, now the largest one-day event in Ohio, includes local festival queens and their royal

Figure 23.2. *Pup in Woolly Bear Costume Contest* from Woollybear Festival Facebook Group. (Copyrighted content used
under US Code, Title 17, Chapter 1, Section 107, Limitations
on exclusive rights: Fair Use)

courts, a mammoth parade with many floats, over two thousand marching
bands, and more than 150,000 spectators. The family- and pet-friendly event,
originally hosted by Goddard, takes place in late September or early October on the first Sunday that the Cleveland Browns football team is playing
out of town. The event features ongoing entertainment, food booths, craft
booths, and merchant sales, including an array of official Woolly Bear Festival memorabilia.

Perhaps best of all, there are a number of competitions for kids, and pets
are also welcome—a clear reflection of Goddard's long-standing efforts as
a muscular advocate for animals. The Woolly Bear Festival in Vermilion is
unique in that kids, teens, adults, and pets not only are welcome but can also
compete for Best Woolly Bear Costume.

Never let it be said that folks on Lake Erie don't know how to mark the
fall season, using woolly bears to predict the oncoming winter weather and,

Figures 23.3 and 23.4. *Woollybear Festival* photos from Woollybear Festival Facebook Group. (Copyrighted content used under US Code, Title 17, Chapter 1, Section 107, Limitations on exclusive rights: Fair Use)

in the process, creating enough warmth and mirth to see them through the long, cold season ahead. Goddard retired from weathercasting after fifty-five years, in November 2016. But for more than forty of those years, Ohioans maintained the lakeshore festival, breaching gaps of generation, gender, and even species to make one and all welcome—including everybody's four-footed, fuzzy-faced family members.

Reference

Vermilion Chamber of Commerce. 2023. "Woolly Bear Festival." https://www.vermilionohio .com/woollybear-festival/.

Figure 24.1. *La Chasse Galerie* (*The Flying Canoe*) by Henri Julien, 1906. (Public Domain)

"LA CHASSE GALERIE," OR "THE FLYING CANOE"

*V*oyageurs is the French word for travelers, but from the 1690s to the mid-1800s, it referred to employees contracted to move furs and trade goods across the five thousand kilometers of rugged wilderness that was once New France. This vast area included all five Great Lakes and numerous other American waterways. Based in the Canadian province of Quebec, some of the Voyageurs were English, some German, and some Iroquois, but the majority were Frenchmen who created their own French Canadian traditions and distributed these tales, along with their goods, up and down their trade routes along Lake Erie's Canadian shore. A representative jewel among such literary treasures is the tale of "La Chasse Galerie," or "The Flying Canoe," still held in French Canadian tradition.

The story may have been influenced by the French tale "The Wild Hunt," in which a nobleman was so devoted to hunting, he stopped attending Sunday Mass. As punishment, he was condemned to fly forever through the night sky, pursued by galloping horses and baying hounds. In real life, French Canadian Voyageurs went to mass regularly, but when they entered the wilderness, the last church they were likely to see was on the island of Montreal, near their home base in Quebec.

French Canada is a historically Catholic part of the nation, and Voyageurs in particular had good reason to stay in divine good graces since their work was physically intense and often life-threatening. Although they seem to have borrowed and modified a motif from the tale of "The Wild Hunt" to fit their own experience, they also may have borrowed the flying canoe motif from a Native American legend, combining these elements into a distinctly French Canadian tale still told today. Like all oral traditions, the story is fluid and differs somewhat from telling to telling, but the core motifs are stable, and the tale, as known to the author (childhood resident of Quebec City, Quebec), unfolds as follows:

"La Chasse Galerie," or "The Flying Canoe"

The Voyageurs were snowed in. The men were three hundred miles from their wives and sweethearts, unable to celebrate the New Year at home. They were feeling glum and passing the rum when Baptiste came through the door with a wintery blast. "*Mon Dieu* [My God]! we can do better than this!" he cried. "Let's go home!"

When the men asked how, Baptiste explained, "I made a pact with the devil. Here's the deal." Baptiste would be allowed to fly a canoe wherever he wanted, but he had to repay the devil by not saying Mass for a full year. In addition, if Baptiste did not return the canoe by dawn, the devil would keep his soul. "And one more thing," Baptiste informed them: once they were in the air, they could not curse or utter the word God, nor could they fly over a church or touch a cross. If they did, the canoe would come crashing down.

Most in the camp refused to go, but seven could not resist. They piled in, and once they were seated, the canoe rose in the air, and they paddled eagerly through the sky. Their wives and sweethearts were so happy to see them! They celebrated well into the night, drinking and dancing. It was close to sunrise when they gathered their wits; after all, Baptiste would lose his soul if they were not back by dawn! They finally found him, drunk and snoring under a table. They bundled him into the canoe, rose up in the sky, and paddled toward camp as fast as they could.

Knowing that Baptiste would start swearing when he awoke, they tied him up and gagged him, just to be sure the word God would not be uttered and they would not be forced to crash. They paddled so fast they nearly capsized to avoid a tall church steeple. Nearing home, they almost tipped over to avoid a cross, perched high on a hilltop. As the canoe came upright, Baptiste awoke. He sat up, struggled with the ropes, and pulled the gag away. "*Mon Dieu* (My God)!" he shouted. "Why have you tied me up?"

At the sound of the word God, the canoe dived, plunging toward the ground. It hit the top of a pine tree in the center of a deep forest. All the men tumbled out,

and not

one was

ever seen

again.

Traditional Motifs

| M211.6 | Man sells soul to devil, for visit home in boat that sails through the sky |
| C495 | Speaking taboo: the one forbidden expression |

Figure 25.1. *Lake Erie Monster Beer*, artwork by Darren Booth from the Great Lakes Brewing Company. (Copyrighted content used with permission)

SOUTH BAY BESSIE

The Lake Erie Sea Serpent

The Loch Ness Monster, a native of Scotland, is fondly known as Nessie. Less known, and less seen, is a similarly monstrous inhabitant of Lake Erie, known as South Bay Bessie. Sightings of Bessie have been variously attributed to ancient myths and modern legends, to ancient sea serpents still lurking in the lake, to an endangered species of famously oversize lake sturgeon, and, perhaps most wisely, to a bit too much to drink.

With a nod to spirit-inspired sightings, the Great Lakes Brewing Company, a popular brewery and restaurant on Cleveland's west side, makes Lake Erie Monster beer, which is bottled with a fierce rendering of Bessie on the label. Still doing swimmingly in local popular culture, she is the namesake of Cleveland's minor league hockey team, the Lake Erie Monsters, and at this writing, she is also memorialized by a local band that calls itself South Bay Bessie. A string of restaurants native to Cleveland, known as Melt University, features a variety of comfort foods made with melted cheese, including the gourmet concoction Parmageddon, named for the once-ethnic, working-class suburb of Parma, honored by adding pierogi and vodka kraut to the basic grilled cheese. But—never to be forgotten—Bessie herself is named in a magnificent melted-cheese and battered-fish creation known as the Lake Erie Monster sandwich.

Sightings in Past Centuries

The first sighting of Bessie is sometimes given as 1793, but this seems to be a fanciful, modern reconstruction of a memoir written by young Oliver Spencer, aged twelve in that year. On an excursion to a snake-infested portion of Middle Bass Island, Spencer and others traveling on the sloop *Felicity* were separated from the captain, who failed in his plan to shoot ducks for dinner. Spencer describes his own experience there and repeats the captain's explanation for returning from the hunt empty-handed:

We spent part of Saturday afternoon on an excursion through the Middle Bass Island on which we killed several large rattlesnakes . . . and the captain, who had gone to a small pond a few hundred yards ahead of us to shoot ducks, returned in a short time, running and out of breath, declaring that a monster, a snake more than a rod [sixteen feet] in length, the moment he shot some ducks issued from the long grass by the edge of the water, made directly towards him, and pursued him for more than twenty rods. On our return to the sloop we caught some fine bass, which more than compensated us for the loss of the captain's ducks. (Spencer [1793] 1917: 151)

It is hard to say whether it was actually a sixteen-foot monster or just bad aim that accounts for the captain's failure to provide ducks for dinner. But sightings of an actual sea serpent, more clearly identified as South Bay Bessie, were periodically reported to newspapers beginning in the nineteenth century. That was when the *Cleveland Gazette and Commercial Register* used a harrowing sea serpent as a metaphor to describe the Second Bank of the United States, which had suddenly demanded the immediate payment of balances due (Carpenter 2019). In a seeming confirmation of nineteenth-century religionist Max Müller, who held that myths are beliefs composed of metaphors taken literally (Dorson 1968: 162), it was only after the *Cleveland Gazette* used the sea serpent metaphor to describe a voracious bank that ordinary folks began spotting the purported monster in Cleveland's South Bay. A twentieth-century sighting by two firefighters from Huron, Ohio, put the sea monster in the newspapers once again.

According to Willis et al., the city of Huron subsequently "declared itself the National Live Capture and Control Center for the Lake Erie Monster. Tom Solberg of the Huron Lagoons Marina offered a $100,000 reward for the safe and unharmed capture of the beast" (2005: 94). According to the city of Huron, the reward has never been claimed.

Bessie in the Twenty-First Century

It seems that sightings of Bessie ceased to be newsworthy in the twenty-first century, but a number of twenty-first-century sightings are still posted to the internet, including this description of a Lake Erie sighting from an online edition of the *UFO Digest*: "At approximately 11 a.m. Thursday August 12th, 2010 I recorded something I cannot explain. . . . It was about 30 to 40 feet in length and made a large swell in the water as well as a wavelike [sic] that of a small boat. It was serpent like and notch and bumps on its back the video speaks for itself. I do not think that my two boys or myself will ever swim in that bay again" (Vander Ploeg 2011).

As in earlier centuries, modern sightings include sincere accounts like the one given above. Yet, like many species that have avoided substantiation in natural science, Bessie is documented only by blurry photographic imagery. Rather than suggesting she never existed, this demonstrates clearly that the belief in South Bay Bessie has not entirely vanished in the twenty-first century, although that belief may yet be overcome by belief in the more modern, mutant monster spawn of nuclear radiation (see "Nuclear Plant Spawns Mutant Monsters," this volume).

Of course, there is always the possibility that Bessie will prevail alongside the irradiated monsters who may come to inhabit the lake. But for now, aside from churning lots of water, defeating all automatically focused cameras, and being clearly visible only in the movies and in imaginative artists' renderings, the surviving sea serpent appears to be one of a species that folklorist Richard Dorson calls "do-nothing dragons" (1982: 65). These are deep-sea denizens long retired from ocean-faring mayhem, living out their golden years as lake-dwelling subjects of reliably blurry surveillance.

References

Carpenter, Kevin. 2019. "CLE Myths: Lake Erie Monster." *Cleveland Magazine*, November 25, 2019. http://clevelandmagazine.com/in-the-cle/articles/cle-myths-lake-erie-monster.

Dorson, Richard M. 1968. *The British Folklorists: A History*. London: Routledge.

———. 1982. *Man and Beast in American Comic Legend*. Bloomington: Indiana University Press.

Spencer, Oliver M. (1793) 1917. *The Indian Captivity of O. M. Spencer*. Edited by Milo Milton Quaife, superintendent of the State Historical Society of Wisconsin. Chicago: Lakeside Press, R. R. Donelley.

Vander Ploeg, Dirk. 2011. "Relaunch of MonsterTracker.com Coincides with Sighting of South Bay Bessie." *UFO Digest: UFO and Paranormal News from around the World*, March 24, 2011. http://www.ufodigest.com/article/relaunch-of-monstertracker-com-coincides-with-sighting-of-south-bay-bessie.

Willis, James A., Andrew Henderson, and Loren Coleman. 2005. "Bessie, the Lake Erie Monster: Horror or Hoax?" In *Weird Ohio: Your Travel Guide to Ohio's Legends and Best Kept Secrets*, edited by Mark Sceurman and Mark Moran, 94–96. New York: Sterling.

BRIG! GEN. ANTHONY WAYNE.

Figure 26.1. *Anthony Wayne* portrait. (Public Domain)

MAD ANTHONY WAYNE

A Lake Erie Ghost Seeks His Lost Bones

General "Mad" Anthony Wayne (1745–96) was a Revolutionary War hero who, after the war, went on to fight Indians in the state of Ohio. In 1771, a soldier arrested for civil disobedience sought Wayne's help, but instead, Wayne recommended that the man be flogged. The disgruntled soldier responded by calling the general "Mad Anthony." Since Wayne's men thought the term suited his fierce combat style, the nickname stuck.

In 1796, when Wayne arrived at Presque Isle, he was quite ill with gout. He died on the shores of Lake Erie on December 5, 1796, and was buried there. But in 1809, his children successfully petitioned to have his body disinterred for reburial and transferred to his home in Radnor, Pennsylvania. When the body was exhumed, however, it was only partially decomposed and loosely intact, in no condition for travel.

The remains were therefore boiled in a cauldron to remove flesh from bone, and the bones were scraped clean before transportation. But according to legend, the cart that carried his remains lurched so badly, the casket frequently bounced open, and bones were lost along the road—a path that now corresponds to State Route 322. As Michael Schellhammer posted online in 2013: "The story goes that every January 1, Wayne's birthday, the ghost of the general rises, along with his horse, and rides the roads of the Keystone State in search of his lost bones. The ghost is often seen along U.S. Route 322 that runs southwest across Pennsylvania. Others have seen the ghost riding in the opposite direction from Radnor to Presque Isle, also along Route 322."

Although Mad Anthony Wayne still rides the road in our own time, he can only be seen once a year, on New Year's Day. Nevertheless, he is far from forgotten. At this writing, the type of cauldron used for boiling his bones, complete with bones afloat and a fake (if cozy) fire, is a favorite exhibition at the Erie County History Center. The stone (fig. 26.3) beside the pot is one of

Figure 26.2. *Anthony Wayne's Pot*, Erie County Historical Society. (Copyrighted content used with permission)

Figure 26.3. *Anthony Wayne's Cornerstone*, Erie County Historical Society. (Copyrighted content used with permission)

the four original cornerstones set in 1795 for what was then a small Pennsylvania town called Erie.

Reference

Schellhammer, Michael. 2013. "The Nicknaming of General 'Mad' Anthony Wayne." *Journal of the American Revolution*, May 3, 2013. http://allthingsliberty.com/2013/05/the-nicknaming-of-general-mad-anthony-wayne.

Figure 27.1. Johnny Appleseed, *Harpers New Monthly Magazine*, 1871. (Public Domain)

JOHNNY APPLESEED
A Folk Hero's Ties to Lake Erie

America has historically been a beacon of freedom, a Promised Land for those seeking freedom of religion. Not surprisingly, a panoply of diverse faiths has arrived at these shores, and many homegrown faiths have emerged here as well. Voltaire's famous French sneer that England had "forty-two religions and only two sauces" could easily be said of America in the years when the frontier went no farther than Ohio. It was on the Ohio Country frontier that John Chapman, a traveling nurseryman and preacher of a new faith, would become an American legend. Known as Johnny Chapman (1774–1845), he was born in Massachusetts in tumultuous times. He grew up to be a nurseryman on the move, planting apple trees across Pennsylvania, Ohio, and Indiana. But according to his obituary, he did have permanent roots: at his sister's home in Cleveland, Ohio, on Lake Erie's shore.

Johnny was a Christian deeply influenced by the writings of Emanuel Swedenborg, founder of Swedenborgianism, a faith also known as the Church of the New Jerusalem, or simply the New Church. The new faith employed hypnotism and introduced people to altered states of consciousness, natural remedies for health, and dream interpretation as part of their spiritual experience. Followers rejected the doctrine of the Trinity but accepted baptism as a requirement for becoming a member. Appleseed, a Swedenborgian preacher, sowed seeds of the faith along with his apple trees, but he pressured no one into conformity, and to almost everyone's delight, he preached the Christian Gospels across the vast, unchurched frontier.

Apples grown from seed are usually unfit to eat, but they were popular with settlers for two good reasons. First, frontier settlers were required by law to plant apple or pear orchards to retain rights to their land. And second, the apples were good for making hard cider and applejack, so Chapman's seeds were doubly welcome, earning him the affectionate nickname Johnny Appleseed. An eccentric fellow, Johnny was known for being as kind and gentle to animals as he was to people, and unlike many settlers, he was also a good friend to Native Americans. He was a strict vegetarian and was easily recognized by his full beard, scraggly clothes, and bare feet—but above all, by the tin pot he wore as a hat.

Whether or not John Chapman was an astute businessman, he was certainly in the right place at the right time to earn a good living and make a lasting impression. As a member of the Chapman family, he maintained close ties with his kinfolk in Ohio, and when he died, he left a large number of productive nurseries, orchards, and landholdings to his sister in Cleveland. But on the frontier, as Johnny Appleseed, he left an invaluable legacy to an entire nation—one of conservation, goodwill, and deep faith.

Figure 28.1. *Fairport Harbor Lighthouse & Marine Museum* by
Paul Comstock. (CC BY 2.0)

HAUNTED LIGHTHOUSES OF LAKE ERIE

The opening of the Erie Canal in 1825, along with the opening of the Welland Canal in 1830, linked the five Great Lakes as a single, oceanic sea and a major shipping resource. But on Lake Erie's relatively shallow, wind-tossed waters, shipwrecks were all too frequent, causing tragic losses of lives, ships, and goods. Lighthouses were built to help ships find the shore and avoid its sandy shoals and rocky outcrops. Some of these structures housed their lightkeepers nearby, and a few housed them within the light tower, but all helped ships navigate through Erie's often life-threatening waters.

With the development of electricity and automated light signals, many lightkeepers were put out of work. Finally, with the development of GPS systems and other navigational advances, lighthouses themselves became obsolete. Perhaps inevitably, some of the now dark and empty towers, once beacons of light and hope, took on a new life, convincing many that they now harbor ghosts of the dark and stormy past.

Ghost stories scare us because at one level they make us glimpse our own mortality, but on another, they reassure us that there is some sort of life after death. A really good ghost story strikes a perfect balance—not reassuring enough to lose that scary edge and not scary enough to dampen the hope of a good afterlife. Ghosts are believed to haunt lighthouses on all five of the Great Lakes, but Lake Erie is home to some of the most unusual ghosts ever to haunt anywhere, let alone on the inland sea.

The Ghost Cat of Old Fairport Harbor

The lighthouse at Old Fairport Harbor was built in 1825. The keeper's house stood beside a sixty-foot tower known as "the light that shone for a hundred years." In its heyday it was a beacon of hope for many escaped slaves traveling the Underground Railroad (see "Underground Railroad," this volume), who were routinely hidden in the tower on their way to freedom in Canada. The structure was rebuilt in 1871, when Joe Babcock became the lightkeeper. The Babcock family lived there uneventfully until the tragic death of their five-year-old son. Thereafter, Mrs. Babcock's own health steadily failed. Eventually bedridden, she would have spent her days alone if not for the number of cats she kept for company. After her death, one small gray cat refused to leave the lighthouse, ever faithful to its departed mistress.

Years later, the lighthouse became a museum. According to several online accounts, the resident curator was working in the kitchen in 1989 when she thought she saw something scurry by. Now and then she would again glimpse movement. Whatever it was, it clearly favored the room where Mrs. Babcock had slept. Once, trying to follow it, the curator caught sight of what appeared to be a cat, scampering off in a flash of gray and vanishing before her eyes. At first, most folks took that claim as more fanciful than factual. But during subsequent construction, workers entered a crawlspace, and to everyone's amazement, they discovered the long-mummified remains of a small gray cat. Apparently, Mrs. Babcock's faithful companion remained there in spirit, along with its mummified body, which to this day can be seen on display at the Fairport Harbor Maritime Museum.

Untimely Deaths and Ghost Noises in the South Bass Island Lighthouse

The lighthouse at South Bass Island was built in 1897 and operated until 1962. The tower is attached to the keeper's residence, putting all who worked there under one roof. In 1967, the lighthouse was purchased by the Ohio State University, which opened the facility for guided tours. If untimely deaths inspire lighthouse hauntings, then this lighthouse is a most likely candidate for uncanny activity. But of the three untimely deaths associated with it, no one can tell which one, or ones, may account for the ghostly noises heard there.

Records exist for all three of the deceased, beginning in 1897 when the lighthouse opened (Cruickshank 1999). Its first keeper was Harry A. Riley, who in 1897 moved in with his wife. In August 1898, Riley hired an assistant named Samuel Anderson. A smallpox outbreak occurred on South Bass Island that summer, but it was mild, and there were no deaths on the island—that is, not from smallpox. Rather, on August 31, only twenty-two days after arriving on the island, Samuel Anderson was found dead at the foot of a cliff. The newspaper reported that he had been terrified of smallpox contagion and had hidden himself in the lighthouse basement, where he lived with several pet snakes. He reportedly emerged one day and threw himself off the cliff, shouting, "God save them all!" Anderson's death was ruled a suicide.

Remarkably, Anderson's employer, the lightkeeper, Harry Riley, was found two days later, raving so madly he was taken into custody. Riley was committed to a state mental health institution, where he was promptly diagnosed as "hopelessly insane." He would die there seven months later. Anderson's suicide, supposedly to avoid an illness that people weren't dying from, seems somewhat less than convincing. So does Riley's overnight descent into "hopeless insanity." But any possible connection between Anderson's death and Riley's bizarre derangement remains unknown. Then, in 1962, tragedy struck the lighthouse a third time. Keeper Charles B. Duggan inexplicably fell to his death from a cliff on the west side of the island. This time, the untimely death was ruled an accident.

Visitors to the South Bass Island Lighthouse report the sounds of footsteps in the basement, doors slamming of their own accord, and an assortment of unexplained noises. Noise coming from the basement suggests the ghost of Samuel Anderson, the first to die and the only basement dweller. But then, no one has ever seen the source of the noises, so none of those who died so tragically can be entirely ruled out. Perhaps the spirits of all three still move about the lighthouse, the last home they would ever know.

The Phantom Keeper of Toledo's Harbor Lighthouse

The Toledo Harbor Lighthouse can only be approached by boat. It stands eight miles northeast of Toledo on an artificial island, built at the meeting point of Lake Erie and Maumee Bay. The lighthouse went into operation in 1904, and in 1966 the light was automated, allowing it to operate without a keeper. When the last Coast Guard crew departed, an unusual strategy was employed to discourage vandalism at the newly empty tower. A nicely mustachioed mannequin was placed at one of the upper windows, nattily dressed in full Coast Guard uniform. As time passed, the fashion-conscious mannequin also acquired a blond, shoulder-length wig.

The keeper in the window is, of course, known to be a mannequin. But despite that fact, tourists who sail out to visit the site have seen him beckon from the lighthouse window. For this reason, the mannequin is thought to be possessed by a ghost: the Phantom Keeper of the Harbor Lighthouse. The lighthouse mannequin has also entered regional Coast Guard tradition; new officers stationed at Toledo make a pilgrimage to the site and sign his shirt as a rite of passage. Moreover, little kids in the region are well aware: if they're not in bed on time, the Phantom Keeper of the Harbor Lighthouse is almost sure to find out.

References

Cruickshank, Nancy. 1999. "South Bass Island Lighthouse" (OHSU-FS-079). Ohio Sea Grant College Program, Ohio State University.

Special thanks are due to Nancy Cruickshank for her support and invaluable help with research for this entry and other maritime segments of this volume.

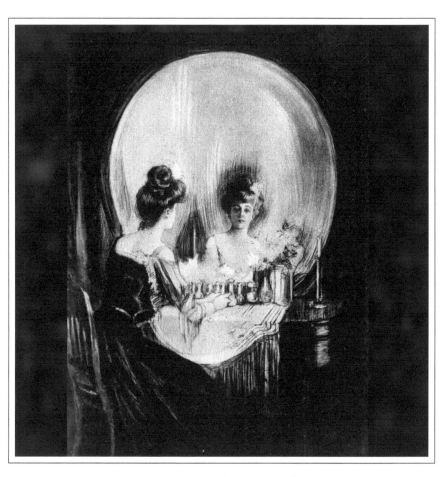

Figure 29.1. *All Is Vanity* by Allan Gilbert, 1892. (Public Domain)

Focusing on the center of this image, you may see a woman at a vanity table looking in the mirror, but try to focus on the whole picture, and instead you'll see a skull. If you see a skull, focus on the center; once again you'll see the woman looking in the mirror. This art style, meant to trick the eye, is called optical art. Combining images of death with symbols of beauty or status is an art genre called vanitas, a symbolic way of showing that we are all alike and that vain persons of beauty and status will be conquered by death, just like everyone else. (Public Domain)

BLOODY MARY IN THE MIRROR
A Lake Erie Variant

"Bloody Mary" is the name of a highly variable tale often involving death and violence. It forms the backstory of a game played mostly by groups of adolescent girls. Bloody Mary herself is almost always a terrifying apparition who appears in the mirror as summoned by a set of ritualized behaviors using a relatively stable oral formula. In earlier times, the object of the game was to glimpse the image of a future husband, who would manifest behind Bloody Mary in the mirror. More recently, glimpses of future husbands have all but given way to a generational power struggle, the object being to face down a bloody matriarchal image without running in fear before it fades. Perhaps the shift in interest from domesticity to defiance was influenced by the egalitarian civil rights and feminist movements of the 1960s and 1970s.

Despite the change in domestic sentiment, summoning Bloody Mary remains a group activity and still requires a mirror. Accompanying rituals may also include walking upstairs backward, lighting candles in a darkened room, and spinning around each time her name is called. Variations in the oral formula involve the number of times the name Bloody Mary must be called and, in some cases, the addition of the ritual taunt "I've got your baby."

An intriguing connection to Mary Tudor, or Queen Mary I (reigned 1553–58) has been suggested, noting that she purportedly suffered a number of fertility issues and miscarriages and was therefore popularly known as Bloody Mary (Ellis 2004). She seems a likely candidate in association with the taunt "I've got your baby." But the only Queen Mary actually known for effusive bloody issue was Mary Stuart, Queen of Scots, who miscarried twins and yet was never known as Bloody Mary. Instead, it was indeed Mary Tudor who was nicknamed Bloody Mary, but the name had nothing to do with miscarriages. Rather, she acquired the *bloody* moniker for her hand in the massacre of roughly three hundred Protestants, in an attempt to defeat the

Reformation. Perhaps these two Marys, swept together, account for a single Bloody Mary figure in folk imagination. But separately, neither of these queens seems a convincing candidate for the Bloody Mary who terrorizes adolescent girls from the mirror.

Another potential inspiration for the Bloody Mary title might include the suitably terrifying Hungarian countess Elizabeth Bathory (1560–1614), known as the Bloody Countess. Tradition holds that Bathory was a sadistic serial killer who thrilled at spilling the blood of young women, inspiring a number of gruesome legends (Melton 2010). Most notably, the middle-aged Bathory is said to have spent hours in front of mirrors checking on her looks and to have bathed in the blood of slain virgins, the better to regain the fading beauty of her youth.

Regardless of who the potential namesake really is, Bloody Mary is the shared moniker of all women seen in the mirror game, who are sometimes known by other names, including but not limited to Mary Whales, Mary Worth, and Hell Mary. The source of the name Bloody Mary remains a mystery and may—or may not—refer to a historical figure.

No matter who or what may have inspired the modern Mary-in-the-mirror game, when the apparition manifests, the point seems to be challenging a domineering female figure, or matriarch. Among girls approaching the age of menses, or bloody issue, who are (or soon will be) mature enough to attract young men (and become pregnant), it seems that facing down the older (postmenopausal) Mary may be a means to transcend maternal authority, eclipsing the older woman's fading youth and supplanting her procreative power (thus, "I have your baby").

Tales of Bloody Mary's past lend a wide variety of backstories to her manifestation in the mirror. Plots range from a clear variant of the ubiquitous "vanishing hitchhiker" legend (Langlois 1980) to different women who come to gruesome ends in a variety of blood-soaked ways. One contemporary tale from Montana depicts a feckless father manipulated by a homicidal stepmother who is jealous of his children. In this variant, the evil stepmother is eventually sucked into the mirror by Mary's bloodthirsty (and in this case helpful!) apparition (Schlosser 2008).

Finding a single thread that unites all Bloody Mary backstories may not be possible. But most are thematically related, featuring a menacing power figure reminiscent of aging fairy-tale matriarchs, past the age of menses, who are threatened by their mirrors—women consumed by vanity who traditionally seek a drop of blood, or a blood-red analogue (e.g., an apple), as a means to prevent youthful rivals from replacing them as "fairest of them all." At this writing, the game is "won" if Bloody Mary retreats from the mirror before a

Figure 29.2. *Two Mirrors* webcomic by xkcd.com, https://xkcd.com/555/. (Copyrighted content used with permission)

player is scared off or sucked into the mirror, clawed, driven insane, or killed with fright.

While the rules of the game have traditionally been passed down, modified, and maintained through personal face-to-face contact, the internet is now an additional source of interest and instruction on how to play. Reflecting the shift in interest from domesticity to defiance, the xkcd.com webcomic upped the ante in 2008 by proposing the use of two threatening mirrors instead of one (fig. 29.2). At the risk of overinterpreting, the cartoon seems to suggest that in an age of blended families, one way to defeat two dominant matriarchs is to set them up for collision with each other.

In any case, the specter of a jealous and menacing old hag, hoping to displace youthful rivals, is evident in a Bloody Mary tale apparently unique to Lake Erie's shore. In this variant, Mary does not appear in the mirror but menaces young women from outside their bedroom windows; those who see her through the window (perhaps a variant of the looking glass) are doomed. The Lake Erie version can be found in print (Gerrick 1982: 42–43):

> Below the waters of Lake Erie around the Sandusky Bay lives an old, ugly hag by the name of Mary. Mary once fell in love with a young man from Huron. He, of course, was not attracted to her. Mary grew more obsessed with this man, and continued to pursue him despite his repeated rejections.
>
> Mary soon turned to black magic to win him over. First she drew a figure of a pretty girl in the sand. Then she stalked and kidnapped young women, taking them to her home where she killed them. To complete her grisly plan, Mary then selected the best body parts from each victim and sewed them together to form a perfect "doll." Mary tried to use the lifelike doll to attract the man. She was almost successful. After luring him on a pier, the man accidently fell into the lake and drowned.
>
> It is said that at night Mary comes up from the bottom of her watery home and roams the shores of Lake Erie looking for new body parts to replace the

rotting ones of her "doll." One variation of this legend states that when the night is stormy, she will creep around the houses along the lake, looking inside the windows for young women. When she finds a suitable candidate for the doll, she will knock three times on the girl's bedroom window. If the girl hears the noise and looks out the window, into the face of "Bloody Mary," she will fall under the witch's spell and be taken away. Another version warns young women against going near the lake at night. If she happens upon Bloody Mary, the witch will drag her under the water.

Although it can't be said with certainty, this narrative's use of gruesome dismemberment on Erie's shore may have found inspiration in the dismemberment of victims in Cleveland's notorious "Torso murders," which stand among the most heinous of unsolved serial killings in American history. Twelve dismembered bodies—the majority never identified because their heads were never found—were apparent victims of the "Torso Killer," who terrorized the Cleveland area from 1935–38. In 1934, a year before serial killing was suspected, the dismembered body of a young woman, never identified, was left near Euclid Beach on the lakeshore, earning her the epithet the Lady of the Lake. Not counting this female victim, the body first traced to the Torso Killer was that of a male, found similarly dismembered in the following year.

The seventh victim (actually the eighth local dismemberment) was a disembodied female found in 1937 at the same spot where the Lady of the Lake was found in 1934. This suggests that the 1934 Lady of the Lake may actually have been the Torso Killer's first victim, bringing the actual total of victims to thirteen. Despite all efforts, no one was ever charged with the crime. Given this history, Lake Erie's "Bloody Mary" variant may have emerged in response to the Torso murders, hoping to discourage young women from venturing out alone at night, especially on the lakeshore.

References

Ellis, Bill. 2004. *Lucifer Ascending: The Occult in Folklore and Popular Culture.* Louisville: University Press of Kentucky.

Gerrick, David. 1982. "Bloody Mary." In *Ohio's Ghostly Greats*, 25–26. Dayton, OH: Dayton Press.

Langlois, Janet. 1980. "Mary Whales I Believe in You." In *Indiana Folklore: A Reader*, edited by Linda Dégh, 196–224. Bloomington: Indiana University Press.

Melton, J. Gordon. 2010. *The Vampire Book: Encyclopedia of the Undead.* 3rd ed. Canton, MI: Invisible Ink.

Schlosser, S. E. 2008. "Bloody Mary Returns." Ghost Stories. American Folklore. http://americanfolklore.net/folklore/2008/10/bloody_mary_returns.html.

Figure 30.1. "The Newfoundland Dog" score by Henry Russell, engraved by George W. Quidor, 1843. (Public Domain)

THE BLACK DOG OF LAKE ERIE

Shipwreck Lore

Belief in black, fearsome ghost dogs appears in the folklore of the English-speaking colonial Americas (see "Buried Treasure and Witchcraft," this volume). Modern tales of "The Black Dog of Lake Erie" trace to a legend involving a black Newfoundland dog, a breed that was prized for saving drowning people from shipwrecks in the nineteenth century. The founding incident reportedly took place at Welland Canal on Lake Erie, near Niagara Falls, where a black Newfoundland was the ship's mascot.

The story says the dog fell or was knocked overboard, and instead of helping the animal, the crew mocked it as it tried to keep up with the ship. The dog was crushed by the gate on the canal lock, and the guilty crew was delayed for hours. Thereafter, it was said their nights were haunted by the howling of the dog they had failed to save.

The Ghost Dog of Lake Erie and Shipwrecks on the Great Lakes

After that incident, the same ghost dog was said to cause misfortune by haunting ships that sailed all five Great Lakes. "Ghost Dog" haunting tales predate "Black Dog" shipwreck tales, but by 1875, the ghostly Black Dog would become the best explanation for the many mysterious shipwrecks that the Great Lakes were known for. In traditional shipwreck tales, the Black Dog appears on a vessel—typically a schooner—and then runs across the deck, leaping to land from the other side. Soon after, the doomed ship goes down.

Circa 1864, Lake Michigan: Haunting of the *Phoebe Catherine*

The tale of the *Phoebe Catherine* is an early haunting story that does not end in a shipwreck. Rather, the ghost dog reportedly followed one of the crew members, even appearing to others. The ghost's presence was used to explain why the schooner ran aground twice and why the captain died in his cabin while the ship was icebound, near the Manitou Islands. Despite these and other misfortunes, the *Phoebe Catherine* was never shipwrecked. But in the next ten years, the ghost dog would transform into the infamous Black Dog, a ghostly apparition used to explain shipwrecks on all the Great Lakes, Lake Erie among them.

1875, Lake Ontario: Wreck of the *Isaac G. Jenkins*, November 30

One night, the helmsman of the *Isaac G. Jenkins* reportedly woke the captain to say he'd seen the Black Dog scamper across the deck and disappear in the darkness. The captain accused the man of being drunk and paid no attention. The helmsman either quit or was put off the ship at Port Colbourne, but he called out warnings from each tow bridge along the way and was finally driven off by the captain's own dog. The *Jenkins* sank on that ill-fated voyage, and afterward, a farmer claimed to have seen a black dog swim ashore and vanish.

1881, Lake Erie: Wreck of the *Mary Jane*, November 19

The Black Dog is said to have caused the tragic wreck of the *Mary Jane*, in which all were lost on Lake Erie. Workers on the wharf at Port Colbourne, Ontario, reported that before it sailed they saw a black dog leap from the schooner and vanish after landing on the dock.

1891, Lake Michigan: Wreck of the *Thomas Hume*, May 21

Some blame the Black Dog for the wreck of the *Thomas Hume*. The schooner had been sailing with the *Rouse Simmons*, which turned back as a gale approached. The *Thomas Hume* sailed on and vanished without a trace. No bodies or wreckage ever washed ashore, and the sunken wreck was not discovered until 2005.

The wreck of the *Isaac G. Jenkins* (whose helmsman claimed to have seen the dog and quit or was put ashore) has been memorialized in a modern folk song, or "story-song," by Tom and Chris Kastle, both of whom have served as crew aboard several Great Lakes schooners. Their folk song, "The Black Dog of Lake Erie," appears on a current CD, confirming the tale's persistence in the twenty-first century. The lyrics appear below.

The Black Dog of Lake Erie

Courtesy of Tom and Chris Kastle, © *1993*

Though the water be calm and the wind it be fair
Don't think it's a safe time to sail

Figure 30.2. The schooner Hattie Hutt, similar to the Isaac G. Jenkins, photo ca. 1908. (Public Domain)

For the storm waits in whispers, a wolf in its lair
And the dog will howl in the gale; a beast will howl in the gale

We were down bound on Erie, the moon lit our way
Like a leaf on the wind we were sent
Bristled black head to tail, it climbed over the rail
And back to the darkness it went; and back to the darkness he went

They thought I was mad for none of them had
Seen it aboard or ashore
It caused such a fright on the Jenkins *that night*
I told them it happened before; warned them of times gone before

It was off Port Colbourne in late '62*
Aboard the old Mary Jane
They all saw him well, that black hound from hell
They've never been seen again; not a soul has been seen again

They threw me ashore and said they'd listen no more
I warned them through moonlight to dawn
From tow bridge to tow bridge I followed and called
But my mates and the Jenkins *are gone; my mates and the* Jenkins *are gone*
I've seen the black dog with his eyes made of fire

I've heard him tread soft in the night
It's not what you think, not the sun nor the drink
I'm cursed because I was right; learned to regret my cruel sight

The lyrics were based on an account in "Schooner Days," *Evening Telegram,* October 20, 1931, by C. H. J. Snyder, found in the Walton Collection, Bentley Historical Library, University of Michigan.

*The *Mary Jane* was built in 1862 and actually sank in November 1881, six years *after* the wreck of the *Isaac G. Jenkins.* The *Jenkins* helmsman who was put ashore in 1875 could not have warned anyone about the wreck of the *Mary Jane* because it hadn't happened yet. Traditional tales—recited or sung—may not be historically accurate since they reflect the fluidity of oral tradition. But their truth-value is inconsequential to folklorists because—if we know how to unpack them—they will always give us accurate information about the spirit and mentality of the people who once held, or still hold, these tales in tradition.

Motifs and "The Black Dog of Lake Erie"

As noted by folklorist Stith Thompson, motifs are the smallest elements of a tale that are striking or unusual and appear in more than one story. "Bone," for example, is not particularly striking or unusual and therefore is not a motif, but "singing bone" is. Motifs are the building blocks of tales, giving us insight into communities that hold specific motifs in tradition. They also help identify what is and isn't a variant of a specific tale type, like "The Black Dog of Lake Erie." Below are motifs listed in Thompson's *Motif-Index of Folk Literature* (1956–58), some or all of which appear in different variants of the "Black Dog" legend over time, up to and including the modern folk song:

F401.3.3	spirit of black dog (demon)
E521.2	ghost of dog
E230ff.	return from dead to inflict punishment
Q285.1	cruelty to animals punished
Q552.12	shipwreck as punishment

Based on motifs in the tale type, we can see that the community believed that cruelty to dogs, as occurred at the Welland Canal, deserves to be punished to right a wrong and symbolically bring justice out of injustice. In the nineteenth century, if not later, belief in the Black Dog's ghost also gave people a way to explain inexplicable shipwrecks, helping them make sense of such tragedies. The tales remain timely and relevant in the twenty-first century, most likely because most people agree that cruelty to animals is unacceptable and many still believe that wronged spirits can return from the dead to punish guilty parties.

As folklorist William R. Bascom (1965) wrote, traditional tales never exist in a vacuum; they perform important social functions for those who hold them in tradition. In the 1880s, "Black Dog" tales had at least two social functions: they were cautionary tales against animal cruelty, and they gave mariners a sense of control over an uncertain fate providing they took proper care of their mascots.

Today, "Black Dog" narratives persist as entertainment and as wonderfully scary ghost stories. But if a ghost story is too bland to hold our interest or too scary to entertain us, it will never be admitted to tradition. Instead, an artfully balanced ghost story—like the modern "Black Dog" folk song—scares us just enough to give the tale a ring of truth. That, in turn, delivers the real prize, for the "Black Dog" folk song assures us of two comforting notions: not only can there be justice in the world, but there is some sort of life after death.

As long as tales of the Black Dog, spoken or sung, perform important social functions and reinforce the shared values of the Great Lakes community, they will remain timely and relevant, and we can expect variants of "The Black Dog of Lake Erie" to persist in tradition.

References

Bascom, William R. 1965. "Four Functions of Folklore." In *The Study of Folklore*, edited by Alan Dundes, 279–98. Englewood Cliffs, NJ: Prentice Hall.

Kastle, Tom, and Chris Kastle. 1993. "The Black Dog of Lake Erie." Ballad from the CDs *Earthways, Waterways* and *Me from the Inland Lakes*. Ballad lyrics, with permission from Tom and Chris Kastle, © 1993. All arrangements by Tom and Chris Kastle unless otherwise noted. Track 15 on *Me from the Inland Lakes*. 1999 Privateer Publishing /Sextant Music, Ltd.

Thompson, Stith. 1956–58. *The Motif-Index of Folk Literature*. 6 vols. Bloomington: Indiana University Press.

Figure 31.1. *The Grave of Johnny Morehouse and His Dog* by Pamela (skitpero) via Flickr. (Copyrighted content used under US Code, Title 17, Chapter 1, Section 107, Limitations on exclusive rights: Fair Use)

JOHNNY MOREHOUSE AND HIS DOG

Inseparable Ghosts on the Miami Erie Canal

The Miami Erie Canal was completed in 1845. It linked Lake Erie in the north to the Ohio River in the south. When the canal was completed, a series of 105 locks raised canal boats to an amazing 390 feet above the lake and 513 feet above the Ohio River. Passengers and goods were carried at four to five miles an hour before the railroad revolutionized travel.

They say that in 1860 five-year-old Johnny Morehouse fell into the Miami Erie Canal at Dayton and drowned. Some claim he froze to death before his dog could bring him to shore, but all accounts agree that whatever the season, his dog was unable to save him. Once Johnny was buried, the faithful dog would not eat or move from the child's grave, and it eventually died of starvation and grief.

In 1861, Dayton sculptor Daniel LaDow completed a special gravestone memorializing Johnny and his loving companion. To this day, people leave toys, candy, and trinkets on the stone—even a hat and scarf in winter, a tender ritual that Woodland Cemetery does not interfere with. The cemetery refrains from any comment, but according to many visitors, the site is haunted by the boy and his dog. One website gives a good synopsis of the haunting legend: "They say that Johnny and his dog, reunited beyond the grave, roam the cemetery after hours. Barking is heard in the vicinity of the grave, and the two of them are spotted sometimes inside the perimeter fence" (Eyes of the Paranormal 2017).

Johnny's haunting times are consistently reported as "after hours" or late at night. Since the cemetery is closed at night, it makes sense that very few people report seeing the inseparable friends, although several websites refer to a purported nighttime sighting in 1997, when police were called to investigate but found nothing (Southern Ohio Supernatural, n.d.). Reports that people hear joyful barking and a child at play are more common; these reports are often attributed to anonymous students at the University of Dayton, which borders the Woodland Cemetery.

Firsthand experiences, posted online, typically come from daytime visitors who report a chilling sense of the uncanny. Others report hearing the child and dog playing at night.

The story is so tragic and touching that it has inspired many different genres of artistic expression. An original bluegrass folk song, "Little Johnny Morehouse," by the Tennessee Firearms, is posted on YouTube:

Little Johnny Morehouse

Courtesy of singer-songwriter Neil Sebree (recorded 2010).

Little Johnny Morehouse had a faithful friend
His dog was always by his side and would be to the end
And would be to the end

Little Johnny Morehouse was only five years old
He fell into the Erie Canal, the water was so cold
Water was so cold

His dog jumped in to save him and brought him to the shore
The icy water sealed his fate and Johnny was no more
Little Johnny was no more

They buried little Johnny, and right beside his grave
The dog laid there until he died, mourning for his friend
He tried to save
Sometimes late at night you can see Johnny play

His dog is always at his side, just like he was that day
Just like he was that day

In 2008, the child's grave was vandalized by persons unknown, who decapitated the dog. But the rest of the population has been caring and respectful for more than 150 years. Since the death of the boy and his dog, a stone carver sculpted a beautiful monument, a musician wrote a skilled bluegrass folk song, countless photographs memorialize the gravestone, reports of sightings still rivet our imagination on websites and blogs, and kindhearted people still pay their respects, leaving tokens of affection for the little boy and his dog.

To this day, some report feeling the presence of Johnny and his dog at the burial site, and after hours, some say they can still hear the boy and his dog, happily at play.

Figure 31.2. *The Grave of Johnny Morehouse and His Dog, with Head Detached* by Justin Masterson via Flickr. (Copyrighted content used under US Code, Title 17, Chapter 1, Section 107, Limitations on exclusive rights: Fair Use)

References

Eyes of the Paranormal. 2017. "Johnny, the youngest son of John and Mary Morehouse, lived with his parents in Dayton, Ohio in the back of his father's shoe repair shop." Facebook, July 31, 2017. https://www.facebook.com/eyesoftheparanormal/posts/1838543552839488?comment_tracking=%7B"tn"%3A"R"%7D.

Sebree, Neil. 2010. "Little Johnny Morehouse." By the Tennessee Firearms. Recorded in Black Creek, FL, January 2, 2010. YouTube. https://www.youtube.com/watch?v=QVYJ2b3ypwg. Lyrics printed with permission of singer-songwriter Neil Sebree.

Southern Ohio Supernatural. n.d. "Haunted Ohio: Woodlawn [*sic*] Cemetery–Dayton." Paranormal Investigations. Accessed October 11, 2023. http://www.sos-paranormalinvestigations.weebly.com/haunted-ohio.html.

THE THREE SISTERS
Occupational Folklore on Lake Erie

Even when people in the same work environment don't work directly with one another, they still share common experiences unique to their shared occupation. Sayings, jests, tales, rituals, songs, foodways, and other traditions that grow out of a work environment are called occupational folklore. Occupational folklore can take many different forms of expression. Often, unique in-group work experiences will give rise to unique in-group ways of expressing them, just as circus people use the term *rube* for an outsider, hospital staff call their uniforms *scrubs*, and police use the term *perps* for perpetrators of crime.

Folklorists are interested in the folk traditions generated, modified, and maintained by groups but also in the social functions of folklore: how items in folklore serve the community that holds them in tradition. Lake Erie anglers form a community built around their occupation, and we can see their folklore working for them in many genres, including tales of narrow escape in confrontation with a deadly wave pattern local to Lake Erie, known as the Three Sisters.

"The Third One Was Always the Pits"

In 1990, fisherman Lewis Keller was seventy-five years old. He told folklorists Timothy Lloyd and Patrick Mullen about a close call he had with the dreaded "Three Sisters": "The roughest spot in the whole Lake Erie is coming right in along that jetty going into Sandusky in a northeaster. I'm telling you boy, I've never been so scared in my life. . . . I'm telling you, to look back there and see those waves, and they would look a mile high. They used to call them the three sisters. There would be one wave that wouldn't be so bad, the next one would be a little bit bigger. The third one was always the pits" (1990: 114–15). According to Lloyd and Mullen, in earlier generations, surviving the Three Sisters was an initiation into mariner manhood. "The implicit sexism of making the dangerous waves female," they wrote, "is a traditional part of a culturally defined male occupation.... once he has gone through this danger in the lake as a young man, he can be fully accepted as a fisherman" (1990: 115). Heroism lay in dominating the waves, although once was always enough. While their informant told his story more than once, he made it clear that no one had to defeat the Three Sisters more than once: "Man, I never wanted to go through that again," he said. "I'll tell you that" (1990: 115).

The Three Sisters belong to a category of wave known as rogues. Rogue waves are typically one-third larger than the biggest of other waves. The added danger with the dreaded Three Sisters is their rapid sequence, since the second wave hits before the excess water from the first can drain away and the third compounds the problem by adding to the backwash and overloading the deck with tons of water. It is theorized that the Three Sisters contributed to the wreck of the SS *Edmund Fitzgerald* in November 1958 (see "The Witch of November," this volume). A ship in the general vicinity witnessed the lead-up to the tragedy, reporting two rogue waves, and possibly a third, headed in the direction of the *Edmund Fitzgerald*, which would have sunk it at the time it was struck.

The danger posed by the Three Sisters persists in the twenty-first century, echoed in a folk song by Don Charbonneau, a fishing guide, artist, and musician from Wawa, Ontario. Folk singers are "singers of tales," and a good folk song will tell a good story. Charbonneau's "Three Sisters" is a tale sung on two CDs: *Songs from the Coastline* and *Gitche Gumee: Songs from the Lake*. This twenty-first-century song reflects the enduring dread of Lake Erie's Three Sisters, but the domination of the (female) waves is no longer the issue, which may reflect a shift in modern gender attitudes.

Three Sisters (Water Coming In)

Courtesy of Don Charbonneau
I fished in wind and I fished in rain
Fished on waves
Fished in fog cause I got bills to pay
I got water coming in, I got water coming in
Old bilge pump she's broken down
I got water coming in, I got water coming in
Brad Buck come and tow me in

Chorus: *Won't be no fishing today*
          I'm adrift here on Mishipicoten Bay

And I hope those three sisters *don't come my way*
I hope those three sisters *stay home today*

I got a six-foot wave pushing me
I see those rocks half a mile away
Brad Buck come and tow me in
I got three nervous guys here on board
A big fog bank moving in
This compass has gone all to hell.

In Charbonneau's ballad, the hero is primarily concerned for the passengers on board. He is focused on rescue from the anticipated Three Sisters by a tow from Brad Buck. His heroism lies in his broader concern for others and in his persistence as conditions worsen. The ballad builds suspense incrementally, or verse by verse; first the bilge pump fails; then the boat is pushed toward rocks; then fog descends as the compass fails; and through it all, the water just keeps "coming in," each moment adding more and more harrowing danger. The song ends with the fishermen still in peril, riveting our imagination because—like the hero at the helm—we can't tell which will come first: rescue from Brad Buck's tow or disaster from the Three Sisters. Preoccupation with rogue waves—and specifically with the lake's infamous Three Sisters—clearly persists on Lake Erie in the twenty-first century, as confirmed by Charbonneau's folk song.

References

Charbonneau, Don. "The Three Sisters (Water Coming ln)." From the CDs *Songs from the Coastline/Safe Harbor* and *Gitche Gumee: Songs from the Lake*. Courtesy of Don Charbonneau, © Don Charbonneau. https://www.doncharbonneau.com.

Lloyd, Timothy C., and Patrick B. Mullen. 1990. *Lake Erie Fishermen: Work, Identity and Tradition*. Chicago: University of Illinois Press.

Figure 33.1. *Harrison Street Cemetery aka Cholera Cemetery*, Sandusky, Ohio, from the Erie County Historical Society. (Copyrighted content used under US Code, Title 17, Chapter 1, Section 107, Limitations on exclusive rights: Fair Use)

CHOLERA CEMETERY
Revenge of Those Buried Alive

Cholera is an infectious, often fatal intestinal disease that rose to epidemic proportions across Europe and the US in the mid-1800s. Forced to cope with a rapid accumulation of infected corpses, some cities dumped dead bodies into mass graves. Fears of being mistaken for dead, only to regain consciousness after burial, were heightened by rumor, by gossip, and probably by the timely publication of Edgar Allan Poe's horrific story "The Premature Burial" (1884), which described supposedly true cases of hasty, live interment.

Even the *New York Times* (1905) reportedly discovered (less than convincing) "evidence" of live cholera burials, as investigated in Kansas: "The principal evidence of burials alive was a large number of cholera victims had been buried. During the cholera scare the health laws required the immediate burial of victims after death. It is supposed that in haste and fright a number of men who were not dead were buried."

In 1899, thousands of men, women, and children fell ill on the shores of the Great Lakes. It is believed that travelers on Lake Erie had carried the disease first from Europe to America's East Coast and from there to the Midwest. The city of Sandusky, on Lake Erie, was among the hardest hit. Half the population fled, leaving two thousand behind, many unable to flee. Of the four hundred who came down with cholera, all died. A burial ground called Cholera Cemetery was quickly built on the lakeside, on Harrison Street (Gerrick 1982: 25). The mass graves were anonymous, but one monument lists the names of the tiny medical staff that courageously stayed to care for the sick. Sadly, their remedies were more likely to harm their patients than save them.

Even today, many believe that in the rush to dispose of bodies, some people were buried too hastily. Supernatural evidence—including inexplicably cold spots and ghost voices, as well as prods, pushes, pulls, and sightings of vengeful spirits wandering in search of retribution for having been buried alive—is still reported at Cholera Cemetery.

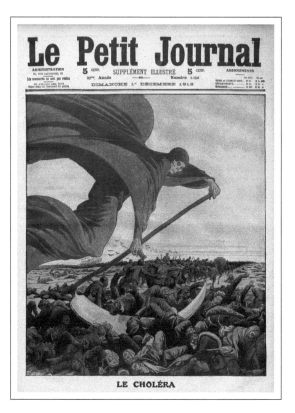

Figure 33.2. *Le Petit Journal* Le choléra, France, 1912. (Public Domain)

In 2007, a reporter for Ghostlytrue described encounters as not clearly vengeful but of the reporter-termed "wondering" variety:

> I had to admit, at first, I didn't feel like the place had any activity of the Paranormal. It's just seemed to look like a place that would be perfect for a mid afternoon picnic. I was wrong. After locating and checking out the cemetery during the daylight hours, we returned to the cemetery that night around 11 pm. We believe the **Cholera Cemetery** may have some wondering souls that may be searching for peace, or unable to let go of their unexpected death. During our Investigation even though the night temperature was 90 degrees, team members reported walking into freezing cold spots, getting poked, touched and pulled.

Among those doing the freezing, poking, touching, and pulling, one male reportedly said hello, one female twice said hi, and a ghostly presence, when asked to identify itself, said "ME!" The narrator added: "We also had activity with dowsing rods. We took pictures but were limited to orb action, which we all know that orbs are not a definite source of evidence, since the possibilities of objects becoming orbs, such as dust. We are planning to visit this location again in the future and we hope to have the same results."

As a matter of common sense, one would expect to hear something more chilling than "hi" from spirits outraged at having been hastily buried alive. It appears that imagination accounts for the encounters described—or else, perhaps, time has mellowed the vengefulness of the ghosts still "wondering" in Cholera Cemetery.

References

Gerrick, David J. 1982. *Ohio's Ghostly Greats*. Dayton, OH: Dayton Press.

Ghostlytrue. n.d. "Cholera Cemetery." Accessed October 11, 2012. https://www.ghostlytrue .com/ghosthunting/investigations.php?recordID-cholera-cemetery.

New York Times. 1905. "Cholera." December 31, 1905, 5. http://newspapers.com/newspage /20562686/.

Figure 34.1. *The Lookout*, Johnson's Island Cemetery, by Counselman Collection via Flickr. (CC BY-SA 2.0)

CONFEDERATE LOOKOUT AT JOHNSON'S ISLAND CEMETERY

In the early twenty-first century, as politics and ideology ripped at the fabric of the nation, controversy erupted over the dismantling of honorific monuments to the Confederacy. Disinformation circulated about a law curriculum known as critical race theory—taught only to adults in law school—prompting a misinformed movement to expunge the history of racism from elementary, middle, and high school classrooms in several states and to punish American teachers for teaching American history. Consequently, at this writing, the future of a Confederate soldier's statue standing lookout over Johnson's Island Cemetery remains uncertain. But by now, if *The Lookout* statue has not carved itself a rightful place in American history, it has certainly carved a place for itself in the folklore of Lake Erie.

The statue is part of a ghostly tradition attending the history of a small island breaking the surface of Lake Erie, two and a half miles from Sandusky, Ohio. Once known as Bull's Island, the site was named for Epaphroditus Bull, its first owner. The island was sold to Leonard Johnson in 1852, and today it is still known as Johnson's Island. But in 1861, Lieutenant Colonel William Hoffman chose the unpopulated site for the construction of a Confederate prisoner of war camp. The Johnson's Island stockade covered roughly sixteen acres and was surrounded by a fifteen-foot-high fence. Inside were thirteen two-story prisoner barracks and a hospital. Prisoners began arriving in 1862, rotating in and out at an uneven pace. Living conditions were horrific, especially during the bitter winters. The prison held roughly 2,500 men at a time, but just over 10,000 Confederate officers and enlisted men were held on Johnson's Island, and more than 260 had died there by 1865–66, when the prison closed.

Once closed, the prison structures were removed, and the island was abandoned, but in 1904 the Daughters of the Confederacy purchased the cemetery site. They replaced the old grave markers with 269 marble headstones, although these no longer mark the actual location of each man's

181

remains. The organization also erected a large bronze statue of a Confederate soldier, called *The Lookout*. He stands facing north, keeping vigil over the Confederate dead. Today, the island is accessed by a causeway built in the 1970s; there are no restrooms or picnic areas, and only the cemetery is open to the public.

But visitors come nonetheless, some sensing connection to those long deceased. Visitors report that the statue's eyes seem to follow them, and many say it comes to life at night and can be seen moving (Willis, Henderson, and Coleman 2005: 238). In addition, visitors report seeing ghosts of Confederate soldiers walking among the gravestones and between trees at the perimeter. Some even claim to have heard the disembodied voices of the long-lost troops. Perhaps most curiously, a group of non-English-speaking Italian immigrants, working at a nearby quarry, are said to have inexplicably learned to sing "Dixie."

The Lookout legend, although brief, is rich in motifs found in Thompson's *Motif-Index of Folk-Literature* (1955–58):

D435.1.1	Statue comes to life
E421	Spectral ghosts
E401	Voices of dead heard from graveyard
D1815.0.1	Gift of tongues received from ghosts

Now and then, anyone can see shadows of things that aren't really there or think a distant sound is something it really isn't. And for many, ghost stories help bridge the gap between those who are lost and those who have lost them, at the same time reassuring the living that there is some sort of life after death. The legend of *The Lookout* certainly performs these functions. But in this case, the "gift of tongues" motif, expressed as non-English speakers singing "Dixie" on an isolated island off Lake Erie's shore, adds a lighthearted element to the legend while lending greater credibility for those who believe.

References

Thompson, Stith, ed. 1955–58. *The Motif-Index of Folk-Literature.* 6 vols. Bloomington: Indiana University Press.

Willis, James A., Andrew Henderson, and Loren Coleman. 2005. "No Retreat for Confederate Soldier." In *Weird Ohio: Your Travel Guide to Ohio's Legends and Best Kept Secrets*, edited by Mark Sceurman and Mark Moran, 238. New York: Sterling.

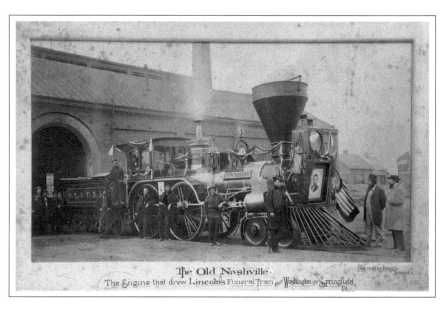

Figure 35.1. View of steam locomotive Old Nashville at the Willson Street Station in Cleveland, Ohio, April 28, 1865. (Public Domain)

THE LINCOLN GHOST TRAIN
Tradition and Transformation on Erie's Shore

Abraham Lincoln's death may have had the greatest and longest impact of all celebrity deaths in American history. In April 1865, his funeral train would make a historic trip from Washington, DC, to his birthplace and burial site in Springfield, Illinois. Mourners lined the tracks of that funereal journey from beginning to end, which included almost the full length of Lake Erie's southern shore from Buffalo, New York, to Cleveland, Ohio. The train, rolling slowly by, stopped in enough towns and cities to allow many ordinary folks to view the casket and pay their respects in person.

Most of us think of tradition as something static, something that doesn't change. But times, places, and generations are so constantly changing that the most stable aspect of any tradition may be its ability to change, just to stay timely and relevant. Traditions that can't remain timely and relevant will be dropped and forgotten, no matter how closely we once held them. For example, where once there were sightings of the ghost train's passing, it seems that changes in travel and technology have reduced the possibility of a modern sighting to the point of extinction. The new, emerging tradition is no longer focused on sighting the ghost train; instead, it seems to focus on waiting for a train that never comes, and in some cases, it actually celebrates the nonevent. A good synopsis of the original ghost train tradition is still carried online (LoveToKnow, n.d.):

> As the story goes, the train will make an appearance along the same railroad tracks, and on the same day, each April. The train is described as having a blue light, and is draped with funeral bunting. The coffin of the fallen president is also visible, draped in the American flag. People who witness this train also mention the dozens of ghost soldiers who appear to salute the train as it passes. After the procession has passed by, clocks in the immediate area are found to be six minutes behind, apparently as a result of the six-minute stop made by the funeral train at some depots along the way.

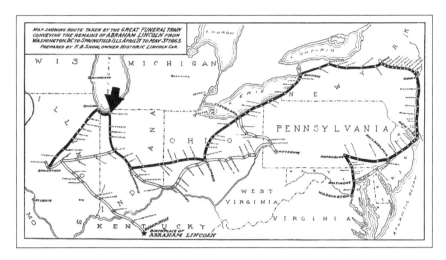

Figure 35.2. *Map of the Route of the Abraham Lincoln Funeral Cortege* by F. B. Snow, 1905. (Public Domain)

As late as 2008, Lorri Sankowsky and Keri Young documented the nationwide loss of train depots in their description of a typical small town in Indiana, although they did not acknowledge the accompanying transformation in the ghost train tradition: "Trains have not visited Irvington since the 1900s. . . . Once a bustling and exciting stop the railway depot is now long gone. The weed-clogged tracks are still visible in some areas. . . . This railway is also the sight [*sic*] of the largest mass ghost sighting in the United States. The phenomenon is known as the Lincoln Ghost train, and it has been seen and heard by hundreds of people for more than 140 years" (2008: 149).

Despite the illusion that Lincoln's ghost train is still being sighted after 140 years, either in Irvington or anywhere else, the authors also speak to another tradition in Irvington's past, as if it, too, is ongoing: "Irvington residents have come to expect the Lincoln Ghost Train. . . . Every April, lights dim and clocks stop, startling newcomers and amusing long-time residents who just shrug and say, 'Must be the spring. That's the ghost train!'" (2008: 149).

Whether or not this report was ever accurate for Irvington, changing technology has long replaced the short-lived light bulbs and wind-up clocks that dimmed, went out, slowed, or periodically stopped back in Lincoln's day. Such dimming, slowing, and stopping were probably as irregular as they were unremarkable, but they clearly happened enough that a clock would now and then coincidentally stop, or a light bulb go out, when the train was expected. The overlap of the two events easily suggested a cause-and-effect relationship and may well have given rise to the tradition. But today, light bulbs and clocks are much longer lasting and are just too reliable to provide enough malfunctions at the right times, and in the right places, to sustain the old belief.

In addition, modern trains come and go with less visual and auditory drama than in Lincoln's day. In the past, engines could arrive surrounded by thick clouds of roiling steam, much like the type of nighttime mist or fog through which a determined observer might see a ghost train passing and even hear the shrill cry of something like a whistle from a dark, deserted train platform. Moreover, because timetables on the internet advertise exactly where the train is supposed to be at each depot's appointed time and because the number of depots is shrinking dramatically, many more people are crowded into far fewer locations, requiring everyone at a given place to see the same thing at the same time to corroborate a purported sighting. Not surprisingly, sightings of the ghost train have dwindled to zero. But remarkably, that's not the case for gathering together to wait for it.

Modern technological advances could have extinguished the ghost train tradition entirely, but as folklorist William R. Bascom (1954) noted long ago, folklore persists because it performs social functions for those who hold it in tradition, and as long as it continues to do so, people will modify and maintain the tradition to keep it timely and relevant. So, instead of disappearing, we see the ghost train tradition beginning to perform more timely and relevant functions, built around a growing number of mass nonsightings. As one observer posted on the Ghosts of Ohio website (2008):

> In April of 2008, *The Ghosts of Ohio* had the unique opportunity to participate in the search for the Lincoln Ghost Train. According to the legend, every April 29th, a ghostly funeral car carrying the body of Abraham Lincoln is supposed to rumble through the town of Urbana, Ohio. . . . Unfortunately, despite setting up all our equipment along the tracks, the ghostly train never showed up, but what did show up were over 90 local residents and students from Urbana University. So while we weren't able to capture any paranormal activity, we were able to become, if only for one night, part of the Urbana community and take part in their annual ritual of waiting for the Funeral Train.

Clearly, the new event is no longer about sighting the ghost train; it's about gathering socially, as a community, to participate in a shared ritual. The posting above added that the Associated Press was present that night, along with forty-three news media, including CNN, *USA Today*, CBS News, the *Chicago Tribune*, and the *San Francisco Chronicle*. Even the *Taipei Times* picked up the story to report the nonevent. Interestingly, widespread confirmation that no one ever sees the ghost train does nothing to dampen the new ritual in any way. Rather, enthusiasts continue to chat and plan all year long at sites online and to gather face-to-face at assorted railroad stations, later posting online descriptions of the train's nonarrival. As one participant posted from New York on All Over Albany (Greene 2012):

> Just as I was about to pack it in for the night at the Rensselaer train station, I saw a weak beam of light. It was bouncing slowly from left to right as it rose up from the ground . . . I heard a deathly creaking . . . a blurry vision came into focus.
> A breathtaking moment, for sure. But short-lived:
> Nay, my friend, this heart-stopping haunt was . . . in fact . . . just some kid on a bike. The illumination was his handlebar headlight. The tyke, all of nine, sneered as he rode past. . . . Feeling silly and defeated, I zipped my hoodie, walked to my car, and let the legend of Lincoln's ghost train disappear into the night.

Most hopefuls are not that eloquent, but they are also harder to discourage. They refuse to let the appointed time of nonarrival go by without doing something to mark the date as meaningful to the community. Most significantly, at some locations, live entertainment has begun to fill the time that would otherwise be spent in unrelieved waiting. For example, in 2010 a Hudson Valley periodical, the *Daily Freeman*, ran the online headline "All Aboard Tonight for the Lincoln Ghost Train." The emerging festivity, held at the Hyde Park train station, promised "a night for children of all ages," including a short discussion of famous American ghost trains, a Civil War reenactment, storytelling, fast food, and live music—and of course, no sighting of Lincoln's ghost train.

There are probably many reasons for the ongoing transformations in the ghost train tradition, two being advances in technology and the shrinking of train depots along the route. But no matter how differently we travel today, no matter how technologically advanced we have become or how electronically anonymous we may be in the twenty-first century, it appears we still need face-to-face contact with other human beings; to be with one another, in person, to perform rituals as a community; and to mark shared experiences as meaningful.

Judging by postings online, gathering to honor Lincoln's memory remains a meaningful reason to be in one another's company at appointed times and places, where the funeral train once passed. Therefore, it is likely that Americans will continue to gather in groups along the same route to pay their respects, just as their forebears did so long ago. In so doing, they form the enduring substance of a like-minded community. By waiting together at the depot, they observe the passing of a fallen hero, although not by sighting the train they wait for.

References

Bascom, William R. 1954. "Four Functions of Folklore." *Journal of American Folklore* 67 (266): 333–49.

Daily Freeman (Hudson Valley, NY). 2010. "All Aboard Tonight for the Lincoln Ghost Train." April 26, 2010. http://www.dailyfreeman.com/articles/2010/04/26/life/doc4bd452277953b980232484.txt.

Ghosts of Ohio. 2008. "The Lincoln Funeral Train." http://www.ghostsofohio.org/lore/ohio_lore_41.html.

Greene, James, Jr. 2012. "Waiting on the Arrival of Lincoln's Ghost." All Over Albany, October 29, 2012. http://alloveralbany.com/archive/2012/10/29/waiting-on-the-arrival-of-lincolns-ghost.

LoveToKnow. n.d. "5 Scary Ghost Stories (That May Keep You Up at Night)." Paranormal. Accessed April 26, 2013. https://paranormal.lovetoknow.com/Scary_Ghost_Stories.

Sankowsky, Lorri, and Keri Young. 2008. *Ghost Hunter's Guide to Indianapolis*. Gretna, LA: Pelican.

Figure 36.1. *Brown Family Vault aka "The Vampire Crypt"* by Justin Waits. (Copyrighted content used with permission)

THE VAMPIRE CRYPT OF ERIE CEMETERY

The Brown family vault is located in Erie Cemetery in the town of Erie, Pennsylvania, on Lake Erie's shore. Above the entry is a small art image, still clearly visible despite exposure to the elements for over one hundred years, just as the crypt itself is unharmed but discolored by more than a century of industrial pollution and acid rain. Some suggest that the image depicts a vampire bat, the discoloration made by demonic flames. But on close inspection, the weathered look is inconsistent with fire and consistent with exposure to the elements, while the image is not of a vampire bat at all but of a flower. If it was not meant to be a stylized funeral lily, it is still some kind of blossom, more clearly than any kind of bat.

Then why is the Brown family vault widely known as the Vampire Crypt of Erie Cemetery?

It seems that, over time, the vault has acquired a number of distinguishing characteristics that might invite such speculation. Three of these characteristics are the most compelling. First, the coffins of four of the seven who lie in the vault were unearthed—or "exhumed"—from other graves and then placed in the vault. Second, popular belief holds that no one in the Brown family vault is named Brown. Third, as noted, some people interpret the carving over the door as a vampire bat. In addition, according to comments posted online, someone once saw a black cat in the vicinity, another person who climbed on the roof saw numbers painted or engraved there, and some people find it uncanny that the door has no handle. But as we are about to see, suggestive material is just that—*suggestive*—and suggestive is not the same as conclusive. Sometimes, even hard evidence won't satisfy everyone. But in this case, the search for hard evidence led to discoveries even more intriguing than suggestive speculation.

Vampires in Pennsylvania

According to current research, vampire beliefs were originally meant to explain why so many people died during epidemics. Contagion wasn't understood, and

Figure 36.2. *Brown Family Vault aka "The Vampire Crypt"* (detail) by Justin Waits. (Copyrighted content used with permission)

it was believed that recently deceased persons would cause others to die by mysteriously sucking their blood (believed to be their life force). The word *vampir* first appeared in tenth-century Slavic Europe, referring to the reanimated body of a buried corpse that somehow drew the blood (or life force) from its victims while they slept.

Similarly, the German term *nachzehrer* means "he who devours after (his death)" (Melton 2011: 283). It, too, refers to a recently deceased person who attacks from the grave, usually consuming the blood of family members and village acquaintances. Disappearance of flesh and clothing due to decomposition was also attributed to the *nachzehrer*'s appetite, which had to be satisfied from inside his coffin; "As a rule, he does not leave his grave, but in a magical way destroys the life of family members who die immediately after him; thus 'he who devours after his death'" (Melton 2011: 284).

According to folk tradition, vampires were capable of consuming the life force of whole populations, but their bodies never left their coffins. That is, they stayed underground unless they were exhumed to be stopped by others. Once they were exhumed, their hearts might be cannibalized to cure illness among the living, and their hungry jaws might be sealed in a number of strategic ways, preventing further blood consumption.

Folklorist Michael Bell notes that both "Slavic and German immigrants brought vampire superstitions with them in the 1700s, perhaps when Palatine Germans colonized Pennsylvania or when Hessian mercenaries served in the Revolutionary War" (Tucker 2012). That would account for vampire exhumations and reburials in New England, practiced there throughout the eighteenth and nineteenth centuries in misguided attempts to contain the spread of contagious diseases. I found no record of vampire exhumations or reburials in Pennsylvania. Yet popular belief in vampirism persists there, especially in connection with the Brown family vault at Lake Erie Cemetery.

Victims and Remedies

Wherever germ theory was not understood, outbreaks of contagious diseases could easily create an inexplicable and terrifying link between those who died and those who lived close by—the most likely to die next. In some ways, it was a reasonable assumption that an insatiable force was draining the life from those still alive, since some elements of normal decomposition could logically suggest that the corpse was gorging on the blood of the living. These elements could include bloating from gases that accumulate in a dead body, "groans" caused by the escape of such gases, brackish or red fluid draining from the mouth, and the seeming growth of hair and nails due to shrinkage of scalp and fingers. In the United States, during the eighteenth and nineteenth centuries, attempts to protect those at risk included exhuming the "guilty" corpse, breaking the ribs, removing and burning the heart, and feeding the ashes to the sick.

If precautions against potential acts of vampirism were not properly taken at burial, then exhumation and extreme measures were required afterward, to end the vampire's nocturnal activity. Such measures included arresting the ability to eat by placing a clump of earth under the chin to hold the mouth shut; some placed a coin or stone in the open mouth, and others blocked the ability to swallow by tying something around the neck or by decapitating the corpse. Yet others drove a spike into the mouth to fix the tongue in place or to pin the head to the ground. Staking the body (which occurred primarily in Slavic countries) was the most practical way to stop a vampire, but it wasn't a good one; in fact, it failed so often that other, more drastic measures normally had to be taken (Barber 1988: 71).

The creation of Count Dracula, the most famous of literary vampires, was probably influenced by events and personalities in history, and certainly by folk beliefs, but the literary Dracula would break from folk tradition in a number of significant ways, perhaps inspired by a source linked to Pennsylvania.

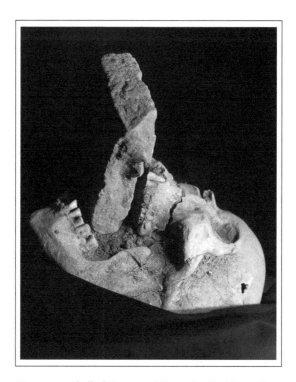

Figure 36.3. *Skull of Vampire of Vienna*, by Dr. Matteo Borrini, forensic anthropologist, Liverpool John Moore University. (Copyrighted content used with permission)

Dracula in a Pennsylvania Barn

The manuscript for *Dracula* (published May 26, 1897) was written by Abraham "Bram" Stoker (1847–1912) and was originally thought to be lost, but it was discovered in a barn in Philadelphia in the 1980s (Miller 2008). Stoker, a young Englishman, was an ardent admirer of the aging American poet Walt Whitman, whom he had visited on a trip to Philadelphia in 1844. While there, Stoker had been introduced to one of Whitman's cohorts and benefactors, Thomas Donaldson. The three men remained friends, and Stoker's *Dracula* manuscript (which he first titled *The Un-dead*) would be found in Donaldson's barn almost a century later. But Stoker kept the notes and outlines for the novel separately, and a year after his death, his widow sold them at Sotheby's auction in London; they are now housed at the Rosenbach Museum and Library in Philadelphia, Pennsylvania.

Scholars working with the Rosenbach material discovered that a year before publication, Stoker had pasted into his *Dracula* notes an American journalist's article on "Vampires in New England," published in *New York*

World (1896). Whether the article inspired Stoker's departures from folk tradition or simply reflects the common knowledge of the time, two of its passages—the first one on staking—give us a possible source for Stoker's use of a stake through the heart to dispatch vampires. Although that isn't *precisely* what is described, the article's wording could have inspired Stoker's use of the stake, his use of a crucifix to deter the vampire, and his decision to invest his Dracula with the ability to shape-shift into a bat. The journalist observed and described a local search for New England vampires:

> The contents of every suspected grave were investigated and many corpses found in such a condition as that described were promptly subjected to "treatment." This meant that a stake was driven through the chest, and the heart, being taken out, was either burned or chopped into small pieces. For in this way only could a vampire be deprived of the power to do mischief. In one case a man who was unburied sat up in his coffin, with fresh blood on his lips. The official in charge of the ceremonies held a crucifix before his face, and saying "Do you recognize your Savior?" chopped the unfortunate's head off.

In his comprehensive study, folklorist Paul Barber found only one report in which someone put a cross over the front door to deter a vampire. He stated, "In general . . . vampires of folklore do not exhibit the violent reaction to the cross that is found in fiction" (1988: 64). Barber also notes, "As important as bats are in the fiction of vampires, they are generally unimportant in folklore" (1988: 33). But in the article read by Stoker, the journalist not only referred to staking the heart and using a crucifix but went on to illuminate a connection between a belief in human vampires and a belief in vampire bats:

> Belief in vampire bats is more modern. For a long time it was ridiculed by science as a delusion, but it has been proved to be founded correctly upon fact. It was the famous naturalist Darwin who settled this question. One night he was camping with a party near Coquimbo, in Chile, when it happened that a servant noticed the restlessness of one of the horses. The man went up to the horse and actually caught a bat in the act of sucking blood from the flank of the animal.
> While many kinds of bats have been ignorantly accused of the blood-sucking habit, only one species is really a vampire. (*New York World* 1896)

In folk tradition, vampires' teeth are unremarkable, and fangs are never mentioned (Barber 1988: 44). But when Darwin confirmed the existence of *Desmodus rotundus*, a bloodsucking bat with menacing canines, he may have solved a problem for Stoker. While Stoker didn't require science to authenticate anything in his blood-chilling fantasy, the announcement of the scientific discovery may have inspired the signature fangs of the fictional vampire and the count's subsequent ability to shape-shift into a bat, which gave him a convenient means to travel incognito, dine out, and leave no mess behind.

Connection to the Brown Family Vault

Perhaps the most notorious American vampire exhumation took place in New England in 1892 (Tucker 2012); it, too, was among the exhumations featured in the *New York World* article that Stoker read in 1896. It seems that when tuberculosis began to spread through a Rhode Island community, the corpse of a nineteen-year-old victim, Mercy Brown (called Lena by her family), was exhumed. In perfect keeping with folk tradition, the ribs were broken, the heart removed, and the body reinterred. The heart was burned, and the ashes were fed to her ailing brother, who died shortly thereafter. The fact that this vampire exhumation was widely publicized and that the deceased's family name was Brown may have forged the first connection between the "vampire" exhumation in Rhode Island and the four exhumations that helped fill the vault of a family also named Brown, in Erie, Pennsylvania.

Adding to the mystique, the four Pennsylvania exhumations took place at the end of the nineteenth century, precisely when vampire exhumations were being sensationalized in the press and *Dracula* came out in print. Today, many on the internet contend (incorrectly) that no one interred in the Brown family vault is named Brown, a "fact" that some consider suggestive of foul play. But records at Erie Cemetery show that between 1884 and 1888, Gertrude (Goodrich) Brown, married to Thomas Brown, interred first her father, George W. Goodrich (1817–84), and then her mother, Mary Ann (Converse) Goodrich (d. 1888), in what was then a handsome vault in one of the loveliest burial sites on Erie's lakeshore.

The record also shows that earlier, George W. Goodrich and his wife, Mary Ann, had lost and buried their one-year-old son, George Converse Goodrich, six years before Erie Cemetery opened. Erie Cemetery opened in 1850, and in 1852, A. C. Goodrich, a relative of George W. and Mary Ann, was buried there, although not in the Brown family vault since there was not yet a relationship between the Goodriches and the Browns. At an unspecified date, a relative listed only as "son of" A. J. Goodrich (thus, probably an infant) was buried in Erie Cemetery, also before the Brown family connection was made. Finally, in 1854, George W. and Mary Ann buried their middle child, twelve-year-old Julia Isadore Goodrich, but not surprisingly, they laid her to rest beside her brother George, wherever he was originally buried in 1844, before Erie Cemetery had opened.

George W. and Mary Ann Goodrich's youngest child, Gertrude, would survive to grow up and become the wife of Thomas Brown, and this is the couple who came to own the Brown family vault in Erie Cemetery. Shortly after her father and mother died, Gertrude reunited her family, arranging for her brother and sister and the two other Goodrich relatives to be exhumed and placed inside the vault with her parents. The last family member to enter the vault was, in fact, named Brown. He is listed as Thomas MacGregor Brown, who died at age two, in 1919, during the great influenza epidemic. It seems reasonable to assume that little Thomas Brown was the baby son of Thomas and Gertrude Brown, although direct family relationships are not indicated in the record. It is clear, however, that Gertrude's interest was in reuniting her relatives, having nothing to do with vampirism and everything to do with memorializing her family together.

While the search for vampire exhumations at Erie Cemetery was unsuccessful, it did reveal fascinating information about vampires in history, folk tradition, and literary fiction. It traced the migration pattern of European vampire beliefs to the shores of Lake Erie, and it helped explain why Erie Cemetery's Brown family vault is still known as, and believed to be, the Vampire Crypt of Erie Cemetery.

References

Barber, Paul. 1988. *Vampires, Burial and Death: Folklore and Reality*. New Haven, CT: Yale University Press.

Melton, J. Gordon. 2011. *The Vampire Book: Encyclopedia of the Undead*. 3rd ed. Canton, MI: Invisible Ink.

Miller, John. 2008. "What a Tax Lawyer Dug Up on *Dracula*." *Wall Street Journal*, October 28, 2008. http://www.wsj.com/article/SB122514491757273633.html.

New York World. 1896. "Vampires in New England." February 2, 1896. Text received as a personal communication.

Tucker, Abigail. 2012. "The Great New England Vampire Panic." *Smithsonian Magazine*, October 2012. https://www.smithsonianmag.com/history/the-great-new-england-vampire-panic-36482878/.

Many thanks and much appreciation are due to the following

Leslie S. Klinger, author of *The New Annotated Dracula* (W. W. Norton, 2008), for informing me of the 1896 article that Stoker pasted into his notes and for graciously sending me the text of that article.

J. Clarke Kuebler, general manager of the Erie Cemetery Association, for kindly sending me a copy of the interment record for the Brown family vault.

Figure 37.1. *Gore Orphanage Rd. Street Sign.* Graphic created for this chapter by Jared Bendis.

GORE ORPHANAGE

Evolution of a Legend on Erie's Shore

In Vermilion, Ohio, a leafy location on Lake Erie's shore, a street sign reads "Gore Orphanage Road." It reads this way because the Swift mansion, once located on Gore Road, has long been misidentified as an orphanage. The mansion's remains have been the site of purported "orphanage hauntings" for more than a century, although the mansion's name was Swift, not Gore, and it was never an orphanage. How are we to interpret such a reconstruction of history?

Rarely do we have an opportunity to witness the separate literary elements of a narrative coming together over time to form a cohesive and enduring legend. But in this case, James A. Willis, Andrew Henderson, and Loren Coleman (2005: 12–14) compiled the history of the imagined Gore Orphanage, helping us follow the tale's development. Willis et al. began by noting that in 1817, four hundred acres of dense Vermilion woodland, located on the old Baldwin Road, were purchased by a fellow named Joseph Swift. Twenty-three years later, in 1840, Swift would build a mansion there—but by that time, Baldwin Road had been renamed Gore Road since it ran along a narrow land formation known as a gore. The change from Baldwin Road to Gore Road apparently set the stage for the future legend.

In 1865, the Swifts sold the mansion to the Wilber family. Tragically, the Wilbers would lose four grandchildren to an epidemic of diphtheria in 1893. Although the children did not reside in the mansion, they lived and died nearby, and all four were buried in the local cemetery. Inspired by the spiritualist fervor then sweeping the nation, the Wilber grandparents held séances in their home, attempting to make contact with the spirits of their dead grandchildren. These séances may account for the mansion's persisting association with the ghosts of dead children (Ellis 2003).

The mansion would pass through two more owners before it was abandoned. In 1895, it was sold to a family named Sutton. In 1903, the property was sold again and purchased by Rev. John Sprunger, who founded the Hope and Light Orphanage, constructing that facility on Gore Road, separate and apart from the old Swift mansion.

Roughly five years later, in 1908 and far from the Hope and Light Orphanage, a devastating fire at Collinwood Elementary School in Cleveland killed more than one hundred children trapped inside. This tragedy may have influenced later speculations on the purported Gore Orphanage tragedy. No such fire ever occurred at the Hope and Light Orphanage, which simply closed its doors eight years later, in 1916. The Hope and Light orphans, along with their caretakers, left the facility unharmed. But at the same time, they abandoned the rest of the property, including the old Swift mansion. Over time, the empty, long-abandoned mansion was popularly mislabeled Gore Orphanage. In 1923, it burned to the ground with no one in it.

After that, the Swift mansion might have been completely forgotten. But the fact that séances had been held there for the Wilber children, combined with the mistaken notion that the mansion was used as an orphanage, contributed to an imagined tragedy thematically linked to the death of the children trapped in the Collinwood school fire, in Cleveland. Over time, as the legend took final form, it entered tradition that the Swift mansion was the Gore Orphanage and that, like the Collinwood school in Cleveland, it had burned to the ground with the children trapped inside.

Even today, some accounts blame the innocent Sprunger for the imagined orphanage fire that purportedly killed the orphans under his care in Vermilion. Other accounts point instead to a mystery villain who set the fire; still others hold that the imagined fire and its imagined deaths were accidents. In any case, it would seem that any children believed to have lived in the mansion between 1893, when the ghosts of the Wilber children were summoned to the Swift mansion, and 1923, when the Gore orphans supposedly died in a fire, were also believed to have died there and, subsequently, to haunt the premises. To this day, roughly a century after the empty Swift mansion burned down, ghost seekers travel to see its one remaining landmark: the charred and crumbling remains of a single sandstone pillar on a street now known as Gore Orphanage Road.

According to Willis et al. (2005), visitors to the site report ghostly images of dead children; some hear flames and calls for help; some even hear horrified screams. Further study shows that some smell burning flesh and catch glimpses of an ominous man lurking in the shadows. Most intriguingly, some report seeing the deceased children's apparitions and even activities.

In modern reports online, orphan ghosts sometimes speak to visitors and give their names, as in the account below, where yet another ghost also leaves a handwritten signature. This vivid account, which opens with sounds of groaning doors and squeaking floors echoing from the long-gone "or-phanage," was posted on forgottenoh.com under the title "Orphans in the Woods." It includes all elements of the traditional Gore Orphanage legend, going on to add both details and "proofs." It was posted in 1999 and appears here slightly abridged:

> We placed the recorder on the sandstone pillar. We then took several pictures. As I took the pictures, mists began to come around. We heard the dull roar of a fire and crackle of the flames. I heard mumbling voices.
>
> As we drove off, I asked my wife to stop the car and I unrolled my window. There stood a young boy. He had blond hair and he was about seven years old. He was wearing ragged old clothes (a red sweater and dark pants). He sneezed. I asked him his name and he said "Jacob." He appeared scared and looking for something. As we left he stood in the middle of the road and waved bye.
>
> Later that day, we had our pictures developed. In the background, you can see 4 children's faces and a man in the distance in the woods. . . . The ominous man showed up in every shot. Later after reviewing the recordings, we heard the dull roar through the whole tape (and no it was not windy) about four minutes into the tape there is about three minutes of mumbling, and somebody saying "Help me" and screams (about six). You can hear the door open in the beginning, "Jacob" saying his name and also Jacob's sneeze. There is no way we could have made those noises.
>
> Later we found on our car tiny handprints. And on the driver's side window there was Richard written from the inside of the car.

But there never was a Gore Orphanage, and the children from the Hope and Light Orphanage never died there, nor did the Hope and Light orphans ever occupy the Swift mansion. The Hope and Light Orphanage never burned down, and even more significantly, the Swift mansion was empty and had been abandoned for several years when it went up in flames. In addition, there were no orphans anywhere near the mansion, in the woods, or even in Vermilion when the empty mansion burned. So how can we account for hauntings like those reported in "Orphans in the Woods"?

One explanation is to deny documented history and insist that an orphanage burned down and that the ghosts of the trapped children are real or—even more cynically—to claim that for some unstated reason a bunch of dishonest people are deliberately making things up. Alternatively, we can speculate with a degree of confidence that there are other ways to explain the experiences reported at the ruined Swift mansion. One possibility may be the influence of the Collinwood tragedy of 1908, in which more than one hundred children died less than fifty miles away. It was an event so horrific and traumatizing that many people, even those with no personal connection to the victims, were shocked, unnerved, and in need of some way to ease their distress.

In such circumstances, one possible coping mechanism is to bring the tragedy physically close to home, into the realm of actual personal connection (e.g., the orphanage on Gore Road), in close association with a similar set of circumstances (e.g., the fire at the Swift mansion). The next step would be to "discover" a manner of survival for the purported child victims (e.g., a ghostly afterlife). After all, ghost stories may scare us, but on another level, they reassure us of life after death, helping us cope with fear, loss, and unspeakable tragedies like the Collinwood school fire. Thus, comfort could come from hauntings, open to confirmation close to home.

Today, there are probably whole populations of differently motivated ghost seekers who visit the site, entirely unaware of the Collinwood fire; some of them may be seeking adventure and others just seeking reassurance of life after death, provided by "child ghosts" associated with the property since the Wilber séances of 1893 and now with the imagined Gore Orphanage. For such hopefuls, that would certainly make the site a tempting destination. It is not so surprising that some people, motivated to find the orphans in the woods, in the mist, in the fog, or in the woodland shadows of the imagined orphanage fire, do find them. Nor is it surprising that some come away convinced they smelled the smoke, felt the flames, heard the screams, and made contact with the spirits of the orphans still among us, sneezing, leaving their names on windows, and waving goodbye.

Regardless of how we attempt to explain peoples' encounters with the victims of a tragedy that never happened, we should remind ourselves that folklore never exists in a vacuum; it performs social functions for the communities that hold it in tradition. If it did not serve the community in some meaningful way, the folklore itself would die (Bascom 1954). We can see how the Gore Orphanage legend may originally have helped the local community cope with a devastating tragedy out of reach and how it may continue to reassure modern ghost hunters seeking the thrill of supernatural discovery or evidence of an afterlife. But we can be certain that the Swift mansion's documented history gives us a very real view of how factual and fictional elements came together, over time, as the building blocks of a local legend, one that continues to function for those who hold it in tradition, on Lake Erie's shore.

References

Bascom, William. 1954. "Four Functions of Folklore." *Journal of American Folklore* 67 (266): 333–49.

Ellis, Bill. 2003. *Aliens, Ghosts and Cults: Legends We Live.* Jackson: University Press of Mississippi.

Forgotten Ohio. 1999. "Orphans in the Woods: The First Story." Accessed December 14, 2013. http://www.forgottenoh.com/Gore/gorestories.html.

Willis, James A., Andrew Henderson, and Loren Coleman. 2005. *Weird Ohio: Your Travel Guide to Ohio's Local Legends and Best Kept Secrets*. Edited by Mark Sceurman and Mark Moran. New York: Sterling.

Figure 38.1. *Creation/Evolution* graphic by Jared Bendis uses *Hand Writing Start-Up on Blackboard* by Marco Verch Professional Photographer via Flickr. (CC BY 2.0)

REMAINS OF NEPHILIM AND MODERN CONSPIRACY THEORIES ON LAKE ERIE

In the nineteenth century, Darwin's theory of evolution challenged the traditional, biblical understanding of human origins. Yet the initial upset many felt toward the notion that humans evolved from more primitive animals changed over a relatively short time (Feder 1996: 50). But not everyone felt the same. During the nineteenth century in particular, when fossil discoveries were confirming Darwin at a rapid pace, a spate of rival discoveries were cited, meant to reestablish the Bible as the natural history of the world. The effort persists to this day in purported discoveries of the biblical Nephilim.

Biblical Sources for Discoveries of Nephilim

At some point, believers in the Bible as natural history must have realized that if we can discover prehistoric hominids with traceable evolutionary histories, we must also be able to discover *biblical* hominids with no traceable evolutionary histories. These would belong to a species that could only have appeared and disappeared by God's hand, thereby challenging Darwin's claim of biological evolution. Thus, throughout the 1800s, across the nation as on Lake Erie's shore, believers began making sensational discoveries of bones believed to be those of Nephilim (Hebrew for "giants"), the giant offspring of mortal women and rebellious angels who fell to earth, as mentioned in Genesis 6:4 and Numbers 13:33.

The King James Version of Genesis 6:4 reads: "There were giants [Hebr. *Nephilim*] in the earth those days; and also after that, when the sons of God [meaning "angels"] came in unto the daughters of men, and they bare children to them, and the same became mighty men, which were of old, men of renown."

The same story appears in the Hebrew Bible, in which Genesis 6:4 reads: "It was then, and later too, that the *Nephilim* [giants] appeared on earth—

205

when the divine beings [angels] cohabited with the daughters of men, who bore them offspring. They were the heroes of old, the men of renown."

In the next verse of both texts, God sees that, over time, the wickedness of these giant offspring has become great. Both biblical accounts tell the same story, stating that the Flood eradicated the Nephilim, along with other beings who, by the time of Noah, had lost their virtue and were excluded from the ark.

The nineteenth-century notion that the bones of giant Nephilim, like those of prehistoric men, lie in caves and crevices or underground offers an opportunity for people of faith to make discoveries as exciting and compelling as those made by people of science. And at the same time, the discovery provides believers with an opportunity to refute Darwin's theory of evolution with a biblical species not accounted for in natural science—one that evolved neither from anything nor into anything but that could only have been created and destroyed by the hand of God.

Giants and Bones on Erie's Shore

The Ohio landscape, once the home of many Native American populations, is now dotted by a number of ancient burial sites. Some pioneer farmers, tilling the land throughout the nineteenth century, unearthed remains they described as "gigantic." Erie's lakeshore communities were a rich site for these discoveries. According to a Mormon website, the Spalding Research Project, "The early settlers of Ashtabula have gone on record that . . . there were over 1000 graves when they came here. . . . A few graves were opened and in some were found skulls and jaw bones of men whose size dwarfed the men who found the graves" (Wright and Spalding 2006).

Writing in the nineteenth century, naturalist Clarence Bloomfield Moore explained that when the ratio of thigh bones (femurs) to body size is not known, amateur impressions can register gigantism. In a footnote, he also records an instance of amateur exaggeration involving a skull. This does not mean that exaggeration always happened, but it confirms that it could, and did, occur. He wrote in the *American Naturalist*: "The thigh bone of a six foot man would be 19.8 inches in length. To those unfamiliar with the relative size of the thigh bone, a femur when found in nearly every case gives the idea of having done duty in a body of abnormal size" (1892: 142–43). The personal experience he recorded gives us an example:

> In 1879 . . . a skeleton [was found] . . . the femur of this skeleton seemed so large that it required the assurance of a professor of Harvard to carry the conviction to the finder then unfamiliar with the ratio existing between thigh bone and skeleton, that the remains of a giant had not been disinterred. . . .

Great pains have been taken by the writer [Moore], and considerable distances have been travelled to inspect the bones of so-called giants and ever with a like result. The bones, if forthcoming at all, have never indicated a greater stature than can readily be found among the white men of today.

Almost as an afterthought, the same naturalist added a footnote on an incident of May 1891, when a well-respected townsman reported a skeleton nine feet tall. He corrected to eight feet toward the end of the conversation, after which he admitted he had not actually seen the skeleton at all. The man who originally informed the townsman was then found, and he in turn claimed that the skeleton was seven feet tall, with a skull large enough to "hold a peck" [two dry gallons]. When the man who actually found the skeleton was interviewed, he considered the deceased to have been large but had not taken measurements. "The skull alone had been kept," Moore noted, but upon inspection, "it proved to be somewhat below average in size."

Twenty-First-Century Conspiracy Theories

When believers in Nephilim fossils are confronted by natural history, as in the example above, they do not adjust their assumptions to fit the facts, as is required of scientists. Rather, they adjust the facts to fit their assumptions, sustaining their belief and simultaneously generating conspiracy theories. The twenty-first-century observation below comes from the CryptoFlorida website, introducing a conspiracy theory involving a demonized version of the Smithsonian Institution and "Darwinian scientists"—a theory apparently held in common by believers across the country: "32 caves within a 180 square mile area were discovered to hold the remains of ancient, strangely costumed 8–9 foot giants. . . . The same burial place had been found 10–15 years earlier by another man who made a deal with the Smithsonian. The evidence of his find was stolen and covered up by Darwinian scientists" (Bennett 2012).

The Lake Erie region, rich in such excavations, is certainly not without modern believers. One individual gives a clear statement of the persistent belief: "I believe they were nephilim and thus acquired vast knowledge through (500+) lifespans and could travel overseas and propregate in many nations. They must have come from the middle east mesopotamia pre deluge era, so they were neither white nor Indian. People were not dumb neanderthals, *the bible is real*, evolutionists are full of bs" (Examiner 2013).

The italicized statement in the last sentence goes to the heart of what is at stake for believers: establishing the authority of the Bible over natural science. Sometimes, perhaps in the heat of passion, supporters of Nephilim discoveries use hateful rhetoric. Many believers in Nephilim fossils, much like UFOlogists (see "UFO Base under Lake Erie," this volume), have adopted conspiracy theories that demonize scientists, such as Darwin, and others who do not share their beliefs.

Since believers see science as the enemy of religion, modern claims that local Native American Mound Builders were Nephilim may reflect a crisis of faith. So it is only fair to comment on what is actually at stake in scientific research, which—although believers in Nephilim fossils are not likely to be convinced—has always been nothing more (or less) than accuracy. For scientists, this is just as true when accuracy supports the Bible as when it does not. Conversely, persistent claims that Lake Erie Mound Builders were gigantic Nephilim suggests a different agenda than accuracy: the reinstatement of the Creation story as natural history.

References

Bennett, Mary Alice. 2012. "Past Blast: Giants in the Americas." CryptoFlorida, August 19, 2012. http://www.cryptoflorida.webs.com/apps/blog/show/18182856-past-blast-giants-in-the-americas.html.

Examiner. 2013. "The Giant Mound Builders of Erie." Accessed September 28, 2013. http://www.examiner.com/article/the-giant-mound-builders-of-erie.html.

Feder, Kenneth L. 1996. *Frauds, Myths and Mysteries: Science and Pseudoscience in Archaeology*. 2nd ed. London: Mayfield.

Moore, Clarence Bloomfield. 1892. "A Burial Mound of Florida." *American Naturalist* 26, no. 302 (February): 129–43.

Wright, Aaron, and Solomon Spalding. 2006. "The Giants of Conneaut." Spalding Research Project. Last modified April 27, 2006. https://solomonspalding.com/SRP/saga2/sagawtoa.htm.

Figure 39.1. "Ohio Grassman" from History Channel's *MonsterQuest*, season 2, episode 4, "Grassman Stalks Ohio," aired June 18, 2008, produced by Whitewolf Entertainment. (Copyrighted content used under US Code, Title 17, Chapter 1, Section 107, Limitations on exclusive rights: Fair Use)

THE OHIO GRASSMAN
A Lake Erie Cryptid

The prefix *crypto-* means hidden or secret. The term *cryptozoology* refers to the study of animals who have remained hidden from—or have simply eluded—discovery by natural science. Those spotted only outside of natural science, along with combinations of species that do not combine in natural science, are called cryptids. Examples include Bigfoot and other varieties of ape-man, as well as other animal-human species not known to occur in nature—such as wolf-men (werewolves) and fish-people (mermaids and mermen).

Sightings of the famous cryptid Bigfoot occur all over the United States although there are distinct regional variants like the northwestern Sasquatch and, in Ohio, the elusive Grassman. Current Grassman sightings are posted more frequently inland but also occur along Lake Erie's shore. At this writing, a quick search found thirteen reported sightings along the lakeshore counties of Ashtabula, Lake, Lorain, Erie, and Ottawa.

The names Bigfoot, Sasquatch, and Grassman are often used interchangeably, all referring to a mute, hairy, gorilla-like biped roughly nine feet tall that does not knuckle-walk like an ape but walks upright like a man. Reports of features that distinguish one from another ape-man are highly unstable, but the Ohio Grassman is unique in three ways: it has an unusually strong odor, lives on the woodland fringes of farms and fields, and, above all, constructs mound-like shelters made of grass.

The traditional medieval Wild Man is not the same as Bigfoot, Sasquatch, or the Grassman, because he was the original inhabitant of the "wild," he can help us understand the Bigfoot phenomenon. Bigfoot and his variants (like the Ohio Grassman) differ from the Wild Man in that cryptids are born and bred in the wilderness or at its borders. According to Bernheimer's (1952) classic study, the medieval Wild Man is native to the civilized world, not the wilderness.

The Wild Man starts out as an ordinary, civilized citizen who has been alienated, either by a heartless woman or by an advancing world indifferent to traditional ways of thinking and doing things. The Wild Man copes by retreating from civilization and regressing into an uncivilized state, living in a physical condition, and geographical area, of wilderness. As Bernheimer wrote: "The spectacle is one which repeats itself at the end of great epochs of history when *traditional* aims and values have become brittle and petrified" (1952: 144–45; my italics). It is precisely when old ways of coping become obsolete that we can expect the Wild Man, as well as cryptids, to crawl out of the woodwork. In other words, when traditional coping tools for living a productive and rewarding life give way, the Wild Man retreats into a primitive state and into areas of uncultivated land that are the natural habitat of the cryptid.

But in the case of cryptids, it may be the hunter who can't keep up with the rapid changes in natural science and who is excluded from scientific exploration and discovery since his traditional ways of seeking and knowing have become obsolete. The cryptid hunter appears to cope like the Wild Man, retreating from the fieldwork of modern natural science into a hunt for species that are supposedly unnoticed or overlooked by natural scientists. The quest stands outside the limitations of seeking and knowing according to the theories, methods, and techniques of natural science.

Bigfoot's Grassman variant seems to have a long history in Ohio. According to James A. Willis, Andrew Henderson, and Loren Coleman, Ohio's Delaware Indians informed early settlers of encounters with a hairy cryptid, and in 1869, a news article reported a gorilla-like attack on a man riding in his carriage, whose daughter caused the strange animal to flee by tossing a rock at it (2005: 88). The media has long broadcast many science fiction and documentary programs on Bigfoot and his various analogues, but in the twenty-first century, programming includes so-called reality TV. In the case of cryptid hunting, the genre involves a night-vision camera and a sound technician that follow cryptid-tracking hopefuls, searching in heightened states of alertness and excitement brought about by signs of purported cryptids in the wild.

According to anthropologist Victor Turner (1967), cryptids like Bigfoot and the Grassman can be seen as liminal beings, by which he meant a state of being that he called "betwixt and between." Turner meant they are neither here nor there, in the same sense that an adolescent is neither a child nor an adult but is somewhere "betwixt and between." Ape-like cryptids, such as Bigfoot, Sasquatch, and the Grassman, seem to fall into a state that is neither man nor beast but is liminal, or somewhere between the two.

As *twilight* refers to a time that is neither dark nor light, liminal beings invariably inhabit liminal zones, in this case meaning uncultivated areas at the borders or margins of farms and fields. These places are found *in* the civilized world but are not *of* it; they are border zones neither impenetrably wild nor penetrably civilized but somewhere betwixt and between. Similarly, combinations of different species that are not known to combine in the natural world, like ape-men, wolf-men, and fish-men, are betwixt and between man and beast. By definition, their liminality stands *above* the laws of nature, and they therefore represent the *super*natura—just as science fiction writer Rod Sterling once reminded us that to enter a liminal or "twilight zone" is to enter a dimension of supernatural experience.

The thrill of exploration, of discovery and conquest, should not be overlooked as a motivating factor among cryptid hunters. It is effectively an armchair, or "walking-distance-from-the-car," departure into the great unknown. Such exploration seems to emulate long-gone days of colonial discovery, when ordinary folks could venture into the uncharted world and discover previously unknown species of flora and fauna—able not only to tell of great adventures but to do so as owners of society's most valuable knowledge. It was a time unlike our own—our own time being one of rapid advances in science and technology that exclude ordinary folks from even understanding, let alone participating in, new ways of discovering and knowing.

As Peter Dendle writes: "To be on to something that even the professors at Harvard do not know about, or to benefit from a cure of which the National Institutes of Health are ignorant, can be very empowering in an age of routine deference to higher bodies of institutional knowledge. It is no great wonder that cryptozoology devotees consciously position themselves in defiance of mainstream science" (2006: 200).

At the same time, however, cryptid hunters legitimate their mission by taking a firm ecological stance (albeit for the protection and preservation of cryptids), and they often use terms from the lexicon of mainstream science. Chuck Klosterman, of the *Akron (OH) Beacon Journal*, described a meeting of Ohio cryptid trackers in 1999. As is fairly common, he refers to Sasquatch and Bigfoot interchangeably in his report (posted online by Dirk Vander Ploeg, 2011):

> During the first weekend of March, about 150 believers drove through a blizzard to Newcomerstown, Ohio, a town with a population of less than 4000. They came to Newcomerstown to sit on metal folding chairs in a tiny elementary school gymnasium, where they drank complimentary Coca-Cola and rapped about the Sasquatch lifestyle.
>
> For 11 years, Newcomerstown has hosted an annual Bigfoot Conference. Among them are a few exceptionally serious Sasquatch searchers who come to Newcomerstown each month to attend meetings of the Tri-State Bigfoot

Study Group, where they analyze recent sightings and discuss the growing body of Bigfoot evidence.

It should be acknowledged that no Bigfoot claim has ever met the test of being actual evidence, while countless Bigfoot claims have more than met the test of fraudulent reporting. But this does not mean there are no undiscovered species in the world, nor does it rule out the discovery of a previously unknown species to account for sightings of Bigfoot and other similarly undocumented animal life.

By the same token, the possibility also exists that for devoted cryptozoologists, the only *good* evidence may be flawed evidence since any genuine discovery would immediately bring the likes of Bigfoot, Sasquatch, and the Grassman under the authority of natural science, the exclusionary realm of academic specialists. Serious cryptid trackers seem highly unlikely to relinquish the adventure of pursuit and discovery, along with the private ownership of privileged knowledge, by ceding it all to the scientific enemy.

It is extremely important to note that at Newcomerstown, as in other places where believers gather to analyze and promote cryptid ecology, no one is ever hurt by this activity. Cryptid seeking is unlike UFOlogy, in which purported alien species (and their evil allies) often become projections of personality disorders or of racism and prejudice. Cryptid hunters show no such tendency. Rather, their claims can be seen as a creative and strategic means of leveling the playing field in conflicts between academic and traditional ways of discovering and knowing things. As folklorist Dan Ben-Amos wrote, human beings normally divide things into categories (creating taxonomies, or classifications) to help us make sense of the world, but traditional sense-making strategies are often quite different from academic sense-making strategies: "Analytical [academic] categories . . . have been developed in the interest of scholarship and serve its varied purposes . . . [traditional] taxonomy, on the other hand, has no external objective. The logical principles that underlie its categorization . . . are those which are meaningful to the members of the group and can guide them in their personal relationships" (1976: 225).

Cryptid hunters are clearly benefiting from, enjoying, and sustaining a close-knit community and a traditional way of knowing that is exciting and personally rewarding and that harms no one. In so doing, they lead an iconoclastic lifestyle committed to challenging a scientific authority that few others dare to question. Trackers of Lake Erie's Grassman stand tall among such challengers. And, since good science never closes the book on unforeseen discovery, someday they may surprise us all.

References

Ben-Amos, Dan. 1976. "Analytic Categories and Ethnic Genres." In *Folklore Genres*, edited by Dan Ben-Amos, 215–42. Austin: University of Texas Press.

Bernheimer, Richard. 1952. *Wild Men in the Middle Ages: A Study in Art, Sentiment and Demonology*. Cambridge, MA: Harvard University Press.

Dendle, Peter. 2006. "Cryptozoology in the Medieval and Modern Worlds." *Folklore* 117 (2): 190–206.

Klosterman, Chuck. 1999. "Believing in Bigfoot." *Beacon Journal* (Akron, Ohio), March 24. l.

Turner, Victor. 1967. "Betwixt and Between: The Liminal Period in Rites of Passage." In *The Forest of Symbols*, 93–111. Ithaca, NY: Cornell University Press.

Willis, James A., Andrew Henderson, and Loren Coleman. 2005. *Weird Ohio: Your Travel Guide to Ohio's Local Legends and Best Kept Secrets*. Edited by Mark Sceurman and Mark Moran. New York: Sterling.

THE LAKE ERIE MIRAGE

Lake Erie spans thirty miles at its narrowest point and fifty-seven at its widest, which makes it impossible for the naked eye to see the opposite side from either shore. And yet people have been "seeing across Lake Erie" throughout history. In 2006, the Associated Press named the phenomenon "the Lake Erie mirage" and began investigating with an account given by a reporter from the *Cleveland Plain Dealer* one hundred years earlier: "The whole sweep of the Canadian shore stood out as if it was only three miles away. The distant points across the lake stood out for nearly an hour and then faded away" (Crystalinks, n.d.).

Although *calm* is not a term usually associated with Lake Erie, when the air is extremely still and certain weather factors prevail, the stage is set for seeing a mirage, something that isn't there. The Associated Press found that mirages occur during atmospheric inversions, when the wind is still and a layer of cold air sits on the lake, covered by layers of increasingly warm air. The inversion causes the light to bend as it filters through the layers across the lake, creating the illusion of distant objects. When the wind begins to stir, the images distort and then "fade away," exactly as described by the Cleveland journalist in 1906.

Seeing across Lake Erie works both ways from either side and is not an artifact of earlier centuries. In 2006, a Canadian reporter from Ontario's *Chatham Daily News* told the Associated Press he had seen Cleveland twice from across the lake, first in 2002 while driving along a road near the shore and again in 2004 while on the same road.

Lake Erie mariners are even more familiar with this phenomenon, but as long as seeing is believing, both seafarers and landlubbers will believe what they see and will "know" they saw the opposite shore, even fifty-seven miles from their location.

Reference

Crystalinks. n.d. "Mirage." Accessed October 12, 2023. https://crystalinks.com/mirage.html.

LAKE ERIE AND THE GREAT LAKES TRIANGLE

The Bermuda Triangle, a section of the Atlantic Ocean that lies off the southeastern coast of the United States, is famous for the unexplained disappearance of more than one thousand ships and planes that have never been accounted for (Fortner and Jax 1997). But the general area of the Great Lakes can also be configured as a triangle, and it may account for even more unexplained mysteries, although it is much shallower and sixteen times smaller than the Bermuda Triangle.

Until the twentieth century, the mysterious disappearance of ships from Lake Erie's surface was attributed to a malevolent water sprite called a storm hag (see "Jenny Greenteeth," this volume). By the twentieth century, the storm hag no longer satisfied as an explanation for the disappearance of ships from the lake's surface, and we now have scientific ways to predict the lake's capricious turbulence and control its consequences. But only on the Great Lakes do ships the size of major freighters, barges, steamships, and ferries sail on fresh water, which best preserves shipwrecks once they go down. That makes it all the more mysterious that many large ships and planes have gone down at specific coordinates on Lake Erie but are nowhere to be found when divers go looking. At least until now. It appears that in the twenty-first century, scientists are solving the mystery of why sunken ships, and even aircraft, disappear from the lake bottom.

The enormous steamer *C. B. Lockwood*, for example, was about 285 feet long and 45 feet wide when it plunged more than 70 feet to the bottom of Lake Erie, just east of Cleveland. More than a century later, it would come to be a perfect example—not just of the lake-bottom mystery but also of its possible solution. The ill-fated steamer sank on October 13, 1902, its location found and charted within days. The wreck was marked with buoys, and the coordinates were recorded. Yet, decades later, divers found only strange markings on the lake bottom and no sign of the sunken ship. But by 2012 it became possible to investigate the site with a subbottom profiler, a device that can highlight structural differences and multiple layers under the seafloor.

Using this new technology, a ship was discovered exactly where the *C. B. Lockwood* was lost, a ship about 285 feet long and 45 feet wide. This ship apparently sank twice: once beneath the lake's surface and once beneath the lake's bottom! The theory is that lost ships like the *C. B. Lockwood* sank beneath the sea floor because of the underwater earthquakes now known to occur on the Great Lakes and to swallow ships whole. "Think of it as a jar of sand with a marble on top," one scientist explained. "When the jar is shaken, the sand shifts, forming air pockets, and the marble sinks" (Blake 2012).

New technology is providing new ways of charting what goes on under the Great Lakes, and specifically at the bottom of Lake Erie. Perhaps this newly discovered seismic activity also accounts for some of the unexplained surges of wave activity on the lakes. New knowledge may also allow the discovery and even recovery of many (if not all) of the ships that sank beneath the waves, only to be lost in the Great Lakes Triangle. Clearly, when a belief can no longer remain timely and relevant in the light of changing times and generations, it will be dropped from tradition. Consequently, not all ships lost from Erie's surface will remain lost beneath the lake. Rather, it is the once-terrifying storm hag who will remain forever lost beneath its depths.

References

Blake, Erica. 2012. "Vanished Shipwreck's Secret Revealed: Sunken Vessel Swallowed Up by Lake Erie Muck." *Toledo Blade*, March 19, 2012. http://www.toledoblade.com/State/2012/03/19/Vanished-shipwreck-s-secret-revealed.

Fortner, Roseanne W., and Daniel W. Jax. 1997. *What Is the Great Lakes Triangle?* Great Lakes Shipping (ES-EAGLS), Ohio State University. https://files.eric.ed.gov/fulltext/ED202716.pdf.

Figure 42.1. *Tiberius* by Lake Erie College. (Copyrighted content used with permission)

LAKE ERIE CAMPUS LORE

Folklorist Simon Bronner tells of his first exposure to campus lore as a college freshman, when he and his fellow students were welcomed by the dorm's resident assistant: "'You know what B.S. stands for, don't you?' Heads turned and glances were exchanged, anticipating where he was going with this off-color reference. 'M.S. is more of the same, and Ph.D.— well, that's it just piled higher and deeper'" (1990: 11).

According to Bronner, the humor helped put newcomers at ease, and sharing a student in-joke boosted a sense of belonging. "For some," Bronner wrote, "it was a refreshing reminder that the job of being a college student is nothing to be afraid of. For others, it was a reminder that if they didn't do well, they needn't feel it was the end of the world. . . . Yet undergirding these views was the assumption drawn from the lore that degrees, represented by those magic letters, hold power" (1990: 11).

Student traditions abound in colleges and universities across the country, including around the periphery of Lake Erie. Campus traditions can be oral, gestured, handcrafted, written, or musical; they can be recited, pantomimed, or costumed; they can involve food, props, and pranks; they can involve buildings, statues, landmarks, and events, as well as personalities, living or dead, real or imagined. Traditions can occur randomly or only at specific times of year. Some traditions are local to specific campuses; some are widespread across the nation. But all of them, Bronner tells us, "arise from the kind of learning we might call informal, typically outside the formal instruction of the classroom" (1990: 23).

Campus lore provides practical instruction, as well as welcome entertainment. It can forge a sense of community, lightening the mood when needed, encouraging students to persevere, and helping them develop the values, identity, and coping skills required to survive, and succeed, in the adult mainstream. Examples below are from the Lake Erie shore; one is local to a specific college, and one is a local variant of a widespread American tradition. Both are representative enough to speak for the genre of campus lore. The first is specific to Lake Erie College in Painesville, Ohio.

Tiberius: The Invincible Mascot

According to journalist Karen Farkas (2013), writing for the *Cleveland Plain Dealer*, Tiberius was a chocolate Labrador retriever owned by Harriet Young, a dean at Lake Erie College at the turn of the twentieth century, when the school was a women's college. Tiberius, who apparently had the run of the campus, attended classes and spent time endearing himself to students.

When Tiberius died, Young memorialized the beloved dog with an iron statue that stood in front of her home. When she retired in 1910, the statue was installed beside College Hall, then the main building on campus. The dog had passed on, but life would be eventful for his statue.

The statue was stolen in the early 1950s, but Tiberius was not forgotten. Seven years later, at 2:00 a.m. on April 13, women in a dorm attached to College Hall were suddenly awakened by loud, frantic barking. The building was on fire, and it was completely destroyed, but the warning came in time for all to escape safely. Since no dog was found anywhere, it was believed—statue or no statue—that the spirit of Tiberius had come to the students' rescue.

A duplicate statue was discovered in a New York antique shop in 1975. It replaced the original and was mounted on a newly installed cement base to prevent another theft. But in 1984 vandals removed the head and smashed the body. Even so, Lake Erie's students were not about to forget their loving mascot. In 2004, graduating students gave the college a small Tiberius statue placed by the gazebo at the center of campus.

There is now a more current replacement. This Tiberius, donated in 2008, stands in the same place as the first Tiberius statue and on the same cement base as the second. And, adding to the legend of the dorm fire, the statue has generated yet another tradition: every football season, before the first game, the team gathers around the invincible mascot and pets him for good luck.

Like most campus lore, Tiberius traditions at Lake Erie College do not teach the subject matter of academic disciplines. But if nothing else, Tiberius legends teach the power of honor to transcend dishonor, along with the power of love and loyalty to transcend the passage of time. Such valuable lessons may be absent from college course listings but are available to all in campus folk curricula.

The Roommate's Death: A Lake Erie "Adolescent Shocker"

Folk traditions can impart knowledge through a variety of expressive genres, including the type of tale that folklorist Jan Brunvand calls an "adolescent

Figure 42.2. *Bloody Handprint* by r. nial bradshaw via Flickr. (CC BY 2.0)

shocker" (1981: 57). The tale of "The Roommate's Death," for example, is widespread across American campuses and appears online in a twenty-first-century variant from Lake Erie's shore. Brunvand points out that "The Roommate's Death" involves young college women alone in their dorms at night or returning to their dorms at night, usually for reasons that are realistic and plausible (1981: 58). The circumstances are those that any female student might find herself in, which suggests that "The Roommate's Death" is a cautionary tale: a warning against actions that women in this tale should not have taken but did or should have taken but did not, both of which led to a tragic end.

Key elements of all variants include the following: a roommate alone in the dorm, who assumes there is nothing dangerous about promiscuity and who will subsequently be murdered. The surviving roommate will come home late and be in the darkened room while the crime is committed; she will hear noises, but like her roommate, she will assume it is "just" promiscuous activity and, therefore, is nothing to worry about. The crime is discovered the next morning, with an important message left by the murderer. The message is usually written on the wall in the victim's blood.

The tale below appears as it was posted online, but with slight changes where the original was confusing. That is, I have called one student "the girl," and the other one "the roommate" since the storyteller uses *girl* and *roommate* interchangeably and also uses *she* for both women, making it unclear who is who as the tale unfolds. The Lake Erie variant is well worth clarifying in this way because it gives us all the key elements of the traditional narrative. The following example was posted to the now defunct Yahoo Answers (n.d.).

> This one is about how this girl's roommate has "it" a lot with her boyfriend. So the girl has to go to sleep every night listening to them. One night the roommate was alone in the room and was flirting with some guy online who she agreed to meet up with. She asked him where he was and he answered "In your room." He grabbed her, pinned her down on the bed and started suffocating her. The girl walks in and hears them in the dark. She thinks it's her roommate and her roommate's boyfriend because of all the squealing. So she goes to sleep. When she wakes up she sees a message on the wall written in blood: "You should have checked on your roommate."

Variants of "The Roommate's Death" have probably been told for as long as women have been living in campus dorms. We know this is a contemporary variant, not simply because it was posted online but rather because the roommate herself is chatting online, although with a predator hiding in her room.

Depending on the variant, as Bronner notes, a question can arise as to who was responsible for the roommate's death: the promiscuous girl who took the fatal risk or the one who was criticized for not checking on her roommate (1990: 171). But in variants that include all elements of the tradition, there is an important lesson for both students.

The tale makes it clear that promiscuity poses serious risks and that flirting with strangers online is far from safe. The tale demonstrates that the doomed roommate would have been fine if she had not been so naively trusting and had taken responsibility for her own safety (in which case she wouldn't have needed anyone to check on her). On the other hand, the girl who didn't check on her roommate was also negligent, because being responsible means recognizing, and speaking up, when someone else is being irresponsible. It also means never doing something both students did: taking a mere assumption for a fact and failing to check before making a decision. Making assumptions without checking, as the tale points out, can easily become a matter of life and death. The tale teaches that acting irresponsibly as one grows into adulthood invites disaster—especially for promiscuous women.

Lessons taught by Tiberius traditions and the legend of "The Roommate's Death" are not part of formal classroom curricula—but wisdom is carried in all of the many types of lore that circulate on college campuses. As long as these lessons remain timely and relevant, they will persist in campus lore, generation after generation, ready to be learned outside the classroom, where important traditional knowledge is available to all.

References

Bronner, Simon J. 1990. *Piled Higher and Deeper: The Folklore of Campus Life*. Little Rock, AR: August House.

Brunvand, Jan H. 1981. *The Vanishing Hitchhiker: American Urban Legends and Their Meanings*. New York: W.W. Norton and Company.

Farkas, Karen. 2013. "Myths and Legends on College Campuses Still Resonate." *Cleveland Plain Dealer*, January 12, 2013. https://www.cleveland.com/metro/2013/01/myths_and _legends_on_college_c.html.

Yahoo! Answers. n.d. Accessed May 28, 2013. http://www.answers.yahoo.com/questions /index?gid=20130124184957AAE02mw.

THE LADY OF THE LAKE
A Haunted Summer Camp

Whenever a cultivated landscape reverts to the wild and public access is denied, any who dare to trespass are thought to risk confrontation with the untamed, the unknown, and the unexplained—even the realm of the supernatural. Typical of such sites is the abandoned Lady of the Lake summer camp.

In 2010, the *Catholic Chronicle* posted a centennial article about the property, once a lakeside children's retreat that one hundred years earlier began serving "orphans and underprivileged youth on Lake Erie's shore, from the Diocese of Toledo" (Stevens Bertke 2010). The property included a full campsite with separate beaches for boys and girls, a playground, a small chapel, and a grotto where every afternoon the children visited a statue of the Virgin Mary. Mother Mary became the orphans' Lady of the Lake, for whom the camp was named and to whom the rosary was prayed every day.

The camp primarily served orphans until modern medicine significantly diminished the number of children left without relatives. The dwindling of that population, added to the problem of running the facility in a challenging economy, forced the camp to close in 1969. With no public record of fire or any other mishap, the site was sold to a local utility company. Happy summers at Camp Lady of the Lake are remembered fondly by former campers, but—perhaps influenced by the lingering memory of a tragic school fire (see "Gore Orphanage," this volume), not to mention the proliferation of modern summer-camp horror movies—the overgrown campsite took on a new and different life among local young people. Those who dared trespass returned to captivate one another with tales of supernatural sightings and encounters. Access was through the camp's old gateway, which was torn down in the early twenty-first century, erasing the point of entry precisely to discourage youthful adventurism. The gateway came down according to plan, but youthful adventurism prevailed.

The current "Lady of the Lake" legend, and its variants, still proliferate and circulate online. Although the oral tradition is extremely fluid, a typical variant would state that around twenty years ago, a lady ran a camp for orphans. One day, when she returned from a walk down the beach, the camp was on fire. All the children died, and the lady committed suicide. Those who go there around midnight can hear screams and see the woman's ghost on the lake.

Motifs for the modern legend appear below, as listed in Thompson's *Motif-Index* (1956–58):

E275	Ghost haunts place of great accident or misfortune
E334.4	Ghost of suicide seen at death spot or nearby
E266.1	Suicide ghost
E587.5	Ghosts walk at midnight

The following query was accessed in 2012 on the now defunct Talk Paranormal (n.d.) website: "Has anyone in here heard of the haunted Camp Lady of the Lake?" In response, two variants were given, both stating that the campers were murdered and adding yet another motif, E225 (Ghost of murdered child). One respondent said, "Yes, I've heard of it. Turn off 75 onto Erie Road north, drive to the end at the gate, continue walking. Haunted by a group of murdered children. Told to be haunted by the 'Lady of the Lake.' I heard the place burned down with the caregiver and the children inside."

A truncated variant, in the same online conversation, keeps the campsite but omits the fire and even the Lady of the Lake. The murder victims are specified as "younger girls," and in this variant, the murderers are identified as "construction workers": "Well, I have heard it is haunted by younger girls that were killed there by some construction workers when they were building more cabins. When you go out there you can hear kids playing on the swing set which is still out there."

Several eyewitness haunting accounts also appeared on the now defunct Weird Michigan website. I have abridged these discussions, limiting my focus to the hauntings only. I have altered spelling or grammar only when required for clarity. Notably, eyewitness haunting accounts tend to fall into two distinct types. The first type focuses on the uncanny nature of the site with no reference to fire, murder, or suicide. This could mean that the camp's legendary history is so well known that it is taken for granted. But it more clearly reflects less interest in suicide and murder and more modern interest in the site as one of "weird and unexplained" phenomena (like "orbs," for instance).

One eyewitness writes, "Hey my name is Joe and me and a few of my buddies who all live in Toledo go up to this camp, Lady of the Lake ... every time we go there something weird and unexplained always happens there." Joe goes on to describe an occasion when he and a buddy left their group of friends to search for campfire kindling. They found some loose clothing and an empty beer case but were interrupted by approaching lights they feared were carried by police. Scouting the intruders, they were much relieved to find only a couple of hikers with flashlights, but when they returned to the spot they'd left, the clothing and the beer case had disappeared. As Joe tells it, aside from their own car, "there were no other cars in the parking lot," marking the disappearance of the objects as a supernatural event. "Me and my friends have many more experiences there," he adds, "as well as pictures with many orbs seen in the pictures."

Joe's narrative departs from the traditional "Lady of the Lake" story, but he adds another traditional motif also associated with the uncanny: F934 (Extraordinary occurrences concerning lake).

Like Joe, another narrator focused on inexplicable activity at the site, which he recognized as supernatural for the same reason: his was the only car in the parking lot. As demonstrated below, this writer separates each sentence or phrase with serial dots and changes the backstory, referring to a pre-campsite, nineteenth-century family and a fire in their home. But his repetition of "the only car in the parking lot" represents more than one telling and for that reason can now be classified as a new folk motif, as defined by Thompson (1977: 114): Narrator's lone car in remote area marks any other presence as supernatural. His narrative reads (my italics):

> And for anyone who has gone up there you know of the path through the woods that leads to the beach. Well if you go left you go where an old house before the camp was built for those that have done the research . . . a house that burnt down and a woman in the late 1800's and her 3 children died . . . well me and my friend went there in the afternoon and someone or something had set up all those bricks . . . probably around 200 or so . . . my friend and I knocked them all down and walked to the mess hall and old playground and then walked back and all the bricks were set back up . . . so in 15 minutes it would have taken six people to set those bricks up again. . . . *and when we walked out only our car was there.*

The second type of eyewitness account at Camp Lady of the Lake describes a direct confrontation with a ghost, or many ghosts. Kaylee, on the same website as Joe, also omits suicide and murder, and she changes the orphans' summer camp to a year-round orphanage. The account retains the fire in which children died and introduces a little girl "glowing white." Kaylee explains that one night she and some friends were bored, so they decided "to go to Lady of the Lake." Kaylee states that she went along to test her disbelief in ghosts:

> We took the path by the woods and thought we'd go where the orphanage was burnt down, but when we got there we were very disappointed, it was . . . [just] a bunch of rocks with cardboard on it. We decided to go into the woods to look around. As soon as we got there we started hearing what sounded like laughter. It started to creep out the guys but it still wasn't enough to make me believe in ghosts, so I went deeper in . . . that's when it started getting worse. We seen what looked like a little girl wearing a dress but she was glowing white. Then we heard twigs snapping all around us and the laughter again.

Kaylee and her friends left quickly, but not before she felt a playful shove from an unseen presence. She ends her story artfully: "That night I went to Lady of the Lake a non-believer in ghosts, and left a believer." Her narrative is built on the traditional motif E275 (Ghost haunts place of great accident or misfortune).

Joe's unexplained "orbs" and Kaylee's "little girl ghost" also appear in other narratives about the campsite; the following two examples, were found on the now defunct *Blogs Monroe* website. The first example, posted in 2009 by Allen, describes orbs: "Hi. . . . I am one of the story believers. I have felt the presence of something there. I have taken pics and seen the orbs (Allen)."

In March 2012, someone called Rah, posting about a little girl ghost, added a tidy little FOAFtale (friend-of-a-friend tale) to the *Blogs Monroe* website. In a FOAFtale, the narrator is never the source of firsthand knowledge—that is, in a FOAFtale, the firsthand observer is always an anonymous friend of the narrator or a friend of a friend of the narrator and is always inaccessible for follow-up. Rah wrote, "My friend experienced paranormal activity here. She froze at one point and then passed out. Once back at the car she didn't remember anything except for a little girl whispering in her ear 'Help me!' Then there were scratches on her neck. No joke! Really happened."

In the early 1980s, folklorist Bill Ellis studied mock supernatural ordeals traditionally set up by counselors to frighten kids at summer camp, almost always at night and often around a campfire. Accounts of hauntings and inexplicable events at Camp Lady of the Lake are not the same as Ellis's mock supernatural ordeals. But as in those ordeals, those who have supernatural encounters at the site tend to "begin with accounts of past happenings, journey into uncanny territory, confront the supernatural, and conclude with intense discussion" (Ellis 1981: 489). In this case, the tales and their discussion do not take place face-to-face around the campfire or in bunkhouses but go back and forth on assorted "Lady of the Lake" websites.

Seeking and describing these encounters appears to be a highly social activity that also reinforces belief in an afterlife through ghostly contact and clearly serves as a youthful form of thrill seeking (or at least relief from boredom, as Kaylee suggested). But above all, narratives of supernatural encounters at the haunted summer camp appear to be sincere efforts by young people to test the limits of their own credulity and courage against the infinite possibilities of the scary, uncharted wilderness.

References

Blogs Monroe. 2009. "Camp Lady of the Lake." Accessed September 2012. http://www .blogsmonroe.com/expatriate/2009/04update-camp-lady-of-the-lake-erie/.

Ellis, Bill. 1981. "The Camp Mock Ordeal: Theater as Life." *Journal of American Folklore* 94 (374): 486–505.

Stevens Bertke, Laurie. 2010. "Camp Lady of the Lake Revisited." *Catholic Chronicle*, June 28, 2010.

Talk Paranormal. n.d. "Camp Lady of the Lake." Accessed September 2012. http://www .talkparanormal.com/thread-3250.html?highlight=camp+lady+of+the+lake.

Thompson, Stith. 1956-1958. *The Motif-Index of Folk-Literature* (6 Vols.). Bloomington, IN: Indiana University Press.

Thompson, Stith. 1977. *The Folktale.* Los Angeles: University of California Press.

Weird Michigan. n.d. "Hauntings." Accessed September 2012. http://www.weirdmichigan .com/hauntings.html.

Figure 44.1. *Lady of the Lake Quilt* by Bonnie K. Hunter. (Copyrighted content used under US Code, Title 17, Chapter 1, Section 107, Limitations on exclusive rights: Fair Use)

THE LADY OF LAKE ERIE QUILT

The word *quilt* comes from the Latin *culcita*, meaning something stuffed, like a cushion. The term *quilting* refers to stitching that holds layers of stuffed clothing or bedding together, as well as to the act of making quilts. The first European mention of quilted bedding occurred in the 1200s, when quilting was a common pastime for wealthy European ladies. I did not find references to American quilting until the 1800s, when it appears that ordinary American women had gained enough leisure time for all social classes to begin quilting as an artistic, as well as a practical, venture.

Notably, labor-intensive quilts and comforters were created in the United States, even when plain blankets were just as warm and even after factories began mass-producing quilted bedcovers. This speaks to a creative impulse that persists across the nation to this day, among both female and male quilters. But the internet has changed the way society expresses itself in general, and as we are about to see, some expressive arts like quilting are changing along with it.

If quilt patterns were unique to specific areas within the United States, such regional patterns would likely have reflected something different about each community; that is, each regional, ethnic, or religious group would need to marshal its own symbols to retain its own specific cultural identity (Royce 1982: 7).

But America has a long history of migration and dissemination of both traditional and innovative quilting, across all regional borders. At present, the rate of cultural exchange has been so significantly increased by electronic publishing it would seem that association with specific geographical areas ought to disappear. Instead, geographical variants are still bubbling up from the roiling cauldron of American creativity, reproduced across all borders but retaining specific regional identification in the pattern title, named for the location that inspired it. The Lady of Lake Erie quilt is one example.

Figure 44.2. Lady of the Lake quilt pattern, traditional.
Graphic created for this chapter by Jared Bendis.

The Lady of Lake Erie quilt is a variant of an older model known as the Lady of the Lake, with no lake specified. The traditional Lady of the Lake pattern is made up of square blocks sewn together. Each block is made from two triangles, each one either blue or white, attached along their bases. The outside edge of each triangle is bordered by a sawtooth pattern, called a bear's tooth, using the fabric of the contrasting triangle. The signature of the Lady of the Lake pattern is that it has a sawtooth border that goes all the way around the outside of the square.

The Lady of Lake Erie quilt differs in its use of the contrasting bear's tooth pattern, which is sewn around only one edge of one triangle in the square. Bonnie K. Hunter is a professional quilter who created the Lady of Lake Erie variant while teaching on the lakeshore. In her regionally inspired quilt, she incorporates the blues, whites, and grays typical of Lake Erie, changing the design in a way that suggests a repeating pattern of white caps and white sails, as well as the colors and rhythms of the lake itself. Both the Lady of the Lake and the Lady of Lake Erie quilts are solid blue on the reverse side and are typically bordered all around by a large bear's tooth hem, just as most skilled artworks are typically framed to their best visual advantage.

Bonnie says she discovered quilting in 1980, in a home economics class in her senior year of high school. She began machine quilting in 1989 and developed a full-time quilting career that included teaching workshops,

Figure 44.3. Lady of Lake Erie quilt pattern, design by Bonnie K. Hunter. Graphic created for this chapter by Jared Bendis.

lecturing to international quilt guilds and clubs, publishing in print and online, and maintaining a quilting business on the internet called Quiltville. com. In an email interview she explained: "'Lady of the Lake' is a traditional patchwork pattern, and I was making this quilt while teaching in Ohio, up along the shores of Lake Erie. That's how I ended up naming my quilt 'Lady of Lake Erie.' My arrangement is a bit different from the norm, but the recognizable traditional elements are still there" (Bonnie K. Hunter, personal communication, 2012, see also https://quiltville.com, Bonnie Hunter's website).

The term *art* derives from the Latin *ars*, meaning "skill." Folk art is all too often demeaned as being unskilled, unschooled, or crude and primitive. But these demeaning descriptions ignore the skill demonstrated by folk art masters: the same skill level demonstrated by fine art masters but never by the mediocre and inferior artists who produce the vast majority of both fine and folk art. Folk art is also frequently demeaned as "utilitarian," as if the perfectly skilled quilt that beautifies the owner's home (in place of an ordinary, equally useful blanket) isn't "art for art's sake," as fine art is said to be. But if we think about it critically, fine art isn't any more or less "for art's sake" than folk art. Fine art may not be beautiful to look at, and there are sometimes legitimate questions as to the skill purportedly demonstrated, but the most skilled fine art is typically purchased as a business or financial investment, and it is hard to imagine anything more utilitarian than that.

When speaking of art, most people feel they don't know what's "good"; they just know what they like. We tend to feel more comfortable with music, and no wonder, since we hear it almost everywhere we go. Not surprisingly, where music is concerned, we know instinctively that a perfectly played fiddle tune is not a failed symphony. Yet, in addition to claiming superior skill, fine art also claims "innovation" and "originality" as its own private property. But when Bonnie says her arrangement is "different from the norm," innovation and originality are exactly what she's talking about.

Bonnie's description recalls the art of the jazz musician; in jazz composition, different artists' arrangements of the same melody will be highly distinct, each artist interpreting in a unique way but in a skilled enough manner that the bounded structure of the melody will still be recognized. As Bonnie says of the Lady of Lake Erie quilt, the arrangement is different from the norm, but the traditional elements remain recognizable. Striking that perfect balance between the transcendent past and the grounded present is much more difficult than simply being "original"; it is the nexus of creative heat in skilled tradition bearing.

Stith Thompson (1977: 415), the grand old man of folklore indexing, defined *motif* as the smallest element in a tale that is unusual or striking. He also determined that if a literary motif appears in more than one telling, that demonstrates its ability to enter, and persist in, tradition. Traditional tales will fall into specific tale types according to similarities in their motifs. And the same may be said of "motifs" in quilting. As with literary motifs, visual elements that are distinct to a specific type of quilt and are repeated in quilt after quilt will constitute a quilt "type" that can be modified into different variants by creating variations in its motif structure.

The innovative Lady of Lake Erie pattern is a current variant of the traditional Lady of the Lake quilt type. The new Lady of Lake Erie pattern may well persist in tradition since it is now repeated by quilters both on and off Lake Erie's shores. The pattern is picked up by countless quilters face-to-face and online or purchased from kits sold online. According to postings on the internet, the pattern is repeated in the blues, whites, and grays of the lake, as well as in a wide variety of different colors and printed fabrics in a kaleidoscopic burst of quilting creativity. Today, quilters display and discuss their work in their blogs and websites; their Facebook, Instagram, and Pinterest posts; and their texts and tweets, instantly disseminating their patterns, techniques, variations, and aesthetics—both in their skilled performances and in their standards of beauty.

Restriction of any quilt design to one locality in the nation, if it ever really existed, has long given way to creativity that observes no regional boundaries at all—at least not in the old geographical sense. Locality is now (or still) memorialized in the names of the places that inspire certain patterns or in variants of those patterns, as with Bonnie K. Hunter's geographically inspired variant of the Lady of the Lake pattern: the beautiful Lady of Lake Erie quilt.

References

Royce, Anya Peterson. 1982. *Ethnic Identity: Strategies of Diversity*. Bloomington: Indiana University Press.

Thompson, Stith. 1977. *The Folktale*. Los Angeles: University of California Press.

Figure 45.1. *Commercial Fishing on the Great Lakes* by Kelly House, published by Bridge Michigan. (Copyrighted content used under US Code, Title 17, Chapter 1, Section 107, Limitations on exclusive rights: Fair Use)

TRADITIONAL FOODWAYS ON LAKE ERIE'S SHORE

C anada and the United States ring Lake Erie's shore with a string of cultural and economic differences that play out in culinary traditions typical of each coast. In multiethnic America, we tend not to fly one another's flags or say one another's prayers, but we happily sing one another's songs, and we eat one another's foods with gusto. Canadian ports on Lake Erie are mostly fishing towns like Port Stanley and Port Dover (the latter also known for its local, nonalcoholic apple wine), while American ports are frequently connected to major cosmopolitan shipping cities like Cleveland. The islands that dot Lake Erie are largely supported by agriculture and tourism, and as a general rule, these islands contribute to wine menus on both sides of the lake.

Whenever one speaks in generalities, detail will be lost, evoking criticism because some things must inevitably be missed or excluded. But what is gained is a broad, overarching example that can't be accessed otherwise. That means some enjoyable foodways that are not widely shared may be overlooked here, but widespread traditions will come to light, and while these examples may not be exhaustive, they will be representative, giving us a broad overview of patterns in regional culinary culture.

While the Canadian fishing shore is similar to Ohio's agricultural shore from Maumee Bay to Vermilion, the Canadian coast is largely composed of towns where one can find French and British influences, less common in the more ethnically diverse populations on the American side. In Canadian coastal towns, one might find street signs posted in English and French, as well as "tea room" restaurants reflecting the afternoon break so cherished in the British Isles. But above all, these are fishing towns, with some regional recipes not common to the United States, particularly for different varieties of pickled fish.

Fishing tends to be a divisive occupation in both countries; Canada has the larger commercial fisheries, typically chafing against quotas and other government controls. On both shores, commercial fishing interests have long been pitted against those of sport fishing. But both nations hold in common Lake Erie yellow perch, a coastal Canadian favorite that is also consumed, along with walleye, on the American side of the lake.

Lake fishing is but one source of sustenance for coastal dwellers. Diverse immigrant communities, particularly in Lake Erie's American port cities, have contributed to ethnic diversity as a general, composite culinary tradition. I will focus on Cleveland's traditional foodways because Cleveland reflects an ethnic heritage largely representative of similar American sister cities. Plus, as a native Clevelander, I know this place best. What I have observed in Cleveland will, in a general way, be true of other American cities on Lake Erie (and in some instances, inland cities on both sides of the lake may also recognize themselves).

Examples of ethnic diversity are visible in Cleveland neighborhoods like Little Italy, Slavic Village, and the area known as Tremont, once a thriving neighborhood of Russian Orthodox immigrants. But historically, children of immigrants tend to move up economically and away from the ethnic neighborhoods of their early settlement. In this way, the city's old ethnic enclaves typically disappear, replaced by waves of different ethnic newcomers. Alternatively, these neighborhoods may become gentrified and homogenized into nonethnic, mainstream communities. Today, the ethnic Tremont community is mostly gone, but the onion-shaped domes of Saint Theodosius Russian Orthodox Cathedral still dominate the neighborhood, and staples of German, Greek, and central and eastern European foodways persist in Cleveland's general menu. Mainstays include kielbasa (a pork sausage), an assortment of savory cabbage dishes, and pierogi (small, fried dumplings filled with meat, cheese, or vegetables).

Vendors at Cleveland's famed West Side Market still offer an array of fresh ingredients and ready-to-eat dishes representing many of the city's ethnic communities, old and new, along with freshly butchered meat, poultry, fish, and seafood; baked goods; and farm and dairy produce. Successive waves of new immigrants from Asia, the Middle East, the Mediterranean, the Spanish Americas, and the Caribbean continue to introduce dishes to tempt Cleveland's palate. African American soul food and dishes from Cleveland's Asia Town are among the different ethnic foodways that vie with older staples for a foothold in local tradition. Barbeque cook-offs and other culinary events spice up Cleveland summers by pitting local restaurants against one another in spirited, outdoor cooking and sampling competitions.

American cities like to brand themselves with certain foods, regional specialties that visitors feel they must sample before leaving. The city of Philadelphia, for instance, is famous for its Philly cheesesteak sandwich, Cincinnati for its three-way chili, and the state of Indiana for its persimmon

Figure 45.2. *The Famed Cleveland "Polish Boy."* Photo by author, Judith S. Neulander.

pudding. A famed Cleveland original is the Polish boy, a bun overflowing with grilled or deep-fried kielbasa, french fries, barbeque or hot sauce, and a layer of coleslaw (smoked kielbasa and sauerkraut can be substituted). In 2009, Chef Michael Symon cited Cleveland's Polish boy as "the best thing I ever ate" on American television's Food Network.

Variants of the native sandwich can be found in other Great Lakes coastal cities; the city of Chicago, located on Lake Michigan, has a worthy rival sandwich involving a hearty helping of Italian sausage and fried peppers. Early in the twenty-first century, growing health-food consciousness began to eclipse many of these traditional delicacies, but the Polish boy can still be found in Cleveland. Like most cosmopolitan cities, downtown Cleveland also offers an array of other ethnic specialties.

Slyman's Restaurant is a downtown Cleveland delicatessen much lauded by culinary critics; *Esquire* magazine (2008) called its towering corned beef sandwich "the best in America." But today, the delicatessens that followed the Jewish community to the eastern suburbs reflect growing health concerns, along with an innovative embrace of other ethnic traditions. Suburban menus now include low-cholesterol dishes like egg-white omelets, skinless chicken dishes, and fabulous combos like popular Mexican variations on Jewish recipes. On the

Figure 45.3. *Slyman's Delicatessen in Downtown Cleveland.* (Copyrighted content used with permission)

east side, Jews and Muslims alike break bread at the tiny Jerusalem Grill, where Israeli dishes (along with a Chinese side bar) meet the dietary restrictions of both faiths with a strictly kosher kitchen.

Away from the large port cities, Lake Erie's American shore is dotted with small fishing and agricultural towns. Canadian pickled fish is not an American commonplace, but the Friday-night fish fry is a regional staple in many American communities, especially on the lakeshore, where fish is abundant. Pancake breakfasts and spaghetti dinners are also typical church and fire station fundraisers.

The fish fry is the centerpiece of countless summer festivals held in small towns along the American shore, where Erie perch and walleye are traditional favorites. Local farms are open to public berry picking in summer, pumpkin picking in fall, and Christmas tree picking in winter. Rural towns often build summer festivals around their pioneer roots, drawing from regional farming traditions. They hold not only fish fry events but corn and apple butter festivals in summer and—like their Canadian counterparts—maple syrup festivals in fall. Some American lakeshore towns expand the delight quotient, as well as the menu, by combining fish fries with other local traditions, as on

Figure 45.4. *Perch, Peach, Pierogi, & Polka Festival* by Jon Stinchcomb for the *Port Clinton News Herald*. (Copyrighted content used under US Code, Title 17, Chapter 1, Section 107, Limitations on exclusive rights: Fair Use)

the annual Port Clinton Labor Day Perch, Peach, Pierogi, and Polka Festival, adding ancestral central European delights (pierogi and polkas) to a number of local cultural and harvest items.

But not every culinary offering on the lake is local or ethnic. The same fast-food restaurants that dot the nation also dot the region, and stadium food is stadium food everywhere you go. But Lake Erie's cosmopolitan coastal cities also offer a full menu of international haute cuisine, including Asian, Italian, and French. By the early twenty-first century, the Travel section of the *Chicago Tribune* had cited Cleveland as a "Hot New Dining City" (Eng 2008). On the whole, Lake Erie foodways appear to be quintessentially American, which is to say, eclectic and experimental—but still laced with the sweet, the savory, and the widely shared traditions of highly diverse ethnic origins.

References

Eng, Monica. 2008. "Hot New Dining City: Cleveland?!" *Los Angeles Times*, January 29, 2008. http://www.latimes.com/travel/la-trw-trvmain3-wk3-story.html.

Esquire. 2008. "The Best Sandwiches in America." February 16, 2008. http://www.esquire .com/food-drink/a4205/sandwiches.

Food Network. 2009. *The Best Thing I Ever Ate*. Season 1, episode 8, "Between Bread." Aired June 22, 2009.

Figure 46.1. *Ice Auger* photo from the US Army Corps of Engineers. (Public Domain)

THE ART OF LAKE ERIE ICE FISHING

Long before the arrival of Europeans, Native American fishermen dug holes in the ice to spear huge Lake Erie sturgeon or catch a variety of smaller fish with shortened fishing sticks held over a hole in the ice. Ancient anglers would often build a small hut over the fishing hole to shelter them from harsh weather. Anglers back then would use handmade tools, bait, and fish decoys to lure curious fish into hooking or spearing range. Today's anglers build upon this history in a number of modern, as well as traditional, ways.

Today on Lake Erie and surrounding waterways, one can find a variety of mass-produced shanties, lures, and decoys. Motorized and electronic tools are also available, but bait, fish decoys, spears, and shortened ice-fishing rods—called jigging sticks—are still skillfully handcrafted; some are made for use and some for sheer artistic pleasure. Ice fishing itself has become an extreme winter sport, an enduring family tradition, and a source of storytelling that generates praise and prompts other storytellers, inspiring appreciative responses on the internet.

The Material Culture of Ice Fishing

Material culture refers to cultural expression in material form, usually—although not always—found in things that are made by hand from natural resources. The first inhabitants of Lake Erie probably used handmade cutting tools, like hatchets, to break through the ice and fish for food in winter. Today's anglers use ice saws or preferably an auger, a large spiral blade that can be driven by hand or motorized. Fishing essentials include what is called a jigging stick, jig (or bait), spears, and fish decoys. All can be purchased from commercial manufacturers, but these essentials are also made by hand.

Beautifully hand-carved jigging sticks, spears, decoys, and related carvings are submitted to contests held by local sports clubs to be judged for technical skill and visual appeal. Some contemporary carvings, along with

247

Figure 46.2. *Fishing Lure (6Q3A0356)* by Ilkka Jukarainen via Flickr. (CC BY-SA 2.0)

surviving antiques, are considered art collectibles; the Smithsonian American Art Museum maintains a collection of these items, some displayed on their website.

Fishing lures are decoys meant to attract and hook specific types of fish that swim at specific depths. These can be manufactured or skillfully handmade, tailored to appear, and sometimes even to move, according to the traits of specific fish.

Fish decoys became popular in the upper Midwest in the 1800s and are often used for spear fishing. During the Great Depression, ice fishing became an important way to put food on local tables, creating a market for decoys that persists to this day. Hand-carved fish decoys are primarily designed to attract predator fish, but they are also valued as artwork, and works by master carvers are prized. Collectors seek whimsical as well as realistic designs, imaginative colors, original patterns, and works by recognized artists.

Fishing with handheld spears, from land or sea, is another ancient practice. Modern anglers on the Great Lakes use spears forged from steel with multiple tines (or forks). These can be commercially manufactured or handmade from forges at home. Skilled handmade spears have a handle on top and are built for the balance and strength required to spear large predator fish. Some spears have hollow centers, allowing a line to pass through for dangling a fish decoy.

A jigging or jig stick is a shortened fishing rod held over a hole in the ice, equipped with a spool, or a top piece, for letting out enough line to reach the desired depth through a perforation at the far end of the stick (jigging should not be confused with gigging, which refers to hunting or fishing with a gig, a small spear). The shape, weight, balance, and aesthetic appeal of a handmade jigging stick will contribute to its value.

The goal of the Great Lakes Fish Decoy Collecting and Carving Association (GLFDCCA) is to collect, preserve, and hand down ice-fishing traditions. Seen in figure 46.4 are two GLFDCCA award-winning handcrafted

Figure 46.3. *Darkhouse Action* by Les C. Kouba from Art Barbarians Gallery. (Copyrighted content used with permission)

natural-finish jigging sticks. First prize went to Brandon Thomas, and second prize went to Tom Vickers.

Ice fishing on a cold winter lake can be a lonely experience, but one rule of survival is to stay off the ice unless you have a companion. Ice anglers tend to obey that rule and are generally a highly sociable group, joining fishing clubs, participating in local ice-fishing events, and often fishing with buddies or with specific family members who share a love of the sport. They refer to themselves as anglers, and while their etiquette includes pranking, it also includes helping fellow anglers, sharing tips, techniques, and, perhaps above all, the art of storytelling.

Multiple ice-fishing websites, like Ohio Game Fishing, exist for the specific purpose of sharing stories and commenting online. A conversation is sometimes started by a lead-in question, generating multiple answers, some of which attract a voluminous number of responses. In response to "What made you like ice fishing?" one angler spoke for a multitude: "My Dad. When you grow up ice fishing you love it before you even know it." Another response similarly refers to the importance of family bonding through ice fishing, along with enjoyment of a good story: "My grandfather done it all, toting me along under his arm—a great outdoorsman—a book full of stories."

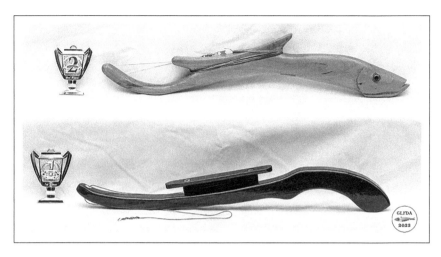

Figure 46.4. Great Lakes Fish Decoy Collecting and Carving Association 2022 award-winning handcrafted natural-finish jigging sticks. (Copyrighted content used under US Code, Title 17, Chapter 1, Section 107, Limitations on exclusive rights: Fair Use)

A Book Full of Stories: The Ice-Fishing Internet

Ice-fishing websites sometimes request personal-experience stories. These are always enthusiastically received, evaluated, and praised by readers. The story below (slightly abridged) is repeated here, followed by the first comment it received among countless others. The narrative belongs to a growing electronic treasure trove, a "book full of stories." This is an online angler's tale from the Comedy Corner of Ohio Game Fishing, as posted in 2004 by its author, Zach Pyles:

ATTACKED! Man-vs-Muskrat

It's Saturday morning, about 30 degrees, overcast skies and a beautiful light snow falling. My father and I are heading out onto the ice just as we do religiously every weekend during the heat of the action [in the] early ice season here in Ohio. . . . You can hear every sound nature has to offer . . . the only foreign noises to be heard is the snow packing beneath our boots and the distant growling of fellow anglers' augers chewing through the ice.

My father and I head straight to the spot where just the morning before we had filled a 5 gallon bucket half full with 8–9" gills, a baker's dozen 9–13" yellow perch and just a few crappies. We pop a few holes and immediately we're on fish! My father being the stubborn person he is, chooses not to sit in the shanty (as usual) so I quickly set up for myself. . . .

About a half hour goes by and I can hear one of those big air pockets that often gets trapped under the ice working its way towards my holes. No bother of course, the air pocket comes up through my ice holes and gurgles a bit. Everything to this point is perfectly normal, but for some reason unbeknown to me till this day, out of pure curiosity I lean way forward down towards the ice holes for a closer inspection. The next thing I know, within a split second, water is being splashed in my face and I'm staring Face-to-Face at the biggest, fattest, meanest muskrat I've ever encountered!!!! This thing didn't have teeth, ooohh no, he had FANGS!

Immediately I jump back, almost falling off my bucket, slamming into the back wall of my shanty, I probably screamed like a girl. In the process of all this ruckus, I managed to kick the access doors to the ice holes shut so I'm trapped in my shanty with this saber-toothed muskrat. Now I learned a few things about muskrats in the process.... They BARK.... They HISS.... They GROWL.... And worst of all, they can JUMP about 3 FEET HIGH.

By this time ... my father being only a few yards away, is hollering "What the hell is goin' on.... What are you doing!!!!?" ... Every time I would reach down to open the access lids or the doors to the shanty, that lil' monster would start barking and hissing at me. If I would use my foot to try to fudge it open he would lunge at me! I'm 'bout ready to gaff this thing by now.

By this time I'm feeling like a little kid being forced to watch a horror flick then being locked in a dark room with the boogie monster!

After a few minutes of WW II inside my shanty, my father finally comes over and opens the shanty door from the outside. My father said he's not sure who came busting out of that shanty faster, me or the muskrat! Once he had realized what it was that was causing the commotion, I'm not sure that I have ever seen him laugh so hard before or since!

Of course now every time we go ice fishing, he never ever lets a moment go by where he can razz or crack a joke about me and that muskrat. Looking back, I too now think that it may be the funniest thing that has ever happened to me and I normally do not pass up an opportunity to joke about the incident either, but rest assured, it sure as hell wasn't funny at the time!

The best thing about this whole situation is that I got to experience that then "nighmarely" now "hilarious" experience with my best friend, my father, and I know that it's a moment that will never be forgotten and we'll be able to share together for all time.

The first comment online said, "That's one of the best stories ever. i bet you never wore them undershorts again!"

Clearly, angling for ice-fishing stories can yield a fabulous catch.

Reference

Pyles, Zach. 2004. "ATTACKED! Man-vs-Muskrat." Reprinted (as: Zpyles_oo # 13 December 15, 2010). https://www.ohiogamefishing.com/threads/whats-your-funniest-ice-fishing-story.161341/#post-1125489.

Figure 47.1. *Walleye Drop* from *Toledo Blade*, December 28, 2011. (Copyrighted content used under US Code, Title 17, Chapter 1, Section 107, Limitations on exclusive rights: Fair Use)

NEW YEAR'S EVE FISH DROP ON LAKE ERIE

It's bird. It's a plane. Oh, wait . . . it's a twenty-foot, six-hundred-pound fiberglass walleye, eclipsing New York's crystal ball for New Year revelers on Lake Erie. The Port Clinton Walleye Drop is the biggest New Year's Eve extravaganza in northwest Ohio. Over ten thousand people turn up every year to watch the fish drop as the New Year arrives; almost as many will log onto the Walleye Drop website to watch the live stream.

It all began in 1996, when former Port Clinton mayor Tom "Big Fish" Brown wondered why, if New York can drop a ball, Ohio can't drop a fish? Good question! Lake Erie produces more fish for consumption each year than the other four Great Lakes combined; in fact, the western end of the lake is known as the Walleye Capital of the World, producing more walleye per hectare than any other lake on the planet.

The original papier-mâché walleye of 1996 had one or two incarnations before it was replaced by the larger fiberglass successor of today, known as Wylie the Walleye. The big fish is the creation of local taxidermist Jim Wendt. Every year, while a work crew is polishing up New York's crystal ball, Jim is sprucing Wylie up for his annual appearance, assuring his readiness to usher in the New Year with equal fun and fanfare.

Figure 47.2. Taxidermist and artist Jim Wendt, working on Wylie. (Copyrighted content used with permission)

Figure 48.1. *Jesus Pierogi* from *Toledo Blade*, August 17, 2005. (Copyrighted content used under US Code, Title 17, Chapter 1, Section 107, Limitations on exclusive rights: Fair Use)

LAKE ERIE AND FAST-FOOD FOLK RELIGION

olklorist Don Yoder (1974: 14) defines *folk religion* as the difference
between what is preached from the pulpit and what is believed in the
pew—not always the same thing. For example, the pulpit, with its
Eucharist hosts and wine libations, festivals, and feast days is no stranger to
both physical and spiritual nurture. But the American pew has historically
relocated spiritual, as well as physical, nurture from the pulpit to the hearth,
which is to say, from the pulpit to the nurturing heart of the home: the
kitchen, or at least the TV snack table (Neulander 2016: 139–41).

Over the years, sacred personalities have appeared across the United
States in many mainstream American food items: in Florida, a Virgin Mary
grilled cheese sandwich; in Texas, a Jesus Cheetos snack; and in Tennessee,
a Mother Teresa pastry, playfully named the "nun bun" (Choron and Choron
2009). In fact, members of the heavenly host have appeared in a full array of
mainstream American fast foods, "value meals," and packaged snacks from
sea to shining sea. But in a nation largely comprised of hyphenated American identities, the sacred also manifests in specifically ethnic American
foodways.

One such example is the southwestern Spanish American tortilla that
broke ground for the phenomenon in 1978, manifesting an image recognized
as Jesus. A local priest was persuaded to bless the flatbread, although he was
careful to inform reporters that he personally was not impressed by what he
saw (Rogo 1982: 140). The Great Lakes area has now joined other parts of
the country where ethnic American culinary apparitions have appeared. The
city of Toledo, on the American shore of Lake Erie, is the site of one such
miraculous manifestation.

Toledo's ancestry is primarily from Germany, followed by Ireland, with
central Europe rounding out the top three. Each line of culinary tradition has
contributed to the regional palate: delectable German strudel dishes, Irish
stews and cabbage dishes, and Polish pierogi, small dumplings filled with

meat, cheese, or vegetables first boiled and then fried to a succulent golden brown. Today, Toledo is a dynamic city known for its industry, its art community, its education, its local sports teams, and more recently, its culinary contribution to American folk religion.

On Easter morning 2005, Toledo lay claim to the Polish American "Jesus pierogi," when a local housewife flipped her sizzling dumplings and came face-to-face with a sacred image in the fragrant mist of her frying pan. Called to the stove, her husband took one look and exclaimed, "What? There's Jesus!" (Choron and Choron 2009). The pulpit may resist authenticating such revelations, but the pew needs no convincing.

Toledo's Jesus pierogi is representative of all sacred imagery that appears in what is aptly described as American comfort food. But culinary apparitions of Mary, Jesus, and the occasional saint differ greatly from historical Virgin Mary, or Marian, apparitions in the type of comfort they provide. Unlike church-approved Marian apparitions, which often appear outdoors or in other places accessible to the public, family food apparitions tend to appear in domestic, indoor settings and are separate from the prophetic, apocalyptic, and politically vocal apparitions that typically promote church objectives. Instead, sacred stove-top images are purely revelatory. They confirm only the comforting notion that sacred beings maintain an ongoing interest and involvement in the everyday lives of ordinary people. They manifest autonomous from the church, require no mediation by religious authority, and are accessible to any believer in possession of a grill or griddle, a skillet, or even a bag of snacks.

Alternatively, American consumers unwilling to wait for a miracle can create a sacred image of their own, on any—in fact on every—piece of

Figure 48.2. *Jesus Toaster* from Burnt Impressions, Instagram, January 7, 2020. (Copyrighted content used under US Code, Title 17, Chapter 1, Section 107, Limitations on exclusive rights: Fair Use)

Figure 48.3. *Jesus Toast* from Burnt Impressions, press release, December 23, 2013. (Copyrighted content used under US Code, Title 17, Chapter 1, Section 107, Limitations on exclusive rights: Fair Use)

homemade toast, by simply purchasing a Jesus Toaster, sold online and shipped by a company called Burnt Impressions. But the commercial toaster is understood to produce an image created by human design. The manufactured image is meant only to celebrate and reinforce the faith and is not taken as a divine emanation from the sacred realm. Conversely, devotion in response to culinary images that emerge by chance should not be underestimated. The phenomenon is understood as what religionist Mircea Eliade (1957: 11) first called a "hierophany": an act of manifestation by the sacred, in ordinary worldly objects. In American folk religion, any sacred image that does not occur by human design occurs instead—by default—as a miraculous manifestation of the sacred.

Substantial benefit may result from the sale of such miraculous foodstuffs, but motivation to sell is not entirely commercial. The American "grilled cheese Mary" spent nine years in a freezer before the sandwich was put up for auction on eBay. It was purchased for $28,000, but only with the promise that it would never be eaten or destroyed. The buyer was the Golden Palace, an online casino that later acquired the Toledo Jesus pierogi for $1,775. In this way, both images managed to enter the bright light of public recognition from the frigid anonymity of dark refrigerator freezers.

The Golden Palace has subsequently added to its collection a Minnesota Madonna pretzel in the shape of the Virgin Mary cradling the baby Jesus. The casino has apparently discovered a form of visual culture that is highly competitive and much less costly than the master artworks favored by brick-and-mortar casinos.

In 1978, a homemade shrine was built to the Spanish American miracle tortilla, and by 1979, over thirty-five thousand visitors had made a pilgrimage to the shed where it rested on a tuft of cotton, as if suspended on a cloud. But lacking a climate-controlled environment, the tortilla eventually became brittle, and the image began to fade. When a grandchild took it to school for show-and-tell, it was accidently dropped and shattered. The shrine closed immediately, but the shattered pieces were safely tucked away in a drawer rather than discarded.

Clearly, the sale of spontaneously generated images of Marian and other sacred personalities leads to their physical protection, preservation, and, in many cases, public display. It consequently brings them to an extended audience willing to make a pilgrimage, or at least to seek out members of the sacred realm in their various culinary contexts. Among the lineup of heavenly hosts that have emerged spontaneously in the United States is a Polish American Jesus pierogi that manifested one Easter Sunday morning on Lake Erie's southern shore.

References

Choron, Harry, and Sandra Choron. 2009. *Look! It's Jesus! Amazing Holy Visions in Everyday Life*. San Francisco: Chronicle Books.

Eliade, Mircea. 1957. *The Sacred and the Profane: The Nature of Religion*. New York: Harcourt, Brace, Jovanovich.

Neulander, Judith S. 2016. "Folk Religion." In *Miracles: An Encyclopedia of People, Places, and Supernatural Events from Antiquity to the Present*, edited by Patrick J. Hayes, 139–141. Santa Barbara, CA: ABC-CLIO.

Rogo, D. Scott. 1982. *Miracles: A Parascientific Inquiry into Wonderous Phenomena*. New York: Dial.

Yoder, Don. 1974. "Toward a Definition of Folk Religion." *Western Folklore* 33:2–15.

Figure 49.1. *Spaceship Leaving an Underwater UFO Base*. Created for this chapter by Jared Bendis. (CC BY-SA 3.0) Source images for collage: *A Flying Saucer That Landed near the Airport in My Town* by Phroziac via Wikimedia Commons (CC BY-SA 3.0); *Cumulus Congestus Clouds over the Atlantic Ocean* by Tiago Fioreze via Wikimedia Commons (CC BY-SA 3.0); *P7277445x (geyser)* by feo90 (CC BY 2.0)

UFO BASE UNDER LAKE ERIE

The acronym UFO stands for "unidentified flying object," usually referring to an unexplained light in the sky. From the beginning of human fascination with the heavens, unexplained lights have never failed to rivet the imagination, their appearance often affirmed by valid and reliable scientific documentation. But at the popular level, imagining where they come from, who is behind them, and why they are here has always been less about scientific inquiry and more about the hopes, fears, aspirations, and animosities of the people doing the imagining.

Historically, there is no scientific basis on which to secure or verify popular imaginings about lights in the sky. But different imaginings in each generation continue to give folklorists access to the spirit and mentality of different imaginers in every age. In Western civilization, for example, world and social order are imagined on a vertical, hierarchical scale that locates good, divine, and heaven "above" and places bad, demonic, and hell "below" (Neulander 1992). So it should not surprise us that in Western civilization one of the most frequent assumptions made about unidentified lights "up" in the sky is their supposedly heavenly, supernatural, and often religious nature.

Fairy Lore and Lights in the Sky

During pre-Christian times, in keeping with pagan beliefs, Europeans of the British Isles imagined these phenomena to be fairy lights. As Christianity gained a foothold across Europe, pagan fairies were repurposed to serve Christianity; they became monitors of unchristian behavior. This allowed fairies to remain timely and relevant as the new faith gained credibility and was probably instrumental in helping the new religion gain followers, especially among those unwilling to fully relinquish their fairy beliefs.

In their new role, fairies were muscular disciplinarians. If a child was not promptly baptized, for instance, it could be stolen by fairies and replaced by a changeling, a malevolent fairy child substituted for one's own human off-spring. Adults believed that fairies could spirit them away should they forget to cross themselves on New Year's morning or before entering an unchurched area, like the forest. Not surprisingly, fairies who made it to America constituted an army of supernatural morality police: the varied goblins, ghouls, and bogeymen of fairyland, who by the 1800s were assigned to the nursery and were out to get naughty children, as in this example from the famous poem "Little Orphan Annie" (using modern spelling), by American author James Whitcomb Riley (1885):

> Once there was a little boy who wouldn't say his prayers,
> And when he went to bed at night, away up stairs,
> His Mammy heard him holler and his Daddy heard him bawl,
> And when they turned the covers down he wasn't there at all!
> And they sought him in the rafter-room and cubby-hole and 'press,
> And they sought him up the chimney flue, and everywhere I guess,
> But all they ever found was just his pants and roundabout,
> And the Goblins 'll get you
>   If you
>   Don't
>   Watch
>   Out!

Once Christianity had become a well-established religion in Europe, lights in the sky were newly associated with sacred Christian personalities—above all, with the Virgin Mary. But it may have been due to nineteenth-century Romanticism that fairy folk—already banished to the nursery—would evolve from goblins, ghouls, and bogeymen into the romantic, miniature royalty of Victorian children's storybooks. Eventually, as the century brought with it life-threatening industrial work conditions, waves of contagious plagues, and the devastation of the US Civil War, romantic fairy lore was eclipsed by a widespread preoccupation with ceaseless death and the furtive hope of a heavenly afterlife (Davies 2007). Globalism, nuclear energy, and burgeoning technology would add to the widespread anxieties of the twentieth century.

War, Globalism, and Ghost Ships in the Sky

The First and Second World Wars brought not only disease, slaughter, and apocalyptic fears but also increased exposure to cultural Others and the fluorescence of modern aviation. Given timely concerns with life after death, it is not surprising that unexplained lights in the sky were linked to "ghost ships"—the specters of war planes lost in battle and never accounted for. Such imaginings helped bereaved families feel closer to those lost by reassuring them of ongoing life for the spirits of their loved ones. With the emergence of commercial travel, weather balloons, missile capability, and manned space flight, sightings of UFOs by both military and civilian pilots increased. In 1947, a pilot reported several objects described as saucer-shaped lights that moved across the sky the way a stone might move if skipped over water. This may well have suggested the possibility of interplanetary visitors, while the iridescent saucer shape of low-flying weather balloons may well have reinforced flying-saucer imagery, used thereafter by the press and media.

According to religionist Robert Ellwood (1995: 394), contemporary belief in the destructive (or even the redemptive) presence of alien-driven UFOs still has religious and often apocalyptic underpinnings. But apocalyptic thinking almost always targets mortal enemies—whether earthlings or space aliens—who must be defeated to save the world from impending doom. Fear and loathing are directed at these purportedly evil sources, who are all too frequently associated with minorities of different religious beliefs or different nationalities, as well as cultural Others who, by virtue of their "otherness," are easily seen as "alien" to the population that shares mainstream "sameness." When anxiety mixes with animosity, UFO beliefs can become prejudicial and radicalizing and can blossom into toxic conspiracy theories.

Conspiracy Theories and UFOlogy

The first American encounters with space aliens were reported in the 1940s by followers of William Dudley Pelley, leader of the Silver Shirts, an American Nazi party promoting racial hatred and inspiring violence against people of color, and specifically against Jews. American Nazis who reported contact with spacemen attributed advanced intelligence to these alien visitors, whose purportedly superior knowledge—oddly enough—always confirmed their Nazi ideology.

Not long after, others not associated with Pelley also became "contactees," some of whom claimed to be repeatedly kidnapped by aliens (Roth 2005). This account would develop into a stable alien-abduction narrative prolific on the internet and on social media. Some abductees became highly spiritualized through these encounters, self-identifying as carriers of messages from above. Like Nazi contactees before them, they repeated and legitimated their personal ideologies, according to the purportedly superior wisdom of many supernatural, and even sacred, beings from outer space.

Political agitator and rabid antisemite Louis Farrakhan was one of the first to discover religious wisdom givers in outer space, describing himself as beamed up to a "mothership" manned by "space angels." These were apparently hovering above the planet in veneration of Farrakhan's own hero, the homicidal fascist, and often bizarrely costumed, dictator Muammar Gaddafi. The space angels informed Farrakhan, who acted as a conduit of supernal information to his earthbound followers, that the Libyan leader had been promoted to sainthood in the sacred realm. Farrakhan easily assumed the role of saint-cum-savior by exploiting the fears and frustrations of his faithful followers, who were all looking toward his supernal self for miraculous relief from a terrifying AIDS epidemic. Deflecting attention from his uselessness as a miracle worker, he targeted a specific faction of the medical community to be the enemy, offering his followers the illusion of prediction and control through the avoidance of the purported villain, informing them that they were dying because Jewish doctors were injecting AIDS into Black babies (Dinnerstein 1994: 221).

Belief that lights in the sky are spaceships manned by space aliens—either sacred or profane—prevails today in a modern folk religion called UFOlogy (see "Lake Erie and Fast-Food Folk Religion," this volume). There are numerous branches of UFOlogy, but the branch that promotes conspiracy theories is largely about exploiting public anxieties and animosities, according to the Farrakhan model. During the twentieth century, public anxiety was typically generated by communism, racism, medical advances (e.g., "test-tube" babies, cloning, and the implantation of tracking devices), pollution, nuclear radiation, and plagues (principally AIDS). Twentieth-century grievances included the loss of white privilege through civil rights movements, the loss of patriarchal privilege through changing gender roles, and a growing gap between those able to keep up with technology and those who feared—or in fact were—being left behind by rapid technological advances (see "The Ohio Grassman," this volume).

Redemption at the End of Time: A Modern Variant of Fairy Lore

According to anthropologist Christopher Roth (2005: 50), folks who see interplanetary enemies, or redeemers, in places where no one can actually see anything—as in the vast, dark heights of outer space or in the vast, dark depths of Lake Erie—are folks with real or imagined reasons to feel threatened by unseen forces in the bright light of day. In fact, the real, underlying reason behind such anxiety may be what is really too hard for the sufferer to see or to pin down with words. Anxiety, cut off from its real source, is called free floating, and through the lens of free-floating anxiety, cultural Others can too easily become targets of aggression, their demise mistaken for a final solution that will end the anxiety.

Among apocalyptic thinkers, the approach of the year 2000 raised anxious fears of an Armageddon that fused contemporary anxieties with expectations of a millennial end-time. One such believer, Betty Luca Andreasson (née Aho), published a representative alien-abduction narrative that includes all motifs attending the core tale in the literary genre (Peebles 1994). Her vision drew from traditional folklore, the popular culture of the time, and apocalyptic sources that pit good against evil, evoking a suspicious white supremacy for those ostensibly chosen by alien scientists to parent a new master race—the new "chosen people." As her narrative evolved, it first assigned hostility to alien genital- and anal-probing kidnappers, who, it turns out, share an astonishing number of motifs with fairies of the British Isles.

Those purportedly abducted by aliens took on the aura of Christian martyrs on two counts. First, by claiming alien-induced sexual trauma, which they suffered for a greater good: the birth of a human-alien master race able to survive the coming millennial Apocalypse. Second, the sexual martyrs suffered the additional trauma of being disbelieved by just about everybody. Betty's narrative embroidered on the concept of wise "Ascended Masters," borrowed from an earlier, nascent branch of UFOlogy called Theosophy, as similarly borrowed by the alien-revering Silver Shirts and by Farrakhan. But, unlike the Indian gurus of Theosophy or the guru-like Space Nazis of Pelley and Farrakhan, Betty spoke of tall, blond, blue-eyed angels called Nordics, here to warn abductees of impending species doom from nuclear pollution and a whole compendium of twentieth-century anxieties. After the Apocalypse, the chosen human parents were to prevail, watching over their superior human-alien hybrid progeny. Notably, Betty also employed terms like *beaming up* and other familiar science fiction dialogue and imagery, lifted verbatim from the most popular TV shows and movies of her own time, in particular *Star Trek, E.T. the Extraterrestrial*, and *Close Encounters of the Third Kind*.

Betty was a Massachusetts housewife whose father was a (Nordic) Finn and whose mother was a "native" New Englander (code for white, Anglo-American). She recalled compelling memories of surveillance by space aliens from her early childhood. As we are about to see, the "watchers" theme in Betty's narrative draws upon an ancient apocryphal text that flourishes in modern popular culture, principally among race-preoccupied conspiracy theorists. Like Betty (who speaks vernacular US English, e.g., "they're *like* all talking"), aliens in her narrative also speak vernacular US English, enriched by the vernacular of her mother's British Isles (e.g., "*wee* little child"). For example, Betty recalls hearing the aliens discussing her during her childhood, describing and quoting them: "They're like all talking together ... [saying] 'Wee little child'" (Fowler 1990: 328).

As her narrative progresses into her adult life, it creates a cosmic duality between good and evil space angels: "They [the good Nordic space angels] are pleased that I have accepted [their wisdom] on my own. . . . I shall suffer many things . . . but will overcome through the Son. . . . *I have been watched since my beginning* . . . my faith in the light will bring many others to the Light and Salvation . . . . the negative voices don't like it . . . bad angels that want to devour man . . . because they are jealous" (quoted in Fowler 1990: 334; my italics).

This apocalyptic good-versus-evil motif is borrowed from the ancient Ethiopic/Aramaic *Book of Watchers*, building on a passage in Hebrew scripture (Gen. 6:4) historically dear to folk imagination (see "Remains of Nephilim and Modern Conspiracy Theories on Lake Erie," this volume). In Genesis 6:4, fallen angels cohabit with mortal women, spawning a hybrid "race" of giant sons. In both Jewish and Christian apocryphal writing, sons of the fallen angels lose their virtue and are subsequently destroyed by the Flood. Yet the revival of fallen angels in Betty's narrative is far from arbitrary, for in the folklore of the British Isles, fallen angels not only survive the Flood but do so as fairies (Thompson 1956–58: Motif V236).

Even with her many personal embellishments, Betty's narrative holds to the core structure of the alien-abduction narrative. This includes gray and "cerebral" (to indicate passionless and unfeeling) aliens the size of small children (like fairies) who have large "eggheads" (a vernacular reference to intellectuals) and whose sexless bodies are no longer capable of reproduction. Abductees all claim to have been beamed up to spaceships by these "Grays" and painfully raped to produce a master human-alien race. Once beamed home, abductees have no memory of the events and typically experience lapses in time they cannot account for, corresponding to the periods in which aliens supposedly tampered with them. These memories are recovered in the process of highly suspect hypnotic sessions, where abductees are placed in heightened states of suggestibility and are given prompts supporting the abduction narrative. Betty also subscribed to UFO beliefs regarding farm animals that die naturally in the field (typically leaving clean lines of demarcation where insects rapidly consume eyes and other soft tissues). In UFOlogy, the animals are believed to have died because they were beamed up and dropped to their deaths from spaceships, having undergone the excision of soft tissues with the "surgical precision" of alien scientists. In the end, all this alien reproductive activity results in the delivery—from "chosen" humans—of a superior hybrid (human-alien) race, able to survive the immanent end-time, believed by many to be the year 2000.

Clearly, Betty's narrative addresses many frightening concerns at the approach of the twenty-first century and combines influences from religion, folklore, and popular culture. But above all, her alien-abduction narrative brings us full circle, back to at least ten literary motifs from the traditional fairy lore of the British Isles, as documented in Stith Thompson's *Motif-Index of Folk Literature* (1956–58):

F239.42	Fairies are the size of small children
F68	Ascent to upper world by magic
F305	Offspring of fairy and mortal
F320	Fairies carry people away to fairyland
F346	Fairy helps mortal with labor (in childbirth)
F357	Mortals as captives in fairyland
F360	Malevolent or destructive fairies
F366	Fairies abuse livestock
F377	Supernatural lapse of time in fairyland
V236	Fallen angels become fairies

Despite the apocalyptic fears of martyred abductees, the millennium year came and went with no effect. It was the alien-abduction narrative that suffered near extinction. But vestiges of UFOlogy do persist today, as indicated below, still projecting conspiracy theories onto unexplained lights in the sky, which brings us to Lake Erie's shore in the twenty-first century.

"Wizard Lights" and the UFO Base under Lake Erie

There have been countless reports of unexplained lights over Lake Erie, beginning with the ancient Native American panther/comet who pierced the lake from above (see "Long Tail," this volume). But Euro-American settlers typically imagined mysterious lights over Lake Erie to have magical rather than sacred origins, referring to them as "wizard lights." Lake Erie's wizard lights seem to have morphed into alien UFOs with the dawn of piloted spaceflight. They acquired a religious connection with fears of Armageddon at the approach of the millennium. It was only after the uneventful turn of the twenty-first century that alien abduction seemed to steadily lose its former hold on local imagination.

But then on March 8, 2007, in an interview with the *Cleveland Plain Dealer*, a variant of the regional sky-into-lake pattern reappeared in association with unexplained lights, echoing the ancient sky-streaking panther who took up residence beneath the lake's surface. It happened when journalist John Lasker interviewed a local UFOlogist (2010:19), writing: "'It's a hot spot' declares local UFOlogist Aron Clark about the beaches of Lake Erie near Cleveland. 'Some believe there's a UFO base on the bottom of the Lake.'"

Given the number of underwater UFO bases now cited on the internet, there is hardly a puddle on the planet that has not claimed its own submersed variant. The Lake Erie claim is—in that sense—unremarkable. What is noteworthy is the traditional formulaic speech pattern of the Lake Erie report. Note that the journalist, John Lasker, identifies the source of his information as the UFOlogist Aron Clark, making it possible for others to secure and verify Lasker's quotes. But the UFOlogist speaks of "some" who believe in a UFO base under the lake, failing to identify the sources of his information and thereby preventing anyone from securing or verifying a single thing attributed to them.

Terms like *some* (as in "some believe"), along with *they* (as in "they say"), *a lot of people*, or even *everybody* (as in "a lot of people know" or "say," etc.), allow nonwitnesses to validate claims in two ways. Speakers gain deniability if they need it later ("I didn't say *I* believe it. I said *some*," etc.). But at the same time, claiming to have received firsthand knowledge allows speakers to claim the same authority as those with firsthand knowledge. Also, by pluralizing an anonymous source of information to *many, some, they, a lot of people*, or *everybody*, nonwitnesses lend credibility to what is reportedly confirmed, not by just one but by a veritable multitude of eyewitnesses.

When a nonwitness speaks directly for unidentified firsthand witnesses to validate a claim of some sort, the speech act is called a "nonwitness validator." At the popular level, speaking from direct contact with eyewitnesses validates what the nonwitness claims, as if the nonwitness is a human bullhorn through which the eyewitness speaks to us. Traditionally, the nonwitness validation formula is always given as a true story, and therefore as "history." But nonwitness validations are not history. Rather, they are the building blocks of three forms of traditional communication: rumor, gossip, and hearsay. It is important to keep this in mind, no matter who the nonwitness may be, to keep us from being manipulated and misled, no matter how charismatic or authoritative the speaker may be.

According to scholars Ralph L. Rosnow and Gary Alan Fine, writing in 1976, people tend to consume rumors, gossip, and hearsay when the topic confirms the peoples' own most cherished biases (e.g., racism). Thus, consumers of rumor, gossip, and hearsay develop their own "brand" loyalties; that is, they become faithful to specific personalities and media outlets that reinforce their biases, especially if the bias is being threatened or a privilege once upheld by the bias is being lost. Rosnow and Fine also point to a codependent relationship between consumers and producers of such speech acts, who need one another to remain empowered. But scholars caution, "Let the buyer beware, because the power dynamics are tilted in favor of the producer and not the consumer. . . . For the producer the reward is money, recognition, and the power to 'manage the news'" (1976: 88, 89). Historically, consumers of rumor, gossip, and hearsay are the losers since producers are always serving their own best interests, largely at the expense of the very same people whose biases they confirm, to keep themselves in power.

Here, it is important to emphasize that the truth-value of a traditional narrative makes no difference to a folklorist. What matters to a folklorist are the greater truths embedded in traditional speech acts and narratives, as expressed by those who generate, modify, and maintain them. One must be able to tell a fictional account from a factual one to conduct a productive study but not to debunk it; only to correctly identify narratives and interpret them correctly (Neulander 2016: 220). That is, if we take traditional "lights in the sky" narratives as factual, or as "history," then at least one of the following statements will be true: fairies account for lights in the sky, lights in the sky are manifestations of the Virgin Mary, Jews are in cahoots with space aliens to take over the world, good and evil space angels are squaring off for an Apocalypse that only a human-alien master race can survive.

If rumor, hearsay, and gossip are recognized as formulaic discourse (e.g., *they, some, everybody* says, does, knows) we find that all UFO narratives tell a perfectly accurate story, not about conspiracy theories involving aliens and UFOs but about the spirit and mentality of the people who hold these narratives in tradition. As folklorist Jan Brunvand notes, contemporary narratives, like those of alien abduction, are contemporary instances of traditional legends, and "like traditional folklore, the stories do tell one kind of truth. They are a unique, unselfconscious reflection of major concerns of individuals in the societies in which the legends circulate" (1981: xii). Folklorists are interested in the greater truth embedded in traditional narratives—not the truth-value of what the narratives claim.

Branches of all religions that lack demonizing, racialized conspiracy theories tend to do what all good religions are supposed to do. To the extent that this influence generalizes to positive belief in space aliens and space angels, it may help some UFOlogists make purposeful sense of the world and gain hope of better worlds to look forward to, before and after death. But religionist Robert Ellwood notes a number of scholars who express discomfort with those branches of UFOlogy that generate bigoted conspiracy theories and discomfort with their racist masquerade as "science." Elwood specifically cites their "promotion of credulity and of authoritarian, even proto-fascist, truth in charismatic contactee figures" (1995: 398). To paraphrase Ellwood and bring us into the twenty-first century, both production and consumption of anxiety-ridden, often racialized rumor, gossip, and hearsay—whether about human cultural Others or their alien proxies—can be seen as "an expression of essentially pathological psychological states that might be better served if treated within the framework of a rational worldview" (1995: 398).

Fortunately, we can distinguish between narrative genres like legends and rumor, gossip, and hearsay. In folklore studies, a legend is defined as a story that has no basis in history but is about a real person, place, thing, or event and is always told as a true story, often with supernatural content (Brunvand 1981: 1, 3, 194). Rumor, gossip, and hearsay seem compatible with this definition since they are also fictions given as truths. And like legends, if items of rumor, gossip, and hearsay die, they can be reborn. But rumor, gossip, and hearsay have relatively short life spans. Unlike legends, they appear, have a period of prominence, and then disappear. They are typically victims of disproof, growing irrelevance, and, finally, dissipation (Rosnow and Fine 1976: 44). Should an item of rumor, gossip, or hearsay demonstrate the power to enter tradition, it can become a traditional genre of fiction—a legend—as described by Brunvand. At this writing, the rumor, gossip, and hearsay of UFOlogy continue to embrace pseudoscience, pop culture, religious themes, and fairy lore, but they have not yet met the test of time. Since such claims are heard less and less frequently in the early twenty-first century, they appear to be receding from popular consciousness, dimming toward invisibility, as into the heights of outer space, or perhaps into the depths of Lake Erie.

References

Brunvand, Jan H. 1981. *The Vanishing Hitchhiker: American Urban Legends and Their Meanings.* New York: W. W. Norton.

Davies, Owen. 2007. *The Haunted: A Social History of Ghosts.* New York: Palgrave Macmillan.

Dinnerstein, Leonard. 1994. *Anti-Semitism in America.* New York: Oxford University Press.

Ellwood, Robert. 1995. "UFO Religious Movements." In *America's Alternative Religions,* edited by Timothy Miller, 393–99. Albany, NY: SUNY Press.

Fowler, Raymond. 1990. *The Watchers: The Secret Design behind UFO Abduction.* New York: Bantam Books.

Lasker, John. 2010. *Technoir.* Limerick: EbookSale.

Neulander, Judith S. 1992. "Creating the Universe: A Study of Cosmos and Cognition." *Folklore Forum* 25 (1): 3–18.

———. 2016. "Conjuring Crypto-Jews in New Mexico: Violating Ethnic, Scholarly and Ethical Boundaries." In *Boundaries, Identity and Belonging in Modern Judaism,* edited by Maria Diemling and Larry Ray, 208–25. London: Routledge.

Peebles, Curtis. 1994. *Watch the Skies! A Chronicle of the Flying Saucer Myth.* Washington, DC: Smithsonian Institution Press.

Riley, James Whitcomb. 1885. *Little Orphant Annie.* Indianapolis: Bowen-Merrill.

Rosnow, Ralph L., and Gary Alan Fine, eds. 1976. *Rumor and Gossip: The Social Psychology of Hearsay*. New York: Elsevier.

Roth, Christopher. 2005. "UFOlogy as Anthropology: Race, Extra Terrestrials and the Occult." In *E.T. Culture: Anthropology in Outer Spaces*, edited by Debbora Battaglia, 38–93. Durham, NC: Duke University Press.

Thompson, Stith, ed. 1956–58. *The Motif-Index of Folk Literature*. 6 vols. Bloomington: Indiana University Press.

Figure 50.1. *Davis-Besse Nuclear Power Station, 6/24/20* by The Sentencer via Nuclear Power Reddit. (Copyrighted content used under US Code, Title 17, Chapter 1, Section 107, Limitations on exclusive rights: Fair Use)

NUCLEAR PLANT SPAWNS MUTANT MONSTERS

Bessie, Blinky, and the Lake Erie Chomper

S pringfield is the fictional town in which the animated TV show *The Simpsons* takes place. "Two Cars in Every Garage and Three Eyes on Every Fish," which aired on November 1, 1990, was the fourth episode in the sitcom's second season. According to the storyline, Bart catches a mutant three-eyed fish in a river downstream from the fictitious Springfield Nuclear Power Station. The episode reflects the widespread American concern with the mutational effects of pollution, which has existed since at least the time of the Industrial Revolution (see "The Lake Erie Cow Monster," this volume).

The Simpsons episode lampooned American politics and questionable nuclear power plant controls, winning the 1991 Environmental Media Award for Best TV Program with an Environmental Message. It had the highest rating of any program shown that week on the Fox network, and it introduced a radioactive fish named Blinky. The mutant fish both reflected and reinforced public distrust in politicians and in the safety of nuclear power stations—a distrust persisting into the twenty-first century.

Local tradition appears to have generated multiple variants of the irradiated Blinky, all of whom—to this day—continue to compete for chief monster status against Lake Erie's traditional old sea serpent, Bessie (see "South Bay Bessie," this volume). Local concerns are primarily focused on the Davis-Besse Nuclear Power Station, located on Lake Erie's shore. This appears to be the case because Besse in the name Davis-Besse is pronounced the same as the name of the notorious sea serpent, South Bay Bessie.

Another irradiated variant, the Lake Erie Chomper, is a mystery fish on Erie's northern shore that took a hefty bite out of three Canadian swimmers in the twenty-first century, eleven years after Bart Simpson pulled Blinky from the fictitious Springfield River. A full account, tagged "Quote: Lake Erie Chomper," was posted online by *Dragonlady Mothman*, drawing fifty-two responses. One voice was primarily concerned with the spawning of irradiated mutant monster fish. Another response connected the Chomper directly to the Davis-Besse Nuclear Power Station on the basis of the similar sounds of Besse and Bessie. The "Lake Erie Chomper" account, and the two responses, appeared as follows on the Unexplained Mysteries website:

Quote: Lake Erie Chomper

Since August of 2001 terror has gripped Lake Erie's coastline communities, as an unknown aquatic predator has been savagely attacking swimmers . . . especially those near Port Dover, Ontario.

Port Dover

Dr. Harold Hynscht has a medical mystery on his hands. He treated three patients recently who suffered major bites on their legs after swimming in Lake Erie beside the Port Dover pump house. All were in about a meter of water when the attacks occurred. Hynscht, a diver with an extensive knowledge of aquatic life, is at a loss to identify the animal that caused them. The bites were not minor. Six inches separated the wounds inflicted by the top and bottom teeth, suggesting the animal has a large mouth.

"That's a big, honking fish," Hynscht said. . . .

Whatever this creature turns out to be, the aggressive nature of the animal in question puts it into direct conflict with the human race . . . and that can only mean trouble ahead.

Of the fifty-two who responded to the online Chomper alarm, almost all speculated on a probable encounter with Bessie, Lake Erie's moldy old sea serpent, or, alternatively, with a large local fish known as a bowfin. There was one exception. *Alien Embryo* posted a query about nuclear mutation, noting, "But there is a nuclear power plant on Lake Erie . . . so maybe that has something to do with it?"

On the Ohio Traveler (n.d.) website, tagged "Under Lake Erie Monster," an unidentified commentor elaborated on this theme, linking the Davis-Besse Nuclear Power Station to the Industrial Revolution, when industrial waste was seen as a menacing source of mutation-causing water pollution. The shared pronunciation of Bessie and Besse clearly strengthened this connection: "My theory is that the toxic pollutants pumped into Lake Erie throughout the Industrial Revolution caused a certain species of eel to mutate into a giant-sized version of its former self. After all, isn't it strange that *Bessie*, the Lake Erie Monster sounds suspiciously similar to Davis-Besse, the nuclear power plant on the Lake Erie Coast of Northern Ohio?"

That's the bad news about potentially irradiated sea monsters populating Lake Erie. But Tom Medlicott, referring to the same issue on the same website, can be lauded for finding something good to post about radioactive fish fries: "The beauty is, you can bar-b-que at night and see what you're doing."

Maybe so, although at this point it's just imaginative speculation. But on an ordinary day in late April or early May 2013, there was an actual event of real concern. Two goldfish were smuggled into the Perry Nuclear Power plant on Erie's shore, forty miles northeast of Cleveland. Both fish died shortly after discovery, but immediately afterward, a headline taken from *The Simpson*'s three-eyed fish episode ran with the phrase "Radioactive Goldfish," which was repeated in columns both in print and online, as in the example below. In this account, the fictional Springfield's radioactive Blinky swims again but through two real-life avatars on Lake Erie's shore: "Two radioactive goldfish were found swimming in a pitcher of nuclear reactor water in an underground steam tunnel at an Ohio power plant."

According to all reports, the unfortunate fish actually died from starvation and neglect, entirely unharmed by the minimal level of radiation they were exposed to. More important was the very real issue of a security breach by the pranksters who got away with it. Security issues have risen more than once at the Perry plant, with no clear action taken, which may have inspired the wake-up call given by whoever planted the unfortunate fish. Repeating the connection to Blinky, one astute observer responded as *Anonymous User* on May 18, 2013, at 12:33 a.m.: "Someone at that plant is a huge fan of the Simpsons."

Not only does life imitate art on our environmentally stressed planet, but on Lake Erie, public concern with radioactive pollution is now imitating *animated* art on TV.

References

Ohio Traveler. n.d. "Under Lake Erie Monster." Accessed October 11, 2023. https://www .ohiotraveler.com/under-lake-erie-monste/

RT. 2013. "Radioactive Goldfish Found in Ohio Nuclear Plant." May 16, 2013. https://on.rt .com/91k290.

Unexplained Mysteries. n.d. "Lake Erie Chomper." Accessed October 11, 2023. https:// www.unexplained-mysteries.com/forum/topic/108755-the-lake-erie-chomper/.

THE LAKE ERIE SALT MINE
An April Fools' Day Prank

According to folklorist Nancy Cassell McEntire (2002), April Fools' Day dates back to the sixteenth century when the Gregorian calendar moved the New Year from late March to January first. In the beginning, the switch away from March may have been missed out of habit, a mistake not caught until a few days later, marked by the change of the month—on April 1. That may account for an association between being fooled and the arrival of April. Since it would have taken time to adjust to the change, there were likely some who noticeably forgot the switch until alerted. Potentially, these were the first to be mocked as "April fools."

Whatever the explanation for April Fools' Day, at some point it became a folk holiday, one that is not designated by church or state but is generated, modified, and maintained by ordinary people. Like all celebrants, folks on Erie's lakeshore are still pulling mild pranks on April 1 and poking fun at those who are fooled. A notable example of an April Fools' prank appeared online in 2011, using humorous satire and social criticism in relation to the spectacular and very real salt mine under Lake Erie.

The mine exists because four hundred million years ago, where the Great Lakes are now located, a drying inland sea left behind a bed of salt sixty feet thick. The salt bed was eventually buried under serial deposits of limestone and shale. Retreating glaciers created the Great Lakes on top of these valuable deposits where the salt lay hidden, like a buried treasure, until the 1950s.

Today, Lake Erie salt miners descend nearly two thousand feet to go to work each day. Intricate webs of underground roadways and caverns pierce the mine area, stretching out for miles beneath the lake bottom, toward the Canadian shore. The lake's two salt mines produce roughly four million tons of salt per year. Both operate from the Ohio shore, one at Fairport Harbor and the other at Cleveland. Some of the salt is for industrial use; the rest adds flavor to our menus.

The salt caves are just as invisible below us as outer space is invisible above us, and both realms seem to generate the same anxiety as do shadows on the ceiling or under the bed. Linking outer space above the earth with inner space below it is commonplace in the language used for online discussions of the salt mines, as in this example: "This underground world deep under Lake Erie's lake-floor is a universe where a galaxy of miners are unknown to so many of us above ground terrestrials" (Embrescia 2010).

Around Lake Erie, apocalyptic speculation—or "end of the world as we know it" narratives—are often inspired by the infinite realm above the earth and the unknown realm below (see "UFO Base under Lake Erie," this volume). Such narratives roil through the region and circulate on the internet, giving no evidence of accuracy, but like all traditional narratives, no matter how fictitious, they perfectly reflect the spirit and mentality of the community and the tumultuous times in which apocalyptic and conspiracy theories tend to gain serious traction.

Below is an April Fools' Day prank, posted online, involving Cleveland's salt mine as a spoof of apocalyptic conspiracies. Folklorist Moira Marsh (2015: 36) has described the traditional formula for such pranking, noting that in an April Fools' joke, the joker will frame his narrative as fact while simultaneously discrediting it as fiction. As long as the target doesn't understand the discrediting message, the target remains fooled and is played for a fool. When the target becomes aware of the deception, "it is the moment of truth, literally," Marsh writes, since realization lets the target in on the joke (2015: 36). The salt-mine prank generated many responses, none of them aware of the joke—except for one wry response by one reader among them all who got the discrediting messages and wasn't fooled.

According to the 2011 report, Lake Erie was leaking and would be gone by 2012. Many readers, apparently ready to believe any and all apocalyptic claims, took this seriously. Skeptics tended to legitimate the claim further by taking it seriously enough to argue, as if there was anything real to argue about. But in one case, the prank was recognized and inspired a humorous response, and—as shown below—it built on the prank's social criticism, trying to match, if not exceed, the delight quotient of the narrative.

The fiction below is framed as fact in part by adopting the style of professional journalism. Like journalistic reporting, it cites sources, using the typical alphabet soup of government agencies. But it simultaneously discredits itself by referring to acronyms like DNR (not a government agency but the medical code for "Do not resuscitate"). As a parody, it jabs at White House politics and at UFO narratives, both closely associated with government conspiracy theories. Typical of such claims, the parody offers photographic "evidence" that is indeed photographic but does not rise to the level of evidence—something also typical of most cryptid photos (see "The Ohio Grassman," this volume). Discrediting its own claim in this manner, the article shows a purported "vortex" that it states began in 2009, with a satellite image actually taken in 2005.

For the more astute, the parody was given as a purported release from the Associated Press, but the date is a strong hint: April 1, 2011. It read as follows, posted by JustOneMoreFish (2011) on the Ohio Game Fishing website:

Salt mines under Lake Erie being flooded

04-01-2011
Reported by Associated Press
Lake Erie is leaking. After two years of relentless rumors the EPPA, DNR, USCC has released top secret information that Lake Erie has been leaking water through a sink hole 30 miles north east of Cleveland to the tune of three (3) billion gallons of water a day and growing.

The sink hole started when the roof of the salt mine located 12 miles under Lake Erie collapsed. At first a trickle of water through a small crack continued to grow in size until today, when the size of the hole is estimated to be 10 feet in diameter.

Large freighters have been reporting the strong clockwise pull of the water as their ships would near the vortex but government officials decided to keep the information secret to guard against panic while they tried to plug the hole. A White House spokesperson said if the leak continues growing at the present rate, Lake Erie is expected to be a dry water bed by July 2012.

The icebergs circling in a clockwise formation north east of Cleveland the past few days convinced the government to come clean and share information with the public. If you look closely at the attached image you can see the icebergs circling. At a closed door meeting at the White House today President Obama stated the problem had started on Bush's watch, and if he had done his job correctly we wouldn't be in this mess.

The White House has scheduled a Presidential spin session at 3 PM today to announce their plan to use this crisis to their full advantage.

An astute online response:

"I heard the real sink hole is in Washington. If it keeps up at this rate, our pockets will all be dry by 2012."

What we see here is an electronic form of thinly veiled political and social satire, a genre once limited only to professionals with credentials that merit journalistic platforms. Today, such publication is open to anyone with access to the internet, in this case using humor to escape censure or other unwanted consequences of doing social criticism (Neulander 2004: 181): "Armed with the built-in escape clause, e.g., 'just kidding,' or 'it was just a joke,' humor has historically been used to deliver criticism that is not only timely, and funny, but as James Scott puts it, also: 'oblique, symbolic and too indefinite to incur prosecution'" (1990: 138).

Clearly, by using humor, words can be safely spoken to power (and peers) by persons who might otherwise suffer negative consequences. This makes funny, cleverly disguised parodies like the salt-mine prank perfect vehicles for political and social criticism.

According to folklorist Marsh, April Fools' Day pranks, like practical jokes in general, can be said to be over when "the fabrication has run its course and been discredited: the target is now 'in on' the joke. It is all over but the shouting" (in this case, literally shouts of "April Fool!"), but Marsh adds: "The shouting can be very significant in social terms" (2015: 36), since there can be postplay to the joke—postplay as occurred in this case, when a target got the joke and joined in on the social criticism, perhaps competing for the best political zinger.

Political satire has historically entertained us, making us aware of both laughable and lamentable patterns in society. But as we can see, on April Fools' Day, 2011, only one—among all who responded online—was *not* made an April Fool!

References

Embrescia, Kendall. 2010. "North East Ohio Salt Mines Are Big Time Producers." http://thegreatworkplace.com/109/north-east-ohio-salt-mines-are-big-time-producers/.

JustOneMoreFish. 2011. "Salt Mines under Lake Erie Being Flooded." Ohio Game Fishing, April 1, 2011. https://www.ohiogamefishing.com/threads/salt-mines-under-lake-erie-being-flooded.169364/#post-1187199.

Marsh, Moira. 2015. *Practically Joking*. Denver: University Press of Colorado, Utah State University Press.

McEntire, Nancy Cassell. 2002. "Purposeful Deceptions of the April Fool." *Western Folklore* 61, no. 2 (Summer): 133–51.

Neulander, Judith S. 2004. "Tchotchkes: A Study of Popular Culture in Tangible Form." In *American Judaism in Popular Culture*, edited by Leonard J. Greenspoon and Ronald A. Simkins, 175–99. Lincoln, NE: Creighton University Press.

Scott, James C. 1990. *Domination and the Arts of Resistance: Hidden Transcripts*. New Haven, CT: Yale University Press.

Figure 52.1. *Round Goby Male* by Dodoman via Wikimedia Commons. (CC BY-SA 4.0)

EVIL FISH
"The Galloping Goby Blues"

The Great Lakes hold one-fifth of the fresh water on the earth's surface, and they cover an area larger than the entire United King-
dom. The lakes are home to 3,500 species of plants and animals, including more than 170 species of fish (Michalak 2017). But since the 1800s,
roughly 200 nonnative species of fish, mollusks, worms, plants, and algae
have become permanent residents of the Great Lakes ecosystem. Many
of these nonnative species are called invasive because they cause harm to
human health, economics, and the environment. Some invasive species
enter the lakes as unwanted pets, but the vast majority arrive through the
release of ballast water by oceangoing or saltwater cargo ships, known as
"salties."

Today, people are discouraged from dumping aquatic pets into natural
waterways, and salties are required to discharge ballast water before entering
the St. Lawrence Seaway, the major gateway to both American and Canadian
waterways. But no matter how an invasive species gets into the lake, once it
manages to take up residence, it is already beyond eradication. Some of these
are, effectively, evil fish. The round goby is one of them.

One voice has been raised against such species in general and the round
goby in particular. The faculty profile of David J. Jude, research scientist
emeritus at Michigan University, notes that his outgoing personality and
sense of humor have engaged many students who are now pursuing successful careers in fisheries biology. In "The Galloping Goby Blues," he composed
a song to entertain his students, these gifts combine with musical talent to
generate a protest of popular appeal. There is probably no song better informed on the reality of invasive species across the Great Lakes. The lyrics
cover more than one lake, more than one waterway, and a spectrum of "evil
fish," but they zero in on the round goby, a pernicious invasive species whose
greatest concentration is in Lake Erie.

The Galloping Goby Blues

Lyrics courtesy of David J. Jude

We got evil fish coming into town
Slippin' in our lakes without a sound
And unless we stop them cold, they'll beat our natives down

There's egg-suckin', fish-bitin', exotics all around
There's ruffe in our largest greatest lake
Zebras, Mitten crabs, it'll keep you awake
There's Bythotrephes in the summer, Dreissena in the fall
If the Quaggas don't get you, you've broken Darwin's law

Round gobies now rule among the rocks
They can live out of water, they'll bite you in your socks
And if we don't stop them soon, there'll only be bad news
I've got those egg-suckin', fish-chewin', galloping goby blues

They're out on the land chasin' hogs
They'll eat cats and especially like dogs
They'll eat your mottled sculpin, have log-perch for brunch
Chew darters for supper, eat trout-perch for lunch

Female gobies have sex everyday
And I can't help but admire their way
They reproduce in beer cans, logs and old TVs
They came across with Dracula from the Black and Caspian Seas

Next they'll be flying 'or our land
Eating birds and pushing contraband
And if we try to sterilize, poison, or eradicate
They'll end up in cyberspace and gleefully mutate

There's gobies in Superior and St. Clair
Gobies running rampant everywhere
Gobies in the bathroom, gobies in the sink
They know where you're going, they know what you think

Illinois made gobies their state fish
Ohio stocked them to honor a fisherman's wish

Minnesota offered refuge to keep the gobies free
Indiana makes money; you can fish them for a fee

Throughout the Great Lakes they've been found
And soon they'll be Mississippi bound
They love vacation cruises, they've paid all their dues
I've got those egg-suckin', fish-chewin', galloping goby blues

Round gobies are the smartest in the lake
They can read, write and even calculate
Soon they'll steal our money and all our women too
Oh, I'm all torn up, despondent, round gobies I eschew

Round gobies are filling every void
Soon they'll become humanoid
I'm getting so annoyed, I just have no clues
I'm depressed, overwhelmed with the gallopin' goby blues
Those gobies are forever, alas what can we do?
I've got those egg-suckin', fish-chewin', galloping goby blues

By volume, Lake Erie is the smallest and shallowest of the Great Lakes. But according to Case Western Reserve University's e-newsletter, the *Daily* (2019): "It is also the most biologically productive, and its watershed is the most populated. Agriculture, urbanization and industrialization draw people to live and work by the water's edge, but they also contribute to many of the environmental problems facing the lake. Making matters worse, changing climatic conditions are exacerbating some of these problems and creating economic and public health concerns for coastal populations."

The general public often lacks access to scientific discussion and publication, but no one can stop good information when it circulates by less formal and more entertaining means, like "The Galloping Goby Blues."

References

Daily. 2019. "Science Café Cleveland: 'Not So Erie Anymore: The Science behind Lake Erie's Most Critical Environmental Issues.'" Case Western Reserve University Internal E-newsletter, June 5, 2019.

Michalak, Anne M. 2017. "Environmental Sciences: Troubled Waters on the Great Lakes." *Nature* 543:488–9. https://doi.org/10.1038/543488a.

Figure 53.1. *Comet Neowise* by Joël Kuiper via Flickr. (CC BY 2.0)

SUPERMAN

Lake Erie's Own

The year was 1937. Dark clouds of fascism roiled over Europe, and the dogs of war began to snarl. But then, like the long-tailed comet of so long ago, something bright streaked across the sky over Lake Erie. It came from the place where hope has always soared against chaos and uncertainty. It wasn't a bird, it wasn't a plane, and it wasn't the long-tailed panther/comet of Native American mythology (see "Long Tail," this volume). It was the Man of Steel—Lake Erie's own Superman!

No one can rightly say how long graphic novels, or their equivalent, have existed. But comic books have been an American literary tradition since at least 1937, when Jack Liebowitz (1900–2000) founded a company that grew to encompass DC, Action, and All-American Comics. The first printing of Action Comics sold out at two hundred thousand copies, with total sales hitting one million in the first thirty days of publication (Neulander 2004). That historic issue featured an alien immigrant child, destined to become a culture hero known as Superman, originally created by Jerry Siegel and Joe Schuster, two Jewish teenagers living in an immigrant Cleveland neighborhood on Lake Erie's shore.

Predictably, some scholars cite as "Jewish" a number of episodes in the Superman saga. One such example is the infant Superman's arrival on earth in a tiny ship dispatched by his desperate family, purportedly influenced by the infant Moses's arrival at Pharaoh's court in a tiny ship dispatched by *his* desperate family. But Stith Thompson's *Motif-Index of Folk-Literature* (1956–58) includes these motifs: S.331 (Exposure of child in boat [floating chest]) and L111.21 (Future hero found in boat [basket, bushes]).

Both motifs predate Jewish tradition. For example, the infant Sargon, a future culture hero and founder of the Akkadian nation, was exposed on a river in a basket of bulrushes many centuries before the infant Moses was set adrift to become a culture hero and founder of the Israelite nation. In turn,

Moses was followed by others, most notably the doomed infant Remus and his surviving twin brother, Romulus, future culture hero and founder of the city of Rome. Rather than a Jewish ethnic marker, the motif of the castaway child is more clearly an ancient literary device for signifying the birth of a future culture hero.

Nevertheless, one could suggest not only that comic book superheroes are of Middle Eastern descent but also that they represent a tradition more ancient than is generally recognized. Most of us have seen pictures of ancient *charuvim* (pronounced *ha-roo-VEEM*), sphinxlike statues of the ancient Middle East with human heads (often crowned and bearded in the manner of ancient culture heroes), also endowed with the powerful bodies of quadrupeds, mighty avian wings, and sometimes gills. Historically, combinations of biological species that can never crossbreed in the natural world are meant to represent the realm that stands *above* nature: in the supernatura, the supernatural realm. These creatures hearken back to the chaos of pre-Creation, which in remote antiquity was believed to persist outside, and beyond, the laws of Creation as ordained by God.

To a great extent, the supernatural otherworld is "other" by virtue of infinite possibilities that exceed the limits of biological law and order. Not surprisingly, we find the ancient *charuvim* stationed at borders between the natural and the supernatural, at the entrances and exits of temples and tombs, or at other junctures between sacred and mundane space. Bearing some characteristics of both realms, the ancient *charuvim* stood with a foot in each, guarding every border—perhaps the first guardian angels—since any misstep, or careless breach, might allow an eruption of chaos into the natural world, disrupting the laws of nature and, in so doing, destroying the order of Creation.

In modernity, the same supernatural mix of species and the guardianship of law and order can be seen in the marvelously caped and costumed heroes of American comic books. These are similarly anthropomorphic beings like Spider-Man, Batman, Aquaman, Ant-Man, and an army of X-Men with enhanced faculties of speed, vision, and strength, not to mention the ability to shape-shift, fly, pass through fire, and breathe underwater. But first among them all was the Man of Steel, conceived in Cleveland when steel reigned supreme. Local lore still cites the art deco AT&T building on Huron Road as the model for the *Daily Planet* building in Metropolis. Suburban Cleveland is where the Maltz Museum of Jewish Heritage has enshrined an issue of the first Superman comic, and a larger-than-life statue of Superman punches through a brick wall above the exhibition hall. Nearby, a commemorative plaque marks Jerry Siegel's house in Glenville, the immigrant Jewish neighborhood where he and Joe Schuster grew up.

Closing in on a century of Superman's adventures, both of his creators have passed away, Glenville has changed unrecognizably, and the Man of Steel has lost his supreme reign to an edgier band of super-rivals. But he may retake his lead as the country once again finds itself faltering in the face of division, chaos, and uncertainty, desperately yearning for Superman's own, inimitable brand: truth, justice, and the American way.

If Superman is to regain his former stature, it will most likely be at the hand of Brian Michael Bendis, who, like Jerry Siegel and Joe Schuster, began his career as a Jewish kid from Cleveland. Bendis, a writer for DC Comics, is an imaginative author who also fictionalized Eliot Ness's hunt for Cleveland's Torso Killer in a graphic novel called *Torso* (see "Bloody Mary," this volume). Bendis has taken over the challenge of reinvigorating the Man of Steel, a character whose principles are easily eclipsed by more startling powers than mere strength, flight, and X-ray vision. In Bendis's favor, Superman's personal brand persists unscathed, and above all, it remains worth fighting for.

Consequently, the Man of Steel is emerging in an edgier, more relatable narrative, reflecting our own time of highly unsettling changes and—according to his antifascist tradition—conducting social criticism in the bargain. Today's Clark Kent is a family man and newspaper reporter who works in a politicized world where the term *fake news* is applied to every truth that threatens the forces of chaos. As a professional journalist striving for accuracy, Kent is labeled an "enemy of the people," and like many newspapers, the *Daily Planet* is in a death struggle with electronic media. On the domestic front, Lois Lane is now his wife and "wants to reset their relationship in a way that makes him uncomfortable," while his dad (who did not die after all) turns out to be "an insufferable, dismissive jerk" (Hannan 2018). In a separate line of DC Comics, his son has left home and has a same-sex lover from a different planet. But through it all, Superman perseveres, striving to justify his relevance on every front, to uphold law and order, and to keep his moral compass at true north (Hannan 2018). "It really is about hope," Bendis told *Cleveland Magazine* in 2018. "Unwavering hope for the future" (Hannan 2018).

Clearly, despite the chaos and uncertainty of the early twenty-first century, something bright still streaks across the heavens above Lake Erie. Hope prevails, following a trail blazed by ancient culture heroes, fairies, cryptids, woolly bears, and wizards, as by the long-tailed panther/comet that long ago fell from the sky, pierced the ice, and gave the lake its name.

References

Hannan, Sheehan. 2018. "Our Superman." *Cleveland Magazine*, September 12, 2018. https:// clevelandmagazine.com/in-the-cle/the-read/articles/our-superman.

Neulander, Judith S. 2004. "Tchotchkes: A Study of Popular Culture in Tangible Form." In *American Judaism in Popular Culture*, edited by Leonard J. Greenspoon and Ronald A. Simpkins, 175–99. Omaha, NE: Creighton University Press.

Thompson, Stith. 1956–58. *The Motif-Index of Folk Literature*. 6 vols. Bloomington: Indiana University Press.

INDEX

Folklorist JUDITH S. NEULANDER has taught at
Case Western Reserve University. She is a prolific
author and speaker whose research has been
featured in the *Atlantic Monthly*, the *New York
Times*, and the *Los Angeles Times*.